A familiar compound ghost

A familiar compound ghost
Allusion and the uncanny

SARAH ANNES BROWN

Manchester University Press
Manchester and New York

distributed in the United States exclusively
by Palgrave Macmillan

Copyright © Sarah Annes Brown 2012

The right of Sarah Annes Brown to be identified as the author of this work has been asserted by her in accordance with the Copyright, Designs and Patents Act 1988.

Published by Manchester University Press
Oxford Road, Manchester M13 9NR, UK
and Room 400, 175 Fifth Avenue, New York, NY 10010, USA
www.manchesteruniversitypress.co.uk

Distributed in the United States exclusively by
Palgrave Macmillan, 175 Fifth Avenue, New York,
NY 10010, USA

Distributed in Canada exclusively by
UBC Press, University of British Columbia, 2029 West Mall,
Vancouver, BC, Canada V6T 1Z2

British Library Cataloguing-in-Publication Data
A catalogue record for this book is available from the British Library

Library of Congress Cataloging-in-Publication Data applied for

ISBN   978 0 7190 8515 4   hardback

First published 2012

The publisher has no responsibility for the persistence or accuracy of URLs for any external or third-party internet websites referred to in this book, and does not guarantee that any content on such websites is, or will remain, accurate or appropriate.

Typeset by Servis Filmsetting Ltd, Stockport, Cheshire
Printed in Great Britain
by CPI Antony Rowe Ltd, Chippenham, Wiltshire

Contents

Acknowledgements vi

1	Introduction	*page* 1
2	Uncanny doubles: part one	19
3	Uncanny doubles: part two	51
4	Ruins	77
5	Reanimation: Orpheus and Pygmalion	112
6	The ghost in *Hamlet*	153
7	A familiar compound ghost: *katabasis* and *The Tempest*	178
8	Afterword: 'You'd think she would remember all this from the first time'	210

Bibliography 214
Index 228

Acknowledgements

I am grateful to Rick Allen, Berit Åstrom, Alex Brown, Ewan Fernie, Eugene Giddens, John Gilroy, Van Leavenworth, John Lee, Lynsey McCulloch, Catherine Silverstone and Rowlie Wymer, all of whom made useful suggestions or commented on individual chapters. I would also like to acknowledge helpful feedback from colleagues and audience members at various conferences and research seminars where I presented earlier versions of some chapters. Finally I would like to thank those at Manchester University Press, as well as the anonymous reviewers of the typescript, for their encouragement and guidance.

1

Introduction

Philip Pullman's *Northern Lights* opens in Jordan College, Oxford, in an England both like and unlike our own. As a talking goose will at one point explain to the heroine, Lyra, 'not further away, but interpenetrating with this one . . . millions of other universes exist, unaware of one another'.[1] Lyra gains her first inkling of such worlds at the beginning of the novel when she listens, safely concealed, to the after-dinner conversation of the Scholars of Jordan College. Her place of hiding is significant:

> She had been crouching. She carefully stood up, feeling around for the clothes-hangers in order not to make a noise, and found that the wardrobe was bigger than she'd thought. There were several academic robes and hoods, some with fur around them, most faced with silk.[2]

Many readers will, at this point, be reminded of the moment in *The Lion, the Witch and the Wardrobe* when Lucy first enters Narnia.[3] She too realises that the wardrobe is much bigger than it seems – for it holds an entire world:

> She took a step further in – then two or three steps – always expecting to feel woodwork against the tips of her fingers. But she could not feel it.
>
> 'This must be a simply enormous wardrobe!' thought Lucy, going still further in and pushing the soft folds of the coats aside to make room for her.[4]

There is nothing supernatural about Lyra's wardrobe and though she will hear of other worlds at this point, it will be some time before she enters one herself. But in a sense Lyra's wardrobe is a portal, for it opens up a kind of channel of communication between Pullman's and Lewis's novels.

The worlds of Narnia and *Northern Lights* collide, interpenetrating like the worlds of Pullman's multiverse, and create numerous moments of intertextual entanglement. Beautiful Mrs Coulter lures children to their doom with 'chocolatl', mirroring the White Witch's temptation of Edmund with Turkish delight. Lyra's ride on the bear, Iorek Byrnison, echoes Lucy's ride on Aslan. When trapped in the sinister Station, Lyra's walk through a narrow attic space resembles Polly's crawl from the attic of her own house to the house of wicked Uncle Andrew in *The Magician's Nephew*. But this is no simple homage to Lewis; Pullman actively distances himself from the Christianity of the Narnia books and embraces the emerging sexuality of Lyra. It is as though he is rebuking Lewis for his treatment of Susan, Lucy's elder sister, who is exiled from Narnia after she begins to be interested in lipstick and parties.

Pullman invokes the idea of a fictional magic portal between worlds, a wardrobe, to create a kind of literary wormhole between the textual universes of an old and a new children's classic. The novel's allusive patterns (and of course *Northern Lights* has points of contact with many other textual worlds, including that of *Paradise Lost*) mirror and reinforce its magical subject matter; just as worlds take their place in the complex, ever-branching multiverse, so, in our real world, do books depend upon each other in an intertextual web. We feel the same pleasurable recognition of sameness and difference when we learn about an Oxford which looks almost like our own (yet in which poppies are consumed after dinner rather than cigars) as we experience when we spot the patterns of difference and similarity between *Northern Lights* and *The Lion, the Witch and the Wardrobe*.

Allusion and the uncanny are both characterised by this blend of the familiar and the unfamiliar. An uncanny effect is created when the membrane separating the natural from the supernatural world appears to be punctured. An allusion is effected by a similar transgression of the barrier separating the enclosed world of the text from its various sources and intertexts. Within literature an uncanny effect is best evoked, not by the entirely strange, but by a disquieting blend of the strange and the familiar. A remote, fantasy setting is unlikely to generate an effective sense of the uncanny, and supernatural elements should remain mysterious possibilities rather than crude certainties.[5] In a text such as Henry James's *The Turn of the Screw* (1898), for example, it is the ambiguous status of the 'ghosts' – the fact that their existence cannot be proved or pinned down – which makes the novel effective, and Jacques Tourneur's 1957 horror film *Night of the Demon* is felt by many to have been spoiled by the inclusion of explicit close-up shots of the monster. Most typically an uncanny story is set in a homely, everyday setting which is then subtly and eerily disrupted by some strange intrusion. The dynamic of allusion is similar in so far as it involves an unexpected intrusion from one (textual) world into another. In a sense allusion reverses the dynamic of the uncanny; rather than being an invasion by an unfamiliar force into a familiar setting, an allusion is characterised by the unexpected presence of the known and familiar within a new, and thus unfamiliar, context. But of course something may be 'known and familiar' and yet not remotely homely; the ghost of Hamlet's father is immediately recognisable to those who witness it, fully familiar, and yet uncanny.

Some allusions are constituted in a way which simultaneously draws attention to their status as allusions and mines the uncanny potential of the allusive moment. This is done through the use of certain clues, motifs which I call 'uncanny allusion markers'.[6] We have already seen one of these in action – the portal between worlds – and other common mechanisms include reanimation, ruins, *déjà vu*, prophecy, excavation, ghosts and doubles. These have the capacity to generate a special allusive charge because they foreground in some way their position within a larger literary network, signalling moments of apparent dialogue between texts far removed in time through a dynamic of doubleness, repetition or return.

Allusion markers, signalling reflexivity, are not always uncanny. Theft, for example, has a pleasingly self-referential potential. In 'The Ministry of Fear', Seamus Heaney quietly filches the phrase 'an act of stealth' from the famous boat-stealing episode in *The Prelude* and, in his translation of Giovanni Battista Guarini's *Il Pastor Fido*, Richard Fanshawe steals lines from Ben Jonson's 'To Celia', a poem about theft in the context of erotic predation. (I have no wish to compound the reflexivity here so I must acknowledge my debts to earlier analyses of these examples by Kerry McSweeney and John Hollander respectively.[7]) Another good example is inheritance, and, in *Allusion to the Poets*, Christopher Ricks explores the reflexive potential of allusive poems about both real and metaphorical parent/child relationships: 'Literary allusions to fathers (or to uncles) are liable to suggest a paternal-filial relationship between the alluded-to and the alluder, since the alluder has entered upon an inheritance.'[8]

To illustrate this point I'll take a well-known example, though not one discussed by Ricks. The topic of inheritance, the relationship between generations, becomes a commentary on the text's own place within a literary tradition in Alexander Pope's 'First Epistle of the Second Book of Horace Imitated'. The idea of poetic ancestry and intergenerational rivalry acquires a fresh significance once Horace's original poem on the topic is brought up to date. Horace had attacked those who value poets simply because they are long dead, pointing out the illogic of such a preference:

> si meliora dies, ut vina, poemata reddit,
> scire velim chartis pretium quotus adroget annus.
> scriptor abhinc annos centum qui decidit, inter
> perfectos veteresque referri debet an inter
> vilis atque novos?[9]

> (If poems are like wine which time improves, I should like to know what is the year that gives to writings fresh value. A writer who dropped off a hundred years ago, is he to be reckoned among the perfect and ancient, or among the worthless and modern?)

Pope's arguments are identical but his 'ancients' and 'moderns' have been updated.

> On Avon's bank, where flow'rs eternal blow,
> If I but ask, if any weed can grow?
> One Tragic sentence if I dare deride
> Which Betterton's grave Action dignify'd,
> Or well-mouth'd Booth with emphasis proclaims
> (Tho' but, perhaps, a muster-roll of Names)
> How will our Fathers rise up in a rage,
> And swear, all shame is lost in George's Age![10]

The fact that his exemplary 'ancient', William Shakespeare, was born hundreds of years after Horace's 'moderns' adds ironic reinforcement to the poem's central thesis.

This instance exemplifies a characteristic common to many examples of reflexive allusion: a shift in roles. Between original and translation, Horace and his contemporaries metamorphose from moderns to ancients. In later chapters we will see characters (and authors) turning from living men into ghosts, from witnesses into objects of scrutiny, as they move from source to later alluding text. Writers describing or addressing some numinous force may themselves actually become that force if their words are picked up and repeated by a later imitator. Indeed it can sometimes seem as though a writer has created such an irresistible urge to imitate that we might describe the earlier work as an 'allusion trigger', a text, or moment within a text, which seems to anticipate or invite future allusions.[11] Elsewhere I have analysed the way in which Ted Hughes subtly adjusts the invocation of the gods which opens the *Metamorphoses*, transforming this into an address to the shade of Ovid himself.[12] Ricks discusses a similar effect created by an echo in Pope's *The Dunciad* of John Milton's description of God as a source of glory and illumination. Even though the immediate context is parodic, in that Pope is actually describing poetic dullness, the simple fact that he has imitated Milton's description of God within the context of poetic rather than divine energy invites the reader to infer a graceful compliment to Milton as an inspirational poet.[13]

Although Ricks's book is witty and erudite, perhaps the most suggestive and sustained exploration of this kind of reflexive allusion – allusion, in other words, which draws attention to itself by means of allusion markers of some kind – is Stephen Hinds's *Allusion and Intertext*. He offers a crisp definition of the phenomenon on the first page: 'Certain allusions are so constructed as to carry a kind of built-in commentary, a kind of reflexive annotation, which underlines or intensifies their demand to be interpreted *as* allusions.'[14] Hinds is interested primarily in Latin poetry and one example he offers of this 'reflexive annotation' is Ovid's description of Corinna's pet parrot as an 'imitatrix ales', an imitating bird. Matrices collide in the epithet, for, as well as being a mimicker of human speech, the parrot represents an imitative repetition of an earlier poetic pet, Lesbia's sparrow in *Catullus*.[15] Hinds goes on to identify references to the acts of recognition and memory in other classical texts, and aligns these with parallel acts of recognition and memory which take place outside the text, in the mind of the reader; the well-read reader at least.

I'd like to offer an analysis of a powerful and well-known example of memory functioning as an allusion marker; one which Hinds does not include in his study. This is an exchange in Euripides's *Electra* which appears to be a direct response to a very similar scene in Aeschylus's *The Libation Bearers*.[16] In Aeschylus's slightly earlier play, Electra is quickly convinced by traces – a lock of hair, footprints and a fragment of cloth – that her brother Orestes has indeed returned. But in Euripides's *Electra*, the heroine marshals logic to refute this 'evidence' in a move which seems to take her outside the text; her voice uniting with that of her creator to issue a challenge to authority and tradition. Euripides's refusal to follow in his precursor's footsteps is matched by Electra's scornful rejection of the old man's invitation to set her foot in her brother's prints:

> You make me angry. How could rocky ground receive
> The imprint of a foot? And if it could be traced,
> It would not be the same for brother and for sister,
> A man's foot and a girl's – of course his would be bigger.[17]

Clearly Euripides's play has a different resonance for the reader or audience who has already encountered Aeschylus. But Euripides doesn't simply tacitly invite the spectator to think of Aeschylus – he, as it were, jabs him in the ribs in case he hasn't noticed the allusion: 'Why do you stare at me like a man who squints / At the bright stamp of a coin? Do I stir your memory?'[18] These words are spoken by Orestes to Electra but they could also be seen as a nudge to us as spectators to remember Aeschylus. An appeal to a character's memory may function simultaneously as an appeal to the literary memories of the reader. The reference to squinting at a coin might invoke some anxieties about quality and authenticity, as though Euripides is at some level engaging with the suspicion that his own play is, if not a forgery precisely, a belated and imitative work at least. This equivocal attitude towards a source, compounded of emulation, admiration, anxiety and bravado, is one we will see in many later alluding texts.

There was nothing uncanny about the example of reflexive allusion I discussed earlier, Pope's imitation of Horace. Euripides's response to Aeschylus perhaps just brushes the 'uncanny' in that it half seems as though Electra and Orestes know more about their situation (as characters, as repetitions) than they should. But the primary effect – and the same is true of the examples of memory being used as an allusion marker discussed by Hinds – is ironic and self-conscious. Although Hinds does touch on at least one potentially uncanny allusion marker, prophecy, he doesn't explore the particular apt richness of allusion markers which are also supernatural motifs. For although any reflexive allusion generates a kind of textual charge, there is a special *frisson* when the allusion marker is uncanny; when the impression of worlds, times or frames of reference colliding within the fiction of a supernatural or spooky text is matched by the parallel collision of textual worlds in the minds of author and reader. Reader and character simultaneously become aware, albeit in different ways, that another voice, perhaps long dead, is trying to make itself heard.

Uncanny allusion markers aren't the only way in which allusion and the uncanny intersect. Another point of contact is the potential for uncertainty when trying to identify the two phenomena, the category confusions in which both may become involved. I shall say a little about the spectrum of effects which might be included within the capacious term 'allusion' before explaining further how these relate to the uncanny. Much has been written on the precise definitions of a whole series of related terms for ways in which texts connect with other texts. Some critics are very concerned to police the boundaries between the different ways in which texts seem to speak to one another and identify set parameters for deciding whether something is an allusion, a quotation or merely an echo. I don't seek to offer a definitive taxonomy, simply a reminder of some of the questions we might ask of moments of apparent interplay between texts.

One of the key questions readers have to grapple with is the issue of 'intentionality'. Some are inclined to brush intentions aside completely, either because it is impossible to establish the intentions of a long dead writer or because a writer's intentions are perceived to be subordinate to larger linguistic or societal pressures. Once again, I find the position taken by Stephen Hinds on this issue particularly helpful. He would agree that we cannot ever be quite sure what a poet such as Shakespeare 'intended' but at the same time he refuses to discount the importance of an 'intentionality-effect' and defends the rhetoric of intentionality from a pragmatic perspective:

> Therefore, while conceding the fact that, for us as critics, the alluding poet is ultimately and necessarily a figure whom we ourselves read out from the text, let us continue to employ our enlarged version of 'allusion', along with its intention-bearing author, as a discourse which is good to think with – which enables us to conceptualize and to handle certain kinds of intertextual transaction more economically and effectively than does any alternative.[19]

Critics who find the idea that a writer might actually have intended something faintly distasteful tend to steer clear of the rhetoric of allusion. The word strongly implies agency; it suggests that a later writer has deliberately referenced an earlier work, inviting the reader to notice and reflect on the connection. Sometimes the echo is so unmistakable, so distinctive, that we experience no doubt in identifying a deliberate allusion. *The Waste Land* is full of this kind of unambiguous allusion, and T. S. Eliot even provides us with footnotes to confirm this. Such an allusion is obtrusive and advertises its status – the fact that its origins lie in a quite different text – for all to see. We are likely to take several factors into account when trying to decide whether an apparent resemblance to an earlier text really constitutes an allusion. Does the allusion rest on a single word or the quotation or near quotation of a more extended phrase? Are the words striking and distinctive? Is the alluded-to text well known – in other words would almost any educated reader identify this as an allusion? Is there some aptness or interest in the fuller context of the alluded-to text which we can import into the new text? Or is the earlier text (to borrow a useful analogy from Ricks) just scaffolding, source material, rather than an integral part of the new work?[20]

Defining an allusion isn't an exact science. Some maintain that an allusion should include a strong verbal component whereas others would accept striking thematic parallels as sufficient evidence.[21] If the allusion is signalled unusually strongly we may want to call it a quotation or reference. If it is systematic or sustained then imitation (or parody) may become a more appropriate term to describe the relationship with the earlier text. And if the questions raised at the end of the previous paragraph don't elicit mostly positive responses then we may want to downgrade the moment of interplay from 'allusion' to 'echo'.

An echo is a more neutral word which doesn't rule out the possibility of conscious borrowing but implies that the connection isn't strong enough to prove deliberate agency or to ensure recognition in the majority of attentive readers. We may compare such echo effects with those identifiable in literary dialogues featuring Echo herself. Many writers have enjoyed playing with the possibilities of Echo's limited capacity for speech, creating dialogues in which, simply by repeating words or parts of words, the nymph is apparently able to articulate her own thoughts and wishes. The following example, from a dialogue between Mercury and Echo in Jonson's *Cynthia's Revels*, is typical:

MER: Farewell, good wag.
Now to my charge, ECCHO, fair ECCHO speake,
Tis MERCVRIE, that calls thee, sorrowfull *Nymph*,

> Salute me with thy repercussiue voice,
> That I may know what cauerne of the earth,
> Containes thy ayrie spirit, how, or where
> I may direct my speech, that thou maist heare.
> ECC: Here.
> MER: So nigh?
> ECC: I.²²

Her responses seem simultaneously involuntary and purposeful as do many literary 'echoes' of one work in another.

We may want to describe these slighter connections in terms of intertextuality, a word which has been used in several different ways. It usually implies a complex and weblike relationship between texts which goes beyond direct influence. Vibrations from different strands of the web will affect how we respond to any work as well as affect (perhaps at several removes) the actual content/composition of that work. A book, and its reception, rests within a complex network of other texts in the same way a single word does within a language. Within the context of a book about allusion the word intertextuality is usually used to connote an absence of clear allusion, as a way of acknowledging that texts can have elements in common, that one may even seem to allude to another, while recognising that these similarities may be entirely involuntary and indeed be produced by a writer who has never read the work he or she seems to reference. Two descriptions of night or a beautiful woman are likely to contain elements in common even if the later writer never saw the earlier work. If you have only ever read two seventeenth-century *carpe diem* poems you will probably think one influenced the other. But the more examples one reads within the same genre, the less certain it will seem that the second poem is alluding to the first, or even echoing it in any meaningful way.

To sum up, sometimes we may feel we can diagnose the status of a moment of textual interplay with absolute certainty. A combination of internal and external evidence may allow us to state with complete security that a writer is alluding to an earlier identifiable text. But there are other occasions when we perhaps sense an affinity between two works but, because it seems comparatively weak and insignificant, don't want to claim it as anything more than an echo, perhaps an intertextual rather than an allusive connection. And somewhere in between lie some particularly intriguing cases where there is genuine uncertainty around the precise nature of the relationship between the two texts but where there is sufficient interesting interplay between them to make the reader dwell further on the link, and perhaps carry out additional research in order to gauge the likelihood that the later writer might have intended the reader to think about the earlier text. There were several moments in my own research when I went through this process. Yet at times I found myself thinking that there was a certain pleasure in not knowing. More specifically, I felt that if some extra detail had been added to the 'allusion' confirming its allusive status, something of its power and interest would actually have been lost. Not being quite sure whether the echo was intentional or just my imagination, purely a coincidence, added to the power of the (possibly) allusive moment.

It is this pleasurable uncertainty which provides that further link between the experience of reading an uncanny text and an allusive one which I mentioned above. The most effective manifestations of the uncanny in literature depend on ambiguity. The events should be strange enough to appear supernatural in origin but should still seem susceptible of some rational explanation – trickery, coincidence or delusion. The reader who has encountered something which may or may not be an allusion is faced with similar choices – either the allusion is a real one or else it is a coincidence, perhaps one whose significance has been magnified or intensified by the preoccupations of the reader. Indeed just as the unfortunate Gothic heroine who feels sure she is in a haunted house will start to think every sound and shadow heralds a ghost, so critics who are interested in allusion (uncanny or otherwise) will be unusually alert to certain patterns in their reading. Thus over the last few years I have become very quick to spot real or imagined allusions to my chosen topics (*Hamlet* and Orpheus for example). John Jervis writes suggestively about the experience of finding unexpected links between texts, the surprisingly uncanny effect of such discoveries on the reader. Here he describes how he first noticed the parallels between E. T. A. Hoffmann's 'The Sandman' and Alfred Hitchcock's *Vertigo*, a pairing I discuss in Chapter 5:

> At the time, I experienced this as decidedly 'uncanny'. Finding such parallels and repetitions *myself*, thus experiencing the findings as *encounters*, as real experiences, marked them as uncanny – irrespective of whether the parallels are 'really' there (whatever that might mean).[23]

Different readers will all have their own preoccupations which cause them to take quite separate paths through the web of literature. But there are certain paths which nearly all readers will feel drawn to; those signalled or opened up by a handful of exceptionally powerful texts. Some allusions are simply more interesting than others and this interest is partly, though not entirely, dependent on the inherent interest of the alluded-to text. Thus a work which presents itself as an adaptation of an indisputably canonical work such as *Hamlet* already has a kind of claim on the reader. If *Hamlet*'s afterlife is of inherent interest so is its source material. In the case of *Hamlet*, the main sources are comparatively few and obscure. The reader will therefore be tempted to cast around for more interesting ancestors, even if their relationship with *Hamlet* is more remote and fugitive. The play is so particularly charismatic that it generates a kind of 'pull' which draws earlier texts into its orbit even if their status as source material is uncertain. We are more likely to look for connections between works which generate a great deal of textual energy than between weaker and less influential works. This urge to identify all possible links between influential and powerful works is perhaps comparable to the allure of the theory of intelligent design or the myth that England was founded by Trojans. We want the things we value – works of literature, our countries, ourselves – to have a meaningful aetiology, to function as the *telos* of a narrative as well as the origin of a new tradition. In my chapter on *Hamlet* I probably betray my own desire to strengthen the play's roots, by giving it a more purposeful relationship with its sources – particularly ones which, though perhaps remote, are equally illustrious.

If there is a degree of delusion or imbalance in this way of reading, it is one which affects creative writers as well as critics, for they too sometimes seem to be trying to make classical texts whose influence on Shakespeare remains unproven part of his heritage, retrospectively. Elsewhere I have analysed the way in which points of contact between Shakespeare and his predecessors have been strengthened, discovered or even invented by later writers. David Slavitt, for example, in his translation of *The Phoenician Women*, makes a link between Lear and Oedipus, a link which seems comparatively chance and uncertain in *King Lear* itself, emerge with a clearer allusive force.[24] Similarly, another text which displays parallels with *Lear*, yet is not generally recognised as a source – Apuleius's version of the Cupid and Psyche story in *The Golden Ass* – becomes far more

Lear-like when it is retold by C. S. Lewis in *Till We Have Faces*.[25] I discuss further examples of the same phenomenon, classical texts being 'Shakespeared', in Chapter 6.

When dealing with complex allusive patterns which accumulate resonance as they move forwards (and sometimes backwards) in time, it is difficult to confine one's scope to a narrow period of English literature. So this book embraces not only a wide range of texts written in English between the fourteenth and twenty-first centuries, but also some of the most influential texts written in other languages and cultures – works by Ovid, Virgil and Dante for example. Clearly any book of this nature is going to reflect the interests and experiences of the writer more transparently than a more narrowly specialised monograph, and there is no scientific basis for my particular choice of texts. When dealing with earlier periods I have been inclined to pay more attention to canonical works which proved most influential as vectors of certain allusive patterns. But even if you are trying to trace a literary tradition chronologically, you can't erase the fact that you are located at the end of the story (so far). A reconstruction of past literary networks, like a costume drama, always bears the stamp of the moment in which it was written – I have inevitably privileged those writers who continue to be influential or fashionable today, rather than those who exerted a great influence for a time but are now little read. Thus I have more to say about Keats and Ovid than I do about Cowley or Statius. It is impossible to know for sure which of today's writers will prove influential and be considered important, so when discussing contemporary literature I have felt free to pursue my personal interests and preferences. My comparatively 'presentist' approach contrasts with that adopted by Helen Cooper in her study of the romance tradition's impact on early modern literature.[26] She actively seeks to recuperate resonances in familiar plays which are inaccessible to modern readers because we no longer know such once popular romance narratives as the story of Valentine and Orson. She is trying all the different entry points to a maze, even those which suddenly reach an impasse. I'm starting with the solution, the end point so far, and working backwards.

I have already mentioned two critics who have helped shape my thinking on allusion, Stephen Hinds and Christopher Ricks. My work has also been influenced by Harold Bloom, Gian Biagio Conte, Thomas M. Greene, Lorna Hardwick, Charles Martindale and David Ross. Within the field of the uncanny I have found Sigmund Freud's famous essay 'Das Unheimliche',[27] Marjorie Garber's *Shakespeare's Ghost Writers: Literature as Uncanny Causality* and Nicholas Royle's *The Uncanny* particularly helpful and suggestive. There are connections between my own study and the field of 'spectral criticism', associated with such critics as Julian Wolfreys and Peter Schwenger, but also differences. Spectral criticism, as David Punter notes, is difficult to define.[28] Rather like queer theory, it embraces a number of different but loosely related impulses. Spectral criticism tends to identify the act of reading as itself uncanny. 'Like writing, ghosts are associated with a certain secondariness or belatedness.'[29] This sense that the act of reading constitutes a kind of dialogue with the dead can be traced back at least to Maurice Blanchot.[30] I find this view of reading suggestive, and I also identify certain reading moments as 'uncanny'. However my own book is concerned with one particular kind of uncanny reading affect, one generated only in certain precise and fairly limited situations. My approach is thus rather different from that taken by Nicholas Royle and Andrew Bennett in the suggestive essays on the uncanny and on ghosts which they include in *Introduction to Literature, Criticism and Theory*. They assert that: 'The uncanny has to do, most of all, with effects of reading, with the experience of *the reader*. The uncanny is not so much *in* the text we are reading: rather, it is like a foreign body within *ourselves*.'[31] For the purposes of my own particular project, I'd instead want to emphasise the importance of the *interplay* between an uncanny phenomenon in the text and an uncanny affect in the reader. The uncanny is both a 'foreign body within ourselves' and something on the page in front of us. In fact it is the simultaneity of these separate but related instantiations of the uncanny which is the most uncanny thing of all.

This simultaneity is very apparent in Chapter 2, a study of nineteenth-century doubles who remind us of their textual predecessors as well as, more immediately, of their own doubled selves. As we move from the uncannily Gothic doubles of the earlier decades (James Hogg and Edgar Allan Poe), through the novels of the mid-Victorian period in which doubles are more usually deployed to drive a sensational plot (Wilkie Collins and Mary Elizabeth Braddon), and arrive at a second, more self-conscious Gothic flowering in the novels of the *fin de siècle* (Robert Louis Stevenson and Oscar Wilde), the tendency to invoke earlier examples of the *Doppelgänger* tradition becomes increasingly pronounced. Mysterious characters, inconsequential plot elements, redundancies and repetitions can all seem more purposeful if we recognise them as symptoms of the *Doppelgänger* text's urge to forge connections with its predecessors, its own 'doubles'. The narrator of the final text discussed in Chapter 2, Joseph Conrad's 'The Secret Sharer', reveals himself to be preoccupied with doubles even before his own encounter with his *Doppelgänger* takes place, and is self-consciously aware of the genre he inhabits. This self-aware, quasi-authorial side to the *Doppelgänger* figure is typical of the later development of the tradition.

Appropriately, this chapter has its own 'double', Chapter 3, which charts the progress of the *Doppelgänger* in later twentieth- and twenty-first-century fiction. As the genre established itself more securely, the possibilities for complexly allusive doubling and redoubling became greater. Some recent writers, such as Sarah Waters and Will Self, find *Doppelgängers* in their Victorian predecessors; others, such as Bret Easton Ellis, respond to the doubles created by their near contemporaries, while Christopher Priest's characters, like those of Daphne du Maurier, seem to be the uncanny doubles of his own earlier creations. When many earlier texts are being referenced, then the clone may also come into play, as a science-fictional subtype of the double as uncanny allusion marker. This is the role played by Sonmi-451 in the final text I discuss in Chapter 3, David Mitchell's *Cloud Atlas*.

Although ruins, the subject of the fourth chapter, are the least obviously uncanny motif in the book, they have often been associated with the supernatural, either because it is believed that ruins are haunted or because the ruins are themselves strongly identified with, or figured as, corpses or ghosts. The ruin has a particular affinity with allusion as both can be described as fragments which invite the reader or viewer to import a missing, whole original to complete the picture. The ruin, when used as an uncanny allusion marker, characteristically enacts as well as describes ruin, dramatising, sometimes resignedly, sometimes more combatively, the later author's sense of belatedness. It is perhaps not surprising that a chapter dealing with the fragments of past civilisations engages with several classical authors: Virgil, Horace and Lucan. Many of the later writers discussed – the anonymous poet of 'The Ruin', Spenser and Shakespeare – also turn back to Rome, and Rome seems somehow present even in depictions of our own civilisation in ruins, such as Mary Shelley's *The Last Man* and J. G. Ballard's *The Drowned World*.

The next chapter, on reanimation, takes as its starting points two episodes from Ovid's *Metamorphoses*, Orpheus and Eurydice, and an inset tale, that of Pygmalion, itself narrated by Orpheus. In later responses to these myths the (re)animated statue and the revenant wife are both used to flag the text's status as an imitation or revival. In many cases this is not all that is being flagged. Both these stories, but particularly that of Pygmalion, are frequently associated with homoeroticism. In earlier texts – including many by Elizabethan writers – this curious connection is often fully apparent. But in other works – including Shakespeare's *The Winter's Tale* and a trio of short stories by Prosper Mérimée, Henry James and Anthony Burgess – homoeroticism is present only as a buried subtext. However the uncanny allusion marker directs the reader to significant textual precursors, and reveals curious repetitions and points of contact which help illuminate the concealed theme. More recent responses to the myths which signal their awareness of the increasingly complex allusive patterns in which they are embedded include Jean Cocteau's Orphic Trilogy, Hitchcock's *Vertigo* and Neil Gaiman's 'Fables & Reflections'.

The ghost in *Hamlet* is the starting point of my penultimate chapter. Ghosts are particularly effective uncanny allusion markers, and the ghost of Hamlet's father first leads us back to one of the text's earliest clear precursors, the story of Amleth as told by Saxo Grammaticus in the *Gesta Danorum*, and then to more remote and uncertain source material in classical literature. The ghostly interplay between these texts has the quasi-incestuous effect of confusing and blurring boundaries between fathers and sons. Ghosts can be seen as representations of a play's own 'ancestors', its sources, but they can also prove to be shades of the future and in some of the later texts discussed in this chapter, such as John Updike's *Gertrude and Claudius* and Tom Stoppard's *Rosencrantz and Guildenstern are Dead*, ghostly figures or visions seem to offer a prophecy of the play's rich afterlife – a word which is itself suggestive of the relationship between allusion and the uncanny. The film versions of the play by Kenneth Branagh and Michael Almereyda also, in different ways, associate the ghost with the future, with the play's afterlife, as well as with the past.

My final chapter opens with a discussion of Eliot's 'familiar compound ghost' in *The Four Quartets*, analysing its reliance on, and re-enactment of, a series of *katabases*, or journeys to the underworld, depicted by Homer, Virgil and Dante.[32] Such journeys typically involve a hero confronting his ancestors (and sometimes his descendents) and such moments often simultaneously dramatise a text's encounter with its own precursors. The compound ghost thus emerges as the sum of all these poets, bearing traces of all these earlier journeys to the underworld. The most recent examples of *katabasis* I discuss, Norman Loftis's *Black Anima* and Derek Walcott's *Omeros*, are also late moments within another allusive sequence, the afterlife of *The Tempest*. Later responses to this play are haunted by memories, corpses and ghosts, which, like the various traces that make up the 'compound ghost', accumulate, coexisting in texts which seem ever more cluttered.

As a wide-ranging and transhistorical study, this book will inevitably not engage with any one period of literary history with the same specialised focus that can be brought to bear on a historicist study of the literature of a single age. Although many readers and critics are sharply alert to the dangers of such an approach, there are parallel dangers, or at least disadvantages, in neglecting the full literary context of a work, a context which includes its sources and later influences, in favour of examining its purely local historical context with scrupulous detail. As Douglas Bruster points out: 'Ironically New Historicism has left us *less* conscious of the fact that literature itself has a history, that it speaks with others' words, talks back to them, and manifests authors' own histories of reading and writing.'[33] Although I don't claim to offer the only way of reading any of my chosen texts, I do aim to show how each is as dependent on texts from its past (or future) as on the cultural context within which it was written, and may well possess certain resonances which remain invisible unless the reader is alert, not just to the immediate historical moment within which it was produced, but to its wider literary context as well.

Notes

1 P. Pullman, *His Dark Materials: Northern Lights* (London: Scholastic Publications Ltd, 1995), p. 187.
2 *Ibid.*, p. 8.
3 For discussions of the relationship between Pullman and Lewis, including Pullman's allusive use of a wardrobe, see B. Hatlen, 'His Dark Materials, a Challenge to Tolkien and Lewis', in Lenz and Scott (eds), *His Dark Materials Illuminated: Critical Essays on Philip Pullman's Trilogy* (Detroit: Wayne State University Press, 2005), pp. 75–94; M. Ward,

'C. S. Lewis and Philip Pullman', in www.planetnarnia.com/assets/documents/74/Lewis_and_Pullman.pdf, accessed 15 June 2010.
4 C. S. Lewis, *The Lion, the Witch and the Wardrobe* (London: HarperCollins Publishers, 2001), p. 14.
5 See S. Freud, 'The Uncanny', in *The Standard Edition of the Complete Works of Sigmund Freud*, trans. J. Strachey (London: Hogarth Press, 1955), 24 vols, vol. 17, pp. 219–52, pp. 236.
6 The phrase 'allusion-marker' is sometimes used by critics to indicate the phrase or line which constitutes and thus signals a specific allusion. However I use the term 'uncanny allusion marker' to signify a motif which may signal the fact or presence of allusion *per se*. It may, but need not, also enable the reader to identify precisely which text or texts is being alluded to.
7 J. Hollander, *The Figure of Echo: A Mode of Allusion in Milton and After* (Berkeley: University of California Press, 1981), p. 73; K. McSweeney, 'Literary Allusion and the Poetry of Seamus Heaney', *Style*, Spring (1999) http://findarticles.com/p/articles/mi_m2342/is_1_33/ai_58055908/pg_2/, accessed 15 June 2010.
8 C. Ricks, *Allusion to the Poets* (Oxford: Oxford University Press, 2004), p. 12.
9 Horace, *Satires, Epistles and Ars Poetica*, trans. H. Rushton Fairclough (Cambridge, Mass.: Harvard University Press, 1978), *Ep.* 2.1.34–7.
10 J. Butt (ed.), *The Poems of Alexander Pope* (London: Routledge, 1993), 6 vols, vol. 6, p. 205, ll. 119–26.
11 See, for example, my discussion of 'Full Fathom Five' in Chapter 7.
12 S. A. Brown, 'Classics Reanimated: Ted Hughes and Reflexive Translation', in R. Rees (ed.), *Ted Hughes and the Classics* (Oxford: Oxford University Press, 2009), pp. 282–99, p. 283.
13 Ricks, *Allusion to the Poets*, pp. 36–7.
14 S. Hinds, *Allusion and Intertext: Dynamics of Appropriation in Roman Poetry* (Cambridge: Cambridge University Press, 1998), p. 1.
15 Hinds, *Allusion and Intertext*, pp. 4–5.
16 This link has been noted by many critics. See for example P. Burian, 'Myth into *Muthos*: The Shaping of the Tragic Plot', in P. E. Easterling (ed.), *The Cambridge Companion to Greek Tragedy* (Cambridge: Cambridge University Press, 1997), pp. 178–208, p. 196.
17 D. Grene and R. Lattimore, *Euripides V* (Chicago and London: University of Chicago Press, 1959), ll. 534–7.
18 *Ibid.*, pp. 558–9.
19 Hinds, *Allusion and Intertext*, p. 50.
20 Ricks, *Allusion to the Poets*, p. 6.
21 Compare E. Cook, *Against Coercion: Games Poets Play* (Stanford: Stanford University Press, 1998), p. 100. Camela Perri also discusses

the limits of allusion in 'On Alluding', *Poetics*, 7 (1978), 289–307. She distinguishes, for example, between allusions which only tacitly indicate an earlier text and those which explicitly identify a source. Some would describe the latter as 'references' rather than 'allusions'.

22 C. H. Herford and P. Simpson (eds), *Ben Jonson* (Oxford: Clarendon Press, 1986), 11 vols, vol. 4, pp. 47–8.

23 J. Jervis, 'Uncanny Presences', in J. Collins and J. Jervis (eds), *Uncanny Modernity: Cultural Theories, Modern Anxieties* (Basingstoke: Palgrave Macmillan, 2008), pp. 10–50, p. 20.

24 S. A. Brown, '"There is No End but Addition": The Later Reception of Shakespeare's Classicism', in C. Martindale and A. B. Taylor (eds), *Shakespeare and the Classics* (Cambridge: Cambridge University Press, 2004), pp. 277–93, p. 286.

25 *Ibid.*, pp. 288–9.

26 H. Cooper, *English Romance in Time: Transforming Motifs from Geoffrey of Monmouth to the Death of Shakespeare* (Oxford: Oxford University Press, 2004).

27 A great deal has been written on this influential essay. A particularly insightful analysis of its own inherently 'uncanny' texture is offered by Robin Lydenberg in 'Freud's Uncanny Narratives', *PMLA*, 112.5 (1997), 1072–86.

28 D. Punter, 'Spectral Criticism', in J. Wolfreys (ed.), *Introducing Criticism at the 21st Century*, (Edinburgh: Edinburgh University Press, 2002), pp. 259–78, p. 259.

29 P. Buse and A. Stott, 'Introduction: A Future for Haunting', in P. Buse and A. Stott (eds), *Ghosts: Deconstruction, Psychoanalysis, History* (Basingstoke: Macmillan, 1999), pp. 1–20, p. 8.

30 Punter, 'Spectral Criticism', p. 259.

31 A. Bennett and N. Royle, *Introduction to Literature, Criticism and Theory*, 3rd edition (Harlow: Pearson Education, 2004), p. 41.

32 The boundaries between the different chapters, like those between the texts discussed, are somewhat permeable. The theme of reanimation is significant in more than one *Doppelgänger* text, ghosts are inevitably encountered in journeys to the underworld, and the compound ghost itself demonstrates many features of the uncanny double.

33 D. Bruster, *Quoting Shakespeare: Form and Culture in Early Modern Drama* (Lincoln: University of Nebraska Press, 2000), p. 3.

2

Uncanny doubles: part one

> What annoyed him most was not so much the loss of his shadow, but the knowledge that there was already a story about a man without a shadow. All the people at home knew that story. If he went back and told them his story they would say he was just imitating the old one. He did not care to be called unoriginal, so he decided to say nothing about it, which was the most sensible thing to do.[1]

In Hans Christian Andersen's 1847 story 'The Shadow' a sensitive young writer becomes separated from his shadow.[2] This interloping shadow first assumes his original's place in society and then has his former owner put to death. The young protagonist's profession is significant, for the relationship between an individual and his replicant becomes, in the passage quoted above, an emblem for the writer's relationship with his source. The hero's horror of bodily duplication and eventual dissolution is matched by his fear of (literary) repetition, of being merely secondary. The hero (and of course Andersen) is well aware that the idea of a man without a shadow had already been taken as the theme of a well-known tale, Adelbert von Chamisso's 'Peter Schlemihl' (1814). However Andersen, like the shadow, ended up usurping the place of this 'original', for it is Andersen's later version which is the better-known story.[3]

A survey of the history of literary doubles reveals a marked tendency for texts which feature doubles to position themselves as the 'doubles' of some earlier textual ancestor, or at least to signal their own reliance on earlier treatments of the theme. The double is thus, as it were, redoubled. Texts, like characters, can be haunted by strange simulacra of themselves, and this 'redoubling' enhances the characteristically uncanny effect produced by the *Doppelgänger* theme. Within the plots of such stories doubles create unease through a *frisson* of *déjà vu*. They are familiar but not in a reassuring way; indeed their homeliness perhaps makes them all the more unhomely.[4] In the 'redoubled' text the disquiet of the character faced with the strangely familiar is shared by the reader who feels that he or she has read something like this before.

In the next two chapters I will explore the use of the double as an uncanny allusion marker which draws attention to a text's status as an act of repetition, to its own 'doubling' of its source material. The first of these paired chapters focuses on nineteenth-century texts, tracing the development of the uncanny double from the Romantic Gothic tradition through to the Victorian sensation novels of the mid century, and concluding with an account of the supernatural tales of the *fin de siècle*. The second chapter of the pair brings the journey of the double up to the present day, identifying patterns of uncannily reflexive 'redoublement' in more recent texts.

Within Western culture it is possible to trace the *Doppelgänger* motif back to the literature of Greece and Rome. The tradition whereby Helen was replaced with a phantom, a perfect counterfeit of herself who remained in Troy while the real Helen lay low in Egypt, is one early example.[5] Going forward to Rome, Plautus's *Menaechmi* and *Amphitryon* both feature significant doubles. In the former play the doubles are separated twins; in the latter the doubling effect is created by supernatural means. Doubles, separated siblings in both instances, can be found in Shakespeare's *Twelfth Night* and *The Comedy of Errors*. In Ben Jonson's *The Sad Shepherd* (left unfinished at Jonson's death in 1637) a witch transforms herself into Maid Marian's double to create mischief. But such doubles are not characteristically invested with a conspicuously uncanny charge; they may have a magical or miraculous provenance but they are rarely radically mysterious. It was not until the rise of the Gothic tradition, in the late eighteenth century, that the double really came into his (or occasionally her) own.[6] The sheer number of *Doppelgänger* texts, as well as the attraction to the supernatural experienced by many writers of this era, provided the right circumstances for the double to become a potent uncanny allusion marker.

A central text for any study of the Gothic double is James Hogg's *The Private Memoirs and Confessions of a Justified Sinner* (1824). The novel's complex plot hinges around Robert Wringhim, who is haunted by a mysterious double, the devilish Gil-Martin. Events in the narrative are shrouded in ambiguity and we are never quite sure whether Gil-Martin simply incites Robert to murder his own half-brother, George Colwan, or actually murders George himself in Robert's form. The text is full of internal splits and doublings, with two voices, those of the editor and the 'sinner', Robert, providing conflicting versions of the story. One of the novel's many uncertainties relates to the ultimate fate of Robert Wringhim whose eventual death by hanging may be either a murder or a suicide:

> This was accounted a great wonder; and everyone said, if the Devil had not assisted him, it was impossible the thing could have been done; for, in general, these ropes are so brittle, being made of green hay, that they will scarcely bear to be bound over the rick. And, the more to horrify the good people of this neighbourhood, the driver said, when he first came in view, he could almost give his oath that he saw two people busily engaged at the hay-rick going round it and round it, and he thought they were dressing it.[7]

This uncertainty is mirrored in other indeterminacies surrounding the corpse. Wringhim is twice exhumed. In one account he is revealed to have had 'fine yellow hair'.[8] But when the 'editor' makes the same experiment he discovers – though without commenting on the discrepancy – that the hair of the corpse is 'neither black nor fair, but of a darkish dusk'.[9] Even the remains of Robert Wringhim have somehow been 'split'.[10]

Although not itself uncannily allusive, *Justified Sinner* provided the springboard for uncanny redoubling in subsequent *Doppelgänger* texts. Wringhim is exhumed twice, yet he fails to come back to life even though his body is raised to an unnatural sitting posture and is reported to be wonderfully well preserved. The refusal to let Wringhim lie parallels Hogg's refusal to let go of his novel, giving us a whole series of 'endings'. In fact even the novel's final lines don't securely effect closure; a few years later Hogg was to pen another tale of a mysterious double, 'Strange Letter of a Lunatic' (1827).[11] This story would make better sense as a pilot for *Justified Sinner* than as a later coda, for it is (though not identical) a pared down version of a very similar scenario. The narrator, James Beatman, accepts snuff from a mysterious old man and is subsequently troubled by encounters with his exact double. Hogg drives home the resemblance to *Justified Sinner* when the 'other' James Beatman even says to the narrator 'you are either a rank counterfeit, or, what I rather begin to suspect, the devil in my likeness.'[12] Like many *Doppelgänger* narratives it concludes with a fight in which the roles of agent and victim are confused. James Beatman and his (apparently equally innocent and indignant) double agree to duel: 'We fired at six paces distance and I fell. Rather a sure sign that I *was* the right James Beatman, but which of the I's it was that fell I never knew till this day, nor ever can.'[13]

The same technique is used here as in *Justified Sinner* to create an ambiguity as to whether a double of some kind was really involved in the text's climactic act of violence. Just as two people were glimpsed by a witness at the scene of Robert Wringhim's suicide, so the doctor confirms that although circumstances point to Beatman's death being a botched suicide in fact the nature of the wound meant it could not have been self-inflicted. This repetition might seem like a failure of invention on Hogg's part; this is certainly the view of Karl Miller.[14] But the very persistence of the duplication perhaps points to a more complex reading of the two texts' relationship.

Once again the doubling effect is not confined to the surface fiction; it also inheres in the story's textual apparatus. Although the whole story is of course written by Hogg he affects to address the 'letter' to himself, as though its fictional author, James Beatman, were real. Hogg thus has a double role in the tale as its real writer and its fictional editor, just as the unfortunate Beatman is split into two, each apparently genuinely convinced that he is the 'original'. Moreover, to confuse the picture, it is hinted that yet a third James Beatman may be performing evil deeds and blackening the names of the other two. Significantly it is of an assault on a lady that the two Beatmans are accused – an offence of which Gil-Martin, in the form of Robert Wringhim, was also guilty. This disruptive additional double, this third James Beatman, might be read as a sign of superfluous proliferation, a reminder that this text enacts as well as depicts doubling. The short story's echoes of the earlier novel's complex doubling dynamic make the later text itself an uncanny double, the shadow of the more celebrated *Justified Sinner*.

In a novel which strongly echoes *Justified Sinner*, *The Master of Ballantrae* (1889) by Robert Louis Stevenson offers yet another story of two rival brothers, Henry and James Durie, one the evil genius of the other.[15] A possible relationship with Hogg is hinted at in his fictional editor's brief preface.[16] In passing, he notes that an earlier member of the Durie family 'had some strange passages with the devil',[17] an immediate clue alerting the reader to look out for affinities between this new novel about Scottish brothers and the earlier *Justified Sinner*, to see parallels between the unnamed ancestor of Stevenson's Master and the celebrated literary ancestor of his *Master*.

Stevenson's treatment of the *Doppelgänger* theme is not of course identical to that of Hogg. This pair of brothers is not troubled by any otherworldly third party. Instead the uncanny qualities of Gil-Martin are transfused into the younger brother, James. A further important distinction can be drawn between Hogg's brothers and Stevenson's. In Hogg's novel introverted, bookish, unpopular Robert is associated with the uncanny whereas extrovert, athletic, sanguine George is presented as an entirely straightforward young man. In Stevenson the situation is precisely reversed. The charming and charismatic James Durie superficially resembles George, but it is James, rather than his quieter, duller and more studious younger brother Henry who is 'uncanny'. Throughout the novel important decisions are made on the toss of a coin, and this action can be seen as an emblem of the novel's play with doubles. *The Master of Ballantrae* plays tails to *Justified Sinner*'s heads. For *The Master of Ballantrae* doesn't just *contain* a pair of uncanny doubles – it is itself the second of a pair of uncanny doubles, the reversed mirror image of *Justified Sinner*.

As well as having a rather devilish disposition, James's credentials as a *Doppelgänger* figure are suggested by his several semi-miraculous returns from death.[18] Reanimation, a topic I return to in more detail in Chapter 5, is as potent an uncanny allusion marker as doubling. Again, as in *Justified Sinner*, the idea of some kind of return from the dead, reanimation or exhumation, mirrors and intensifies the sense of *déjà vu* or repetition inherent in the *Doppelgänger* theme. So is Stevenson's combination of the two themes a move which is designed to draw attention to the novel's allusive processes or simply coincidence? It is now widely acknowledged that Stevenson, once thought of as a writer of straightforward boys' adventure stories, is a tricky and self-consciously sophisticated novelist.[19] And there are various clues in the novel which invite us to interpret the theme of resurrection within an inter- and extratextual framework of allusion rather than simply as a realistic, or even realistically uncanny, device.

The novel's subtitle, 'A Winter's Tale', may invoke only the simplest meaning of that expression. A winter's tale means a fireside yarn and the subtitle can thus be read as a straightforward description of Stevenson's own engrossing adventure story. But it is difficult to read the phrase without thinking of Shakespeare's play. On the surface there is little to connect *The Master of Ballantrae* with *The Winter's Tale*. However the theme of reanimation is common to both works. Hermione's apparent death and miraculous reappearance are comparable with similar 'resurrections' undergone by Stevenson's 'Master', James Durie.[20] James seems to cheat death not once, but three times, and the novel itself can of course be seen as a 'resurrection' of Hogg's earlier treatment of a similar theme. If the novel's subtitle does gesture towards the theme of resurrection it does so, admittedly, rather obliquely. But (although it makes authorial intention more difficult to determine) an uncertain allusion, as I suggested in the introduction, can be more effective than an unambiguous one. As we have seen, the most effective instances of the uncanny are those which raise genuine problems of definition or interpretation. In this novel we are never fully certain whether James's resurrections from the dead are completely 'canny'. Similarly the hint at a significant allusion to Shakespeare's own play of resurrection suggested by the phrase 'a winter's tale' and the demand it places on the reader to fill in the blanks, is more effective than a more explicit paratextual detail – for example the use of a quotation from Hermione's 'resurrection' scene as an epigraph – could ever be.

A further possible hint at resurrection requires the reader to import knowledge, not of a text, but of a famous Scottish scandal, into the narrative of *The Master of Ballantrae*. James's first 'resurrection' follows his supposed death while fighting for the cause of Bonnie Prince Charlie. The news is brought to his family by James's companion, the Chevalier de Burke. If the novel's subtitle gestures towards the theme of resurrection then so perhaps does his naming of this character. Stevenson had already treated the theme of grave robbing in his 1883 short story 'The Bodysnatcher', and it may be no coincidence that 'dead' James is brought back home by a man who shares the name of one of the two notorious Scottish resurrectionists, Burke and Hare. As well as thus representing a kind of 'resurrection' of the author's own work, the name Burke intensifies the aura of the supernatural around James by hinting that he may really have lain in the grave.

James's second false death is rather more dramatic. Here, if there is an allusion, a suggestion that more is being resurrected than a fictional character, it is perhaps best characterised as a more generic allusion to the conventions of *Doppelgänger* fiction. James's flirtation with his brother's wife forces Henry to challenge him to a duel in which James is apparently killed. Yet his body mysteriously vanishes from the scene and we later learn that he was only badly wounded and was spirited away by free traders. The account of the 'fatal' stroke, offered by a witness to the duel, Henry's secretary Mr Mackellar, is somewhat imprecise and confused. His narrative is consistent with an entirely realistic fight yet also invokes a common feature of *Doppelgänger* narratives, one we have already seen at work in Hogg's treatments of the theme, the confusion between agent and object:

> For it is beyond doubt he now recognised himself for lost, and had some taste of the cold agony of fear; or he had never attempted the foul stroke. I cannot say I followed it, my untrained eye was never quick enough to seize details, but it appears he caught his brother's blade with his left hand, a practice not permitted. Certainly Mr. Henry only saved himself by leaping on one side; as certainly the Master, lunging in the air, stumbled on his knee, and before he could move the sword was through his body.[21]

Later Mackellar explains that James was killed 'in the very act of a foul stroke'[22] and the impression is given that he was aiming for his brother but somehow stabbed himself by accident. Mackellar's apparent innocence of the uncanny traditions he is tapping into enhances the effective ambiguities attendant on James's fall. This is yet another example of the uncanny – like allusion – benefiting from understatement. We have already seen a confusion between suicide and *Doppelgänger* murder in both of Hogg's tales, and in several other texts, including Edgar Allan Poe's 'William Wilson' (1839) and Oscar Wilde's *The Picture of Dorian Gray* (1891) – both discussed below – there is an elision between an attack on oneself and an attack on one's double. The 'vanishing corpse' is another hallmark of *Doppelgänger* literature and, here too, Stevenson hovers on the threshold between the natural and the supernatural in his account of James's improbable but not impossible disappearance from the scene of the duel.

The reader's credulity is stretched still further by James's final resurrection, which can perhaps be seen as an echo of the exhumation in *Justified Sinner*. Here he does literally rise from the grave, having learnt certain mysterious Eastern techniques which have allowed him to mimic the appearance of death. Once again an improbable but rational explanation for 'resurrection' collides with an alternative explanation, an appeal to the uncanny: 'This man has the name of my brother,' says Henry, 'but it's well understood that he was never canny.'[23] James is briefly revived by his Indian servant but barely regains consciousness. His final act is to cause the (almost instantaneous) death of his brother Henry, who expires from apparent shock. The near simultaneity of the two brothers' deaths compounds the narrative's flirtation with the uncanny and its self-conscious awareness of those *Doppelgänger* texts in which a man's fate is tied up with that of his double. However the novel ultimately refuses explicitly to suggest an uncanny or supernatural explanation for its many improbable events despite the odd teaser. By invoking the atmosphere and conventions of 'uncanny' *Doppelgänger* literature but then negating the supernatural as a possibility Stevenson forces the reader to become more self-conscious about the way he or she tackles the novel. Stevenson withholds from the reader a full immersion in the story of the Master, instead inviting us to place it within a wider intertextual network of texts and discourses, and through doing so to gain a heightened awareness of the instability of the novel's fictive world.

Two further fractured allusions, one to an earlier novel by Stevenson and one to the 'real' world, are characteristic of his strategies. In these cases no double appears in the novel. Instead characters turn out to be doubles of someone outside the text. Towards the beginning of the Chevalier de Burke's inset narrative he refers to a quarrel and then a race between James Durie and one 'Alan Black Stewart (or some such name . . .)'.[24] It is distracting enough to have one of Stevenson's most famous characters, the romantic swashbuckler from *Kidnapped* (1886), dragged into the novel, and still more distracting when an editorial note is offered: '*Note by Mr Mackellar.* – Should this not be Alan *Breck* Stewart, afterwards notorious as the Appin murderer? The Chevalier is often very weak on names.'[25] Still more outrageously obtrusive is the following note Mackellar offers on the name of the pirate with whom James briefly serves:

> *Note by Mr Mackellar.* – This Teach of the *Sarah* must not be confused with the celebrated *Blackbeard*. The dates and facts by no means tally. It is possible the second Teach may have at once borrowed the name and imitated the more excessive part of his manners from the first. Even the Master of Ballantrae could make admirers.[26]

A mistake over a name and the imitation of a name are moves ascribed to Burke and 'Teach' respectively but in reality both are part of Stevenson's own playful and self-conscious manipulation of the text's increasingly permeable boundaries, and of its place within a literary tradition characterised, like the aspiring 'Teach', by the urge to imitate and repeat.[27] 'Teach', Alan Black Stewart and of course Burke are all in a sense 'doubles'. But we have to look outside this novel to find each man's *Doppelgänger*.

Stevenson's *fin-de-siècle* novel invokes, even if it doesn't securely inhabit, the much earlier traditions of Romantic Gothic. The novels produced in the intervening decades, in the mid-Victorian period, are associated more readily with realism than with the supernatural.[28] Yet they too often deploy the double to mysterious and almost uncanny effect. Dickens's novels are full of doubles. Sometimes (as is the case with the likeness between Sydney Carton and Charles Darnay in *A Tale of Two Cities*) they are little more than a handy plot device. Resemblance (between Esther and Lady Dedlock) operates more mysteriously in *Bleak House*, although the reader will soon guess that the two women are really mother and daughter. More potentially uncanny are the paired doubles in *Dombey and Son*. Malevolent old Mrs Brown and her haggard daughter Alice are ominously similar to scheming, bedizened Mrs Skrewton and her despairing daughter Edith Dombey. Yet the effect of the doubling is a moralising rather than a truly uncanny one and, once again, any uncanny effect is softened when it turns out that Alice and Edith are cousins.[29]

It is in the 'sensation' novel of the 1850s and 1860s that the most striking mid-Victorian doubles can be found. The best known example is Wilkie Collins's *The Woman in White* (1859). Rather than analyse this much discussed text's own use of the motif, I will demonstrate how two slightly later texts signal reliance on Collins's best known work through their own handling of doubles; doubles which operate as uncanny allusion markers revealing a debt to Collins's defining intervention into the sensation novel genre. *The Woman in White* pivots around Count Fosco's despicable plot to defraud the heroine Laura Fairlie of her wealth and identity. Fosco, with Laura's own villainous husband Sir Percival Glyde, arranges for Laura to be exchanged with a simple minded girl whom she strongly resembles, Anne Catherick. When Anne (eventually revealed to be Laura's half-sister) dies naturally, Glyde pretends that the body is Laura's and claims her wealth as his inheritance. Laura meanwhile is incarcerated in an asylum, and her claim to be a rich lady rather than a poor lunatic only makes her appear to be more decisively mad.

A slightly later sensation novel, Mary Elizabeth Braddon's *Lady Audley's Secret* (1862), as well as being spectacularly successful in its own right, can be seen as a kind of response to *The Woman in White*, its 'double'. Rather than signalling its relationship with Collins by featuring truly significant *Doppelgängers*, Braddon encourages the reader to notice the interplay with Collins by introducing a 'double' for the protagonist, Lady Audley, whose role is comparatively negligible. This is Phoebe Marks, her watchful and ambitious maid. When Braddon reveals her likeness to Lady Audley the reader is encouraged to anticipate a plot twist hinging on this coincidence. Everything seems ripe for an exchange of identities:

> The likeness which the lady's maid bore to Lucy Audley was, perhaps, a point of sympathy between the two women. It was not to be called a striking likeness; a stranger might have seen them both together, and yet have failed to remark it. But there were certain dim and shadowy lights in which, meeting Phoebe Marks gliding softly through the dark oak passages of the Court, or under the shrouded avenues in the garden, you might have easily mistaken her for my lady.[30]

Many reading the novel for the first time will detect a clear significance in the traits which Phoebe does *not* share with her mistress:

> 'Not at all, Phoebe,' said the little lady, superbly; 'you *are* like me, and your features are very nice; it is only colour that you want. My hair is pale yellow shot with gold, and yours is drab; my eyebrows and eyelashes are dark brown, and yours are almost – I scarcely like to say it, but they're almost white, my dear Phoebe. Your complexion is sallow, and mine is pink and rosy. Why, with a bottle of hair-dye, such as we see advertised in the papers, and a pot of rouge, you'd be as good-looking as I, any day, Phoebe.'[31]

These differences, as Lady Audley herself informs us in what many readers must imagine to be a rather clumsy prolepsis, are precisely those which can most easily be erased. And a further inconsequential detail again seems to serve to build Phoebe up into a convincing simulacrum of the well-educated former governess, Lady Audley, in some future intrigue:[32]

> 'But they say traveling makes people genteel, Luke. I've been on the continent with my lady, through all manner of curious places; and you know, when I was a child, Squire Horton's daughters taught me to speak a little French, and I found it so nice to be able to talk to the people abroad.'[33]

And yet Lady Audley's double remains inert and undeveloped and thus, paradoxically, draws more attention to herself. What is Phoebe for? Perhaps simply to trigger memories of *The Woman in White*. It is not only in being a young female *Doppelgänger* that Phoebe recalls Collins's novel to the reader. She is described in a way which might bring Laura Fairlie herself to mind through a further effect of physical resemblance, of intertextual doubling. Laura's colouring is delicate to the point of deliquescence:

> Her hair is of so faint and pale a brown – *not flaxen*, and yet almost as light; *not golden*, and yet almost as glossy – that it nearly *melts*, here and there, into the *shadow* of the hat. It is plainly parted and drawn back over her ears, and the line of it ripples naturally as it crosses her forehead.[34] (my italics)

Although Phoebe's colouring is not in fact the same as Laura's, and although she is presented in a much less appealing way, the lexical and rhetorical patterns themselves draw the two girls together:

> She might have been pretty, I think, but for the one fault in her small oval face. This fault was an absence of colour. *Not* one tinge of crimson flushed the waxen whiteness of her cheeks; *not* one *shadow* of brown redeemed the pale insipidity of her eyebrows and eyelashes; not one glimmer of *gold* or auburn relieved the dull *flaxen* of her hair. Even her dress was spoiled by this same deficiency. The pale lavender muslin faded into a sickly gray, and the ribbon knotted round her throat *melted* into the same neutral hue.[35] (my italics)

The description of Phoebe as a bride reinforces her uncanny, even ghostly, appearance and invites further recollections of *The Woman in White*:

> A very dim and shadowy lady, vague of outline, and faint of colouring, with eyes, hair, complexion and dress all melting into such pale and uncertain shades that, in the obscure light of the foggy November morning a superstitious stranger might have mistaken the bride for the ghost of some other bride, dead and buried in the vault below the church.[36]

Lynda Hart identifies the apparently gratuitous doubling between maid and mistress as a 'curious excess' and argues that it hints at a relationship which is narcissistic and homoerotic. She goes on to suggest that the slightly sinister reference to Phoebe's likeness to another bride is an allusion to Lucy Audley's previous existence as

Helen Talboys, a bride who pretends to be dead in order to carve out a new life for herself.[37] But if we look outside the text, we might instead identify 'some other bride' as Laura Fairlie, who is 'buried' and yet returns from the dead to be married once again. In a strange vision Laura's sister Marian imagines Laura as a literal revenant: '[Walter] was kneeling by a tomb of white marble, and the shadow of a veiled woman rose out of the grave beneath and waited by his side.' [38] This vision will be uncannily fulfilled when Walter encounters the veiled Laura standing next to 'her' tomb. Of course these two alternatives, Lynda Hart's suggestion and my own, are complementary rather than mutually exclusive. Helen's return from apparent death (as Lucy), after being mourned by the man who loves her, clearly echoes the similarly miraculous 'rebirth' of Laura, although the latter heroine is the victim of a crime rather than its perpetrator.

The link between these two revenant wives is just one of many parallels between the two novels. When we read *Lady Audley's Secret* against *The Woman in White* other common themes and plot elements are immediately obvious.[39] An illegal exchange of spouses is attempted, there is a dramatic fire, a woman is thought to be mad and is locked up in an asylum.[40] But the elements have been completely reconfigured. Here it is a woman, Lady Audley, who is the novel's villain. She marries bigamously and then attempts to murder her first husband when he returns. When the nephew of her second husband tries to investigate her past she tries to murder him as well, burning down the inn at which he is staying. She is finally unmasked and locked away in a lunatic asylum after it is revealed that she inherited madness from her mother. (This emphasis on inheritance is perhaps itself a further allusion marker, as madness can be seen as a function both of her genetic and her textual ancestry.)

By introducing a double with no role to play in the plot the text perhaps encourages us to probe the relationship between the two novels rather more closely. *Lady Audley*'s own narrative, like that of *Justified Sinner*, can be shown to be 'double' though not because of any obvious devices such as a change of narrator. Rather, its many points of contact with *The Woman in White* invite the reader to uncover an alternative narrative, a concealed double as it were of *Lady Audley*, hiding beneath the text's surface, waiting to be unveiled or exhumed, like the secret stories Natasha Sajé describes in her poem 'Tongues':

Some stories float; others are held under
until someone sees a small series of bubbles and knows
there's a body to be dredged.[41]

The novel's hero, Robert Audley, is an attractive *flâneur* in the tradition of Dickens's Sydney Carton or Eugene Wrayburn, an apparently indolent young man who is revealed to have hidden strength of mind and moral purpose. But, looked at through a *Woman in White* lens, Robert might be read differently. On the surface, he is acting on behalf of his friend and his uncle, Lady Audley's first and second husbands respectively. But if we import the motivating force of Collins's villains, financial gain, into the story we might start to wonder if Robert Audley is really so disinterested. He surely has a lot to lose if his uncle's young wife has a male heir, and his hunt for the 'truth' about her might seem sinister. His near death by fire (started by Lady Audley) is also significant because it seems to echo the death of the unscrupulous Percival Glyde, himself killed in a fire.

An allusion's combination of sameness and difference from the original text raises questions about its intention and effect. In this instance the repetition of the fire and other parallels between these two sensation novels force the reader to ask whether Robert Audley is Percival Glyde's opposite or his secret double. Approached in this way Lady Audley's eventual confinement in a lunatic asylum becomes more sinister. Even without any possible pressure exerted on the novel by *The Woman in White* the ending is ambiguous as there is a disquieting informality in the processes which condemn Lady Audley to a life imprisonment without trial. Although the motives for secrecy are more or less benign – the wish to spare her elderly second husband distress for example – there are uneasy echoes of other novels – and *The Woman in White* is only the most famous example in a long tradition – in which the innocent and sane are maliciously accused of madness.[42] We cannot of course claim that Lady Audley is 'really' innocent. Instead what the novel does, via its 'redoublement' of *The Woman in White*, is encourage its readers to think about the way different stories, different definitions of madness in women for example, compete for our attention and problematise the idea of a definitive version of events. Robert Audley himself gives us the clue that his own 'reality' (itself of course a fiction) might be the double of some earlier story:

He remembered a story – a morbid, hideous, yet delicious story, which had once pleasantly congealed his blood on a social winter's evening – the story of a man, monomaniac, perhaps, who had been haunted at every turn by the image of an unburied kinsman who could not rest in his unhallowed hiding-place. What if that dreadful story had its double in reality? What if he were henceforth to be haunted by the phantom of murdered George Talboys?[43]

It is significant that Robert seems here to be remembering Wilkie Collins's own tale 'Mad Monkton', and on the next page we are given a still stronger nudge towards *The Woman in White* when Robert remarks, 'I haven't read Alexandre Dumas and Wilkie Collins for nothing.'[44] And perhaps it is Dumas's account of that famous switched and imprisoned double, the Man in the Iron Mask (in *Le Vicomte de Bragelonne*, 1847–50) which is on Robert's mind at this point.

Just a few years later, in 1866, a further novel, also featuring doubles, and pursuing similar themes to both *The Woman in White* and *Lady Audley's Secret* was published. Its most arresting if not its central character is an unscrupulous adventuress, Lydia Gwilt, who, like Lady Audley, wants to profit from being thought the wife of one man while being legally wedded to another. To compound the similarities with both earlier texts, this novel includes a climactic scene in an asylum in which the wicked heroine tries to kill a man so that she can pose as his widow. This scenario operates in counterpoint to that of *Lady Audley's Secret*. Lady Audley thought she had killed a man, her legal husband, and is desperate that no one should guess they were ever married. The heroine of this later text also mistakenly thinks that she has killed a man but, by contrast with her literary predecessor, she goes to great lengths to give the (false) impression that they were married so that she can inherit his money.

What makes the novel still more striking is that this further allusive copy of *The Woman in White* is in fact Collins's own *Armadale*. The audacity of the repetition, not just of his earlier novel but of the intervening and equally well known *Lady Audley's Secret*, is mirrored in the audacity of the novel's use of doubles. The novel opens with the story of two Allan Armadales, family connections, one of whom is driven to murder the other when his prospective wife is effectively stolen from him. Both Allans have sons and both are also called Allan Armadale, though one of this younger generation goes by the name of Ozias Midwinter. To have a pair of doubles who share a name threatens our credulity and the further identical doubling of the sons' names betokens some bravado on the author's part, and also gestures towards the novel's own reliance on its two famous predecessors. A purely internal 'redoubling' echoes the intertextual redoubling. *Armadale* is in a sense a triple rather than a double, given that it mirrors so closely not one but two earlier texts. This tripling might be paralleled with an otherwise rather inconsequential reference by Allan Armadale to a magic trick involving three brothers:

> Deuce take the pounds, shillings, and pence! I wish they could all three get rid of themselves, like the Bedouin brothers at the show. Don't you remember the Bedouin brothers, Mr. Brock? 'Ali will take a lighted torch, and jump down the throat of his brother Muli; Muli will take a lighted torch, and jump down the throat of his brother Hassan; and Hassan, taking a third lighted torch, will conclude the performances by jumping down his own throat, and leaving the spectators in total darkness.' Wonderfully good, that – what I call real wit, with a fine strong flavour about it. Wait a minute! Where are we? We have lost ourselves again.[45]

The obtrusiveness of the over-weighty simile is compounded by Allan's rather reflexive praise of the trick's wit followed by the reference to being lost.

If *Armadale* in any way fuses as well as simply repeats the two earlier *Doppelgänger* novels then it does so through the person of Lydia Gwilt. *The Woman in White* and *Lady Audley's Secret* present us with two antithetical females, innocent victim and evil murderess; Lydia Gwilt offers a subtle synthesis between the two extremes, a two-sided coin which continues to spin. Her love for her real husband, Ozias Midwinter, is genuine, and her plan to pose as the widow of the other Allan Armadale is so ill thought-through (because it fails to take Ozias's reactions into account) as to seem almost unreal. It is to the complex Lydia that Collins allows a moment of strange self-knowledge: 'How unnatural all this would be, if it was written in a book!'[46] This classic instance of dramatic irony would seem to forge a knowing complicity between author and reader which bypasses the fictional and thus unconscious Lydia. But Lydia *is* writing in a book, albeit only her journal, and thus can be said to be the co-creator, not just the butt, of irony.

Despite the great popularity of sensation novelists such as Collins and Braddon, later nineteenth-century writers seem to have taken their inspiration from earlier and more explicitly 'uncanny' treatments of the double. We have already seen traces of a relationship between Hogg and Stevenson. The affinities between Oscar Wilde's *The Picture of Dorian Gray* (1891) and Edgar Allan Poe's 1839 tale 'William Wilson' are still more striking. In Poe's story, as in *Armadale*, the narrator and his double share a name.[47] William Wilson first meets his double at school and gradually reveals to the reader an astonishing string of coincidences – they share a birthday as well as a name and even look nearly identical, although the double, unlike the narrator, is only able to speak in a whisper. As the narrator grows up he falls into a life of crime and debauchery and the other William Wilson, like Dorian's portrait, acts as his conscience, warning him and intervening to prevent him from carrying out evil deeds. Eventually the double follows Wilson to a masked ball where Wilson is driven to stab his stalker. He seems to see himself in a mirror splattered with blood but this is only an illusion and the double retains a clearly separate identity, even though with his dying words he claims that Wilson has murdered himself in murdering his double, his better half.

The *Doppelgänger*'s role as a depraved man's conscience, the elision of murder and suicide, anticipate the way the double is deployed in Wilde's novel. But the portrait is only one of Dorian's doubles, and Poe is not Wilde's only source. I have already suggested that *Doppelgänger* texts seem particularly permeable to outside influences and, in Wilde's novel, Dorian appears to experience direct encounters with his own literary sources and even with his author.

Dorian Gray's slide into evil culminates in the brutal murder of his devoted friend Basil Hallward, creator of the fatal portrait. Dorian needs to get rid of the body in a hurry and enlists the help of a former intimate friend, the scientist Alan Campbell. The relationship between the two men, which we only learn about in retrospect, is a mysterious one:

> They had been great friends once, five years before – almost inseparable, indeed. Then the intimacy had come suddenly to an end. When they met in society now, it was only Dorian Gray who smiled; Alan Campbell never did.[48]

Like almost all the male friendships in the novel it has a homoerotic dimension although, on Campbell's side at least, attraction has turned to horror by the time he enters the novel.[49] He is only persuaded to help his former friend, using a mysterious chemical process to destroy all traces of Basil's body, because Dorian has some strange hold over him, knowledge of a secret which would ruin him if it were revealed.

It is easy for the reader to forget Alan Campbell. His only use for Wilde, as for Dorian, seems to be to dispose of an inconvenient corpse. But Dorian's thoughts return to his former friend just before his own death: 'As for Alan Campbell, his suicide had been his own act. He had chosen to do it. It was nothing to him.'[50] It is tellingly difficult to disentangle the pronouns here. Apparently it is only in the last short statement 'it was nothing to him' that Dorian is thinking of himself, yet Wilde's failure to signal the change from Alan to Dorian creates a curious confusion between the two. This draws attention to Dorian's own culpability in Alan's suicide despite his attempt to deny any responsibility for the act. It also, within the context of a novel which pivots around a sinister double, suggests that Alan is in some sense a further 'double' of Dorian.

If we only focus on the surface fiction of the novel there is nothing particularly suggestive in this fleeting confusion between Dorian and Alan. They can scarcely be described as 'doubles' in any meaningful way for the only thing Alan has in common with Dorian is an (unspecified) secret. But *The Picture of Dorian Gray* actively encourages the reader to go beyond the surface of the story and, like the Pompidou Centre in Paris, displays its inner workings for all to see. The processes of artistic creation, and particularly the operations of influence, are flagged throughout the novel, often to metafictional effect. To take a well known example, Joris-Karl Huysmans's *À Rebours* (1884), a major influence on Wilde, has a prominent role within the novel for it has an equally profound influence on the young Dorian. The text confuses its fictional influence (on Dorian) with its actual influence (on Wilde), particularly in chapter 11 when the atmosphere and detail so closely resemble those of Huysmans's novel. It opens:

> For years, Dorian Gray could not free himself from the influence of this book. Or perhaps it would be more accurate to say that he never sought to free himself from it. He procured from Paris no less than nine large-paper copies of the first edition, and had them bound in different colours, so that they might suit his various moods and the

changing fancies of a nature over which he seemed, at times, to have almost entirely lost control.⁵¹

This seems to be a direct echo of the long description of how Huysmans's decadent protagonist, Jean Des Esseintes, experiments with different paints to discover the best colour scheme for his rooms.⁵² Is Dorian being influenced by this incident, or is it only Wilde who is aware of this particular link between the two characters? The sense that Dorian has been subsumed by Des Esseintes, for this chapter at least, is teasingly suggested by the reference to him losing control over his nature, although this detail can of course be explained more simply with reference to his moral decline. But Wilde makes sure that we don't lose sight of his own presence within the text as creator of a Huysmans-inspired dandy: 'And, indeed, the whole book seemed to him to contain the story of his own life, written before he had lived it.'⁵³ The glimmer of an (impossible) possibility that this book is *Dorian Gray* itself may just flash into the reader's mind.

So how can this confusion of the boundaries which separate Dorian's fictive universe from the 'real' world of Wilde himself help us explain the brief 'doubling' of Dorian and Campbell? One answer might be located in another of the novel's sources. Alan Campbell has a conspicuously Scottish name, and he followed the Natural Science Tripos at Cambridge and has since made a study of both chemistry and biology: 'Every day he seemed to become more interested in biology, and his name appeared once or twice in some of the scientific reviews, in connection with certain curious experiments.'⁵⁴ With his Scottish antecedents, scientific curiosity, notorious experiments and mysterious secret, Campbell can be seen as a kind of avatar of one of the key precursors of Wilde's novel, Stevenson's *Dr Jekyll and Mr Hyde* (1886), which also deals with a man's destruction by his malevolent double, although the doubling mechanism is quite different, a chemical compound rather than a supernatural painting. A further clue to such a reading of Campbell's role is offered by the information that Dorian had been close to him 'five years before'.⁵⁵ A similar length of time separates *Dorian Gray* from Stevenson's own *Doppelgänger* novel. (*Dorian Gray* was published in novel form exactly five years after *Jekyll and Hyde*, but it first appeared a year earlier in *Lippincott's Magazine*.) *The Picture of Dorian Gray* could be seen as *Jekyll and Hyde*'s evil twin, as its decadent atmosphere and moral uncertainties contrast with Stevenson's apparently more upright novel. It is therefore significant that Dorian should play Hyde, as it were, picking up again the theme of blackmail which also haunts the earlier text. But if we interpret Alan Campbell as an emblem of the novel rather than simply a reincarnation of Jekyll we might probe the relationship a little further. Wilde's decadent tale threatens to expose the secrets of its textual 'double', and its overt homoeroticism casts a new and more lurid light on the homosocial world of Jekyll and his bachelor friends.[56] Thus the fleeting appearance of a further 'double' for Dorian is in fact a double not merely of the character but of the novel itself.

Campbell is not the only character who sometimes seems to usurp the uncanny portrait's role and become Dorian's double. Towards the beginning of the novel Basil Hallward describes how he first met Dorian at a party: 'When our eyes met, I felt that I was growing pale. A curious sensation of terror came over me.'[57] This seems a strikingly uncanny affect, and resembles the sensation experienced by someone encountering their own double. The bond between the two is further suggested by Basil's portentous insistence that he has put too much of himself into Dorian's portrait. A final significant hint that Basil is in some sense Dorian's double can be identified in the way his horrific death is associated with Dorian's violent interactions with his portrait. In between Basil's own attempted stabbing of the fateful portrait and Dorian's final accomplishment of that task comes a third stabbing, Dorian's murder of Basil. Just as Basil's first glimpse of Dorian was accompanied by a curiously negative charge, so, in their final encounter, do we learn that Dorian experienced a similar inexplicable feeling of aversion. He looks at the portrait and feels 'an uncontrollable feeling of hatred for Basil Hallward . . . he loathed the man who was seated at the table, more than in his whole life he had ever loathed anything'.[58] Even in the cold light of day when Dorian wakes to deal with the body, 'the same curious feeling of loathing . . . came back to him'.[59] The inexplicability of the sensation creates an uncanny *frisson* especially when we remember the odd emphasis on the mechanics of disposing of the body. Through Campbell's skill the body is made to 'disappear' much as the doubles disappear at the end of both of Hogg's *Doppelgänger* tales or as James Durie's body is mysteriously removed from the scene of the duel. By inhabiting the 'vanishing body' trope, Basil cements his position as one of Dorian's doubles.

The links between Dorian and Lord Henry Wotton are equally striking. At an early stage in their acquaintance the two men discuss the nature of influence. Lord Henry warns Dorian that all influence is immoral:

> Because to influence a person is to give him one's own soul. He does not think his natural thoughts, or burn with his natural passions. His virtues are not real to him. His sins, if there are such things as sins, are borrowed. He becomes an echo of some one else's music, an actor of a part that has not been written for him.[60]

Given that Dorian does go on to fall heavily under Lord Henry's influence, this would seem to make Dorian both his double and his creature. The older man muses on the charms of this process in penetratingly erotic terms:

> There was something terribly enthralling in the exercise of influence. No other activity was like it. To project one's soul into some gracious form, and let it tarry there for a moment; to hear one's own intellectual views echoed back to one with all the added music of passion and youth; to convey one's temperament into another as though it were a subtle fluid or a strange perfume.[61]

The concrete physicality of the process, as seen by Lord Henry, is almost vampiric. Later he tells Dorian, 'I represent to you all the sins you have never had the courage to commit',[62] again invoking the discourse of doubling, and indeed foreshadowing the relationship between Dorian and his most obvious double, his own portrait.

Both Basil Hallward and Lord Henry Wotton help 'create' Dorian, Basil through his art and Henry through his seductive doctrines of amorality. We have already seen that this text's boundaries are highly permeable, allowing in artefacts from outside its fictive world, such as *Jekyll and Hyde*, and, through the presence of *À Rebours*, confusing the boundary between influences on Dorian and on *Dorian*. Basil and Henry can both be seen as similar intruders. On the surface, they are simply part of the novel's purely fictive world. But they can also be seen as doubled avatars of Wilde himself, representatives of his own capacity for good and evil. The devoted and passionate adorer of Dorian and the cynical aesthete who corrupts him are two sides of the same coin. Typically uncanny, Basil's 'disappearance' has a rational explanation which yet doesn't quite seem to tell the whole story. Did Basil vanish because he wasn't quite 'real', because he was only an aspect of Dorian's psyche? Or, by contrast, was he only too 'real', as an extension of the author, and thus unable to sustain coexistence with his own creation?

There is some aptness in two of Dorian's doubles also being aspects of his creator. A book can be seen as a kind of 'double', an extension of one's personality which echoes one's own thoughts and feelings and yet has the capacity to move away from its creator and sustain a semi-independent existence, just like Andersen's sinister shadow.[63] Thus as well as harking back to fictional doubles such as those of Poe and Stevenson, *Dorian Gray* also invokes a more subtle real life 'doubling' between a man's life and his art. The novel's central conceit, the portrait which is also one's uncanny double, maps readily onto this analogy between a book and its author. A portrait, like a book, remains an unageing testament to one moment of one's existence. In the case of this novel, it may be remarked that *Dorian Gray*, like Andersen's shadow, helped destroy its creator. Edward Carson, the barrister who cross-examined Wilde at the trial which led to his conviction for gross indecency, claimed that *The Picture of Dorian Gray* was an immoral and perverted book, invoking it as evidence on which to convict its author.[64]

As well as offering an ironic anticipation of Wilde's own destruction by his novel, his 'double', the ending of *Dorian Gray* strongly echoes 'William Wilson'. William Wilson thinks he sees himself in a mirror at the tale's climax; Dorian Gray looks into the mirror of his soul when he gazes with rage on the portrait. Yet Wilde seems to offer us a mirror image of Poe, rather than a simple repetition. Whereas William Wilson feels certain he has killed himself, taking his bloody double for his own reflection, Dorian confidently seeks to kill his double but, like James Durie, harms only himself. Unexpectedly, although his double dies, William Wilson survives to narrate the tale. In *Dorian Gray*, by contrast, the portrait remains intact while its owner perishes. It is as though the texts, as well as their heroes, are staring at their own reflections.

Like many of the *Doppelgänger* texts so far discussed, *The Picture of Dorian Gray* is highly self-conscious. Dorian wonders how he would respond to Sibyl Vane's death had he read about it in a book, and compares her sad end to a beautiful Greek tragedy.[65] One moment at which Dorian comes particularly close to breaking down the barriers completely and realising that he is in fact himself a fictional character comes when he studies the portraits in his country house and, first musing on his resemblance to his ancestors, goes on to reflect:

> Yet one had ancestors in literature, as well as in one's own race, nearer perhaps in type and temperament, many of them, and certainly with an influence of which one was more absolutely conscious . . . It seemed to him that in some mysterious way their lives had been his own.[66]

Dorian seems for a moment almost capable of foretelling his own fate, of knowing that he has been inscribed in a series of *Doppelgänger* texts, of recognising that he is doubled in more ways than one.[67]

So far we have seen how the *Doppelgänger* tradition, as it runs through a sequence of texts over the course of the nineteenth century, becomes increasingly self aware. Both writers and readers bring their knowledge of existing *Doppelgänger* texts to bear on each new text creating the special *frisson* of redoublement. But the characters themselves seem largely excluded from that knowledge. Dorian, as we have just seen, does experience a moment of self-awareness, but it is a comparatively vague and fugitive one. And, though he may have read Huysmans, there is nothing to suggest he has read Hogg, Poe or Stevenson.

The fictional narrator of our next text, Joseph Conrad's 'The Secret Sharer' (1909) reflects a further stage of self-awareness, although at the same time he is one of the most self-deluding protagonists discussed in the chapter.[68] Nevertheless he is in an important sense the author as well as the victim of his curious tale. This narrator, who remains nameless, appears to have internalised the figure of the double as a literary motif, using his implicit familiarity with *Doppelgänger* literature as a way of interpreting his own adventures. He would appear to be aware, in a self-conscious way, of the textual tradition into which he is being inscribed – or indeed is inscribing himself. Hans Robert Jauss observes of the workings of genre that a text 'evokes for the reader (listener) the horizon of expectations and rules familiar from earlier texts, which are then varied, corrected, changed, or just reproduced'.[69] Within the context of the *Doppelgänger* genre, characters as well as readers seem to have a 'horizon of expectations'. In this particular text the double is an uncanny allusion marker pointing back at the tradition as a whole, rather than, as was the case with *Dorian Gray* or *The Master of Ballantrae*, at a specific earlier text or texts. Although it thus represents a slightly less striking instance of the charged relationship between allusion and the uncanny, it illustrates an important moment of transition within the genre, and develops themes, such as homoeroticism, which are central to the twentieth-century progression of the *Doppelgänger*.

The narrator is a young ship's captain, new to command, who is voyaging in the South China seas. One night on deck he sees what he at first takes to be a dead body but turns out to be a living man, a fugitive called Leggatt who has escaped from another ship where he was being held on a charge of murder. The captain is drawn to Leggatt and agrees to hide him, although the stranger has no compelling excuse for his crime except that it was committed in a fit of temper. The narrator manages to keep his new friend hidden but Leggatt's only real hope of escape is to be marooned on a nearby shore – but this will involve the captain in a dangerous sailing manoeuvre which will put the lives of all his men at risk. However – though at the expense of making his crew think him quite mad – it is successfully achieved and Leggatt escapes to freedom.

A bald description of the narrative doesn't make it sound very uncanny – indeed there is nothing in the tale which requires any special explanation, nothing as bizarre as the events in *Justified Sinner* or even in the more realistic *Master of Ballantrae*. Instead the effect of doubling is a function of the narrator's perspective rather than of objective events. In the light of the tale that follows, the focus on liminality in the narrator's opening description of the Gulf of Siam is significant and repays a little further attention. Initially he describes the near seamless divide between land and sea:

> And when I turned my head to take a parting glance at the tug which had just left us anchored outside the bar, I saw the straight line of the flat shore joined to the stable sea, edge to edge, with a perfect and unmarked closeness, in one leveled floor half brown, half blue under the enormous dome of the sky.[70]

The next phase of the description may thus wrong-foot the reader:

> Corresponding in their insignificance to the islets of the sea, two small clumps of trees, one on each side of the only fault in the impeccable joint, marked the mouth of the river Meinam we had just left on the first preparatory stage of our homeward journey.[71]

This might at first seem to be a continuation of the description of a mirror image along the same join, that separating land and sea. But as we read to the end of the passage it becomes clear that the narrator is describing two separate and entirely real clumps of trees, one on each side of the river mouth. In other words the narrator has moved from talking about a horizontal divide between sea and sky – in effect a threshold between illusion and reality – to describing a vertical and quite concrete divide between two similar but not identical halves of the seascape. The same confusing elisions inhere in the story as a whole. The narrator encounters a man with, there is every reason to assume, an entirely real and separate identity and seems to want to recast him as a mysterious alter ego or mirror image, dependent upon himself. In other words he interprets as a reflection a man who is every bit as concrete as himself, just as he makes us think for a moment that one of two similar clumps of trees is the other's reflection rather than an equally real and solid object.

The young captain's response to Leggatt can be at least partially accounted for. It is clear from the beginning of the story that he has a rather unstable and divided sense of his own self, and dwells self-consciously on this aspect of his personality: 'But what I felt most was my being a stranger to the ship; and if all the truth must be told, I was somewhat of a stranger to myself.'[72] This marked self-consciousness aligns him more with the authors of earlier *Doppelgänger* texts than with their characters. It is as though he is a writer trying his best to write a tale of the uncanny but forced to work with intractably realistic raw material. The narrator recounts his first sighting of Leggatt with atmospheric detail, describing how the fugitive seems dead, or even unreal, perhaps recalling Narcissus's view of his own reflection in the water:

> As he hung by the ladder, like a resting swimmer, the sea lightning played about his limbs at every stir; and he appeared in it ghastly, silvery, fishlike. He remained as mute as a fish, too. He made no motion to get out of the water, either. It was inconceivable that he should not attempt to come on board, and strangely troubling to suspect that perhaps he did not want to. And my first words were prompted by just that troubled incertitude.
> 'What's the matter?' I asked in my ordinary tone, speaking down to the face upturned exactly under mine.
> 'Cramp,' it answered, no louder. Then slightly anxious, 'I say, no need to call anyone.'[73]

The literary sensibility of the narrator equips him well to create an uncanny atmosphere. There seems something mysterious in Leggatt's stillness and muteness and the word 'exactly' (when the narrator observes that Leggatt's face is upturned 'exactly under mine') nicely hints at a doubling without being explicit. However, as the narrator is obliged to report events as they happen, the sense of mystery is inevitably undercut once Leggatt opens his mouth. His humdrum explanation for his stillness, his colloquial 'I say' and his entirely pragmatic concern for his own safety destroy the narrator's attempt to write a *Doppelgänger* text. Bathos, as *Northanger Abbey* demonstrates, is the enemy of the uncanny.

Thus here, as with the opening mirrored seascape, Conrad is giving the reader clues to the narrator's personality and, indirectly, to his reliability. We don't have to take the narrator's perspective on events at face value and may not feel inclined to take seriously his statement that 'a mysterious communication was established already between us two – in the face of that silent, darkened tropical sea'.[74] The narrator lends Leggatt a sleeping-suit, just like the one he himself is wearing. This simple fact makes him articulate a feeling that Leggatt is his double – he first says he 'followed me like my double on the poop' and then describes how 'it was, in the night, as though I had been faced by my own reflection in the depths of a sombre and immense mirror'.[75] Over the course of their relationship the narrator seems to become increasingly convinced that he and Leggatt are uncannily indistinguishable and imagines that, if the mate were to see them together, 'he would think he was seeing double, or imagine himself come upon a scene of weird witchcraft; the strange captain having a quiet confabulation by the wheel with his own grey ghost'.[76]

The narrator's odd insistence on the idea of the double may be explained partly by his apparent immersion, typical of an educated reader of the period, in the literature of the *Doppelgänger*. At one point he grumbles to Leggatt, 'We are not living in a boy's adventure tale'.[77] We may assume that he has read Stevenson, at the very least, and that his reading habits have infected his perception of the world and the way he writes. I've already suggested that he is the most authorial 'double' we have yet encountered, largely because the 'doubling' is so clearly a figment of his imagination. Perhaps we can even go further and claim that he has a bent not just for fiction but for literary criticism. Here for example he reiterates his sense of inhabiting the *Doppelgänger* role – 'I felt doubly vexed. Indeed, I felt dual more than ever.'[78] The link between 'doubly' (extremely) and 'dual' (split) is a surely a purely rhetorical one, and reflects the narrator's fondness for over-reading not just words but situations.

But some readers and critics have suspected that there is another reason for the narrator's fascination with the double. A double is someone with whom one has a secret bond. A double implies a transgression of the usual rules of nature. Transgression and secret bonds also characterise homosexual acts in a society which proscribes same sex desire.[79] A queer reading of 'The Secret Sharer' is consistent with many of its oddnesses, for example the unearned tensions in the following exchange:

> 'A pretty thing to have to own up to for a Conway boy,' murmured my double, distinctly.
> 'You're a Conway boy?'
> 'I am,' he said, as if startled. Then, slowly . . . 'Perhaps you too . . .'[80]

The rhythm of the discovery that the two men have something in common – the hesitancy – the ellipsis – of 'Perhaps you too . . .' seem misplaced if all that is being discussed is the fact they trained on the same ship. Ellipses are deployed to similarly suggestive effect when Leggatt gives his own account of being discovered by the narrator:

> 'I didn't mind being looked at. I – I liked it.' [. . .]
> 'I don't know – I wanted to be seen.'[81]

Perhaps the narrator is resituating the danger, the forbidden quality of homosexual attraction as the parallel though quite different danger of supernatural encounter; one kind of transgression of the laws of nature is being used to figure another (perceived) deviation. The narrator of 'The Secret Sharer' begins the story feeling strangely different from everyone else on the ship. His apparent discovery of a supernatural bond with a *Doppelgänger* seems to offer an explanation for his sense of singularity but the real solution may be more mundane. There are certainly some curious undercurrents in the narrator's account of their tense proximity in his cabin, their continual fear of being found out. The bedroom location, yet again, might suggest that the concealment of Leggatt (because he is a murderer) figures concealment of criminalised sexual activity.

Here is a final and particularly telling combination of sexual suggestion with elliptical punctuation:

> He was by my side in an instant – the double captain slipped past the stairs – through a tiny dark passage . . . a sliding door. We were in the

sail locker, scrambling on our knees over the sails. A sudden thought struck me. I saw myself wandering barefooted, bareheaded, the sun beating on my dark poll. I snatched off my floppy hat and tried hurriedly in the dark to ram it on my other self. He dodged and fended off silently. I wonder what he thought had come to me before he understood and suddenly desisted. Our hands met gropingly, lingered united in a steady, motionless clasp for a second . . . No word was breathed by either of us when they separated.[82]

However rather than simply reinforcing a much canvassed homosexual interpretation of the story I want to emphasise that a queer reading draws attention to the tale's immersion in earlier *Doppelgänger* texts, an immersion, or redoublement, which is itself already an established pattern in the literature of the double. *The Picture of Dorian Gray* is overtly homoerotic, the slightly earlier *Jekyll and Hyde* more covertly so. It isn't hard to see why male doubles and homoeroticism might go hand in hand, and it is quite possible simply to see 'The Secret Sharer' as a further example of this easy congruity. But there is an important distinction between Conrad's tale and the earlier queer doublings of Wilde and Stevenson. In *The Picture of Dorian Gray* and *Jekyll and Hyde* we are forced to suspend our disbelief in the supernatural and believe in the existence of doubles. But in 'The Secret Sharer', unless we read against the grain of the text, nothing supernatural has occurred. Thus once again the fictional narrator of Conrad's tale may be aligned with the authors of earlier doubles texts. If we accept queer undertones in the *Doppelgänger* texts of Stevenson and Wilde then we must ascribe the conjunction of these two motifs to the novelists. Whatever the sexual interests of Jekyll and Dorian (in so far as it makes sense to speak of these), the doubling phenomena they experience have a separate and 'real' existence which has no objective connection with sexuality within the fiction of the novel. The case of Conrad's narrator is quite different for here we are invited to speculate that his fancy that Leggatt is his double is fundamentally bound up with his implied attraction to the other man. If there is, or was within a certain cultural moment, a link between homoeroticism and the double, then 'The Secret Sharer' seems to represent a conscious articulation of that perceived affinity, and in the character of the unnamed narrator offers the reader a case study of a man who creates a *Doppelgänger* narrative in the manner of Stevenson and Wilde rather than endures a *Doppelgänger* experience in the way Dorian and Jekyll are forced to do. The capacity for self-delusion and the repression of homosexual feeling that can be identified in Conrad's narrator will both prove to be key ingredients in later twentieth-century reprisals of the *Doppelgänger* theme.

Notes

1. H. C. Andersen, *Longer Stories*, trans. Jean Hersholt (New York: Heritage Press, 1943), p. 53.
2. Much has of course been written about the *Doppelgänger* in literature. See for example M. Atwood, *Negotiating with the Dead: A Writer on Writing* (Cambridge: Cambridge University Press, 2002), pp. 31–57; K. Miller, *Doubles: Studies in Literary History* (Oxford: Oxford University Press, 1985); O. Rank, *The Double: A Psychoanalytic Study*, trans. H. Tucker Jr (London: Karnac, 1989); N. Royle, *The Uncanny* (Manchester: Manchester University Press, 2003), pp. 187–204.
3. On 8 June 1846 Andersen wrote: 'In the evening, began writing the story of my shadow.' Maria Tatar claims that this means Andersen identifies completely with his young writer hero, but it may be, rather, that it is the *writer* (rather than the writer's shadow) to whom he refers when he writes 'my shadow'. (M. Tatar and J. K. Allen (eds), *The Annotated Hans Christian Andersen* (New York and London: W. W. Norton, 2008), p. 263.
4. S. Freud, 'The Uncanny', in *The Standard Edition of the Complete Works of Sigmund Freud*, trans. J. Strachey (London: Hogarth Press, 1955), 24 vols, vol. 17, pp. 219–52, pp. 226–7.
5. Both the *Palinode* of Stesichorus (only a fragment of which has been preserved) and Euripides' 412 BCE *Helen* are predicated on this scenario.
6. For an account of the rise of the literary *Doppelgänger* at this period see J. Herdman, *The Double in Nineteenth-Century Fiction* (London: Macmillan, 1990), pp. 11–20.
7. J. Hogg, *The Private Memoirs and Confessions of a Justified Sinner* (Peterborough, Ontario: Broadview Books, 2001), p. 223.
8. *Ibid.*, p. 225.
9. *Ibid.*, p. 229.
10. In Emma Tennant's 1978 rewriting of Hogg's novel, *The Bad Sister*, the equivalent exhumed corpse offers a new take on Hogg's confused account of Wringhim's hair colouring: 'It was black for about three inches – it had grown that length in the grave, I suppose – and yellow for another three, suggesting the wearer, at the time of death, had had extremely short dyed blonde hair.' E. Tennant, *The Bad Sister* (Edinburgh: Canongate, 2000), p. 165.
11. For a brief account of this tale see Herdman, *The Double in Nineteenth-Century Fiction*, pp. 85–7. I would like to thank Sakiko Reuterskiold

for drawing my attention to this tale, and for other insights into the *Doppelgänger* motif.
12 J. Hogg, *Selected Stories and Sketches* (Edinburgh: Scottish Academic Press, 1982), p. 165.
13 *Ibid.*, p. 166.
14 Miller says the story 'stands in invidious relation to the *Confessions*' and asserts that it is 'one of his less welcome duplications'. (K. Miller, *The Electric Shepherd: A Likeness of James Hogg* (London: Faber, 2003), p. 347).
15 The affinities between the two tales are briefly noted in Herdman, *The Double in Nineteenth-Century Fiction*, p. 128. N. Abi-Ezzi discusses the *Doppelgänger* motif in *The Master of Ballantrae* in *The Double in the Fiction of R.L. Stevenson, Wilkie Collins and Daphne du Maurier* (Oxford: Peter Lang, 2003), pp. 84–90.
16 Eric Massie explores the relationship between the two novels, establishing the fact that Stevenson read and was struck by *Justified Sinner* and describing the texts' shared plot elements. (E. Massie, 'Scottish Gothic: Robert Louis Stevenson, *The Master of Ballantrae*, and *The Private Memoirs and Confessions of a Justified Sinner*', in W. Jones (ed.), *Robert Louis Stevenson Reconsidered: New Critical Perspectives* (Jefferson: McFarland & Co Inc, 2002), pp. 163–74.)
17 R. L. Stevenson, *The Master of Ballantrae* (London: Penguin, 1996), p. 6.
18 O. S. Buckton analyses the theme of reanimation in the novel in *Cruising with Robert Louis Stevenson: Travel, Narrative and the Colonial Body* (Athens: Ohio University Press, 2007), pp. 59–62 and also offers a fuller account of the theme in Stevenson's works in 'Reanimating Stevenson's Corpus', *Nineteenth-Century Literature*, 55.1 (2000), 22–58.
19 Douglas Gifford offers a useful account of this novel's ambiguities in 'Stevenson and Scottish Fiction: The Importance of *The Master of Ballantrae*', in H. Bloom (ed.), *Robert Louis Stevenson* (Philadelphia: Chelsea House, 2005), pp. 53–78. Alan Sandison discusses the sly self-consciousness of the novel in *Robert Louis Stevenson and the Appearance of Modernism: A Future Feeling* (London: Palgrave, 1996).
20 Adrian Poole notes the Hermione link in his edition of the novel (R. L. Stevenson, *The Master of Ballantrae* (London: Penguin, 1996), pp. xii–xiii) although his own emphasis is on the mismatch between a play which focuses on renewal and regeneration and a novel which closes down such possibilities. He does not comment on the presence of mysterious reanimations in both works. A fuller account of the Shakespearean resonances of the subtitle is given by Jean-Claude Amalric in 'Un Conte d'hiver? Note sur un sous-titre', *Cahiers Victoriens et Edouardiens*, 40 (1994), 121–5.
21 Stevenson, *The Master of Ballantrae*, p. 96.

22 Ibid., p. 99.
23 Ibid., p. 209.
24 Ibid., p. 33.
25 Ibid.
26 Ibid., p. 47.
27 An interesting, related analysis of the textuality of the novel is offered by Alexander B. Clunas in '"A Double Word": Writing and Justice in *The Master of Ballantrae*', *Studies in Scottish Literature*, 28 (1993), 55–74.
28 An extended discussion of the wider European tradition of the *Doppelgänger* is outwith the scope of this study. The single most important such work is Dostoevsky's *The Double* (1846) which is discussed in K. Miller, *Doubles*, pp. 132–5.
29 See also M. C. Paganoni, *The Magic Lantern: Representation of the Double in Dickens* (New York and London: Routledge, 2008).
30 M. Braddon, *Lady Audley's Secret* (London: Penguin,1998), pp. 108–9.
31 Ibid., p. 60.
32 Helena Michie offers a good account of Phoebe as an inert double. She suggests that Phoebe seems doomed to be a victim of scheming Lady Audley, although in fact the power dynamic between the two women might make the reader equally likely to assume that Lady Audley herself is to be duped. (H. Michie, *Sororophobia: Differences among Women in Literature and Culture* (Oxford: Oxford University Press, 1992), pp. 64–5.
33 Braddon, *Lady Audley's Secret*, p. 30.
34 W. Collins, *The Woman in White* (London: Everyman, 1969), pp. 39–40.
35 Braddon, *Lady Audley's Secret*, p. 29.
36 Ibid., p. 114.
37 L. Hart, *Fatal Women: Lesbian Sexuality and the Mark of Aggression* (Princeton: Princeton University Press, 1994), p. 45.
38 Collins, *The Woman in White*, p. 245.
39 For discussions of the links see J. B. Taylor, *In the Secret Theatre of Home: Wilkie Collins, Sensation Narrative, and Nineteenth Century Psychology* (London: Routledge, 1998), pp. 10–13 and L. Pykett, *The Sensation Novel: from The Woman in White to The Moonstone* (Plymouth: Northcote House, 1994), pp. 55–6.
40 *Jane Eyre* is of course another suggestive intertext, and one in which some readers and critics have identified the *Doppelgänger* motif.
41 N. Sajé, *Red under the Skin* (Pittsburgh: University of Pittsburgh Press, 1994), p. 26.
42 Examples of this motif include Mary Brunton's *Discipline* (1814) and Mary Wollstonecraft's *Maria: or, The Wrongs of Women* (1798).
43 Braddon, *Lady Audley's Secret*, p. 394.
44 Ibid., p. 395.
45 W. Collins, *Armadale* (London: Penguin, 1995), p. 62. J. B. Taylor also

sees a connection between the three brothers' trick and the novel itself: 'Armadale is a story which "jumps down its own throat."' (J. B. Taylor, 'Armadale: The Sensitive Subject as Palimpsest', in L. Pykett (ed.), *Wilkie Collins* (Basingstoke: Macmillan, 1998), pp. 149–74, p. 153.)
46 Collins, *Armadale*, p. 565.
47 See Herdman, *The Double in Nineteenth-Century Fiction*, pp. 95–8.
48 O. Wilde, *The Picture of Dorian Gray* (Oxford: Oxford University Press, 2008), pp. 305–6.
49 The connection, or perceived connection, between the motif of the double and homoeroticism has long been recognised. See for example O. Rank, The Double, pp. 71–3.
50 Wilde, *Dorian Gray*, p. 335.
51 *Ibid.*, p. 276.
52 This process takes up much of the first chapter of Huysmans' novel. Christa Satzinger notes the repetition of the colours motif but does not comment on its potential to destabilise our sense of Dorian's identity. (*The French Influences on Oscar Wilde's The Picture of Dorian Gray and Salome* (Lampeter: Edwin Mellen Presss, 1994).)
53 Wilde, *Dorian Gray*, p. 276.
54 *Ibid.*, p. 306.
55 *Ibid.*, p. 305.
56 Many have identified an apparent homoerotic subtext in Stevenson's novel. See for example E. Showalter, *Sexual Anarchy: Gender and Culture at the 'Fin de Siècle'* (London: Bloomsbury, 1990), pp. 105–26.
57 Wilde, *Dorian Gray*, p. 173.
58 *Ibid.*, pp. 229–30.
59 *Ibid.*, p. 303.
60 *Ibid.*, p. 183.
61 *Ibid.*, p. 199.
62 *Ibid.*, p. 236.
63 See p. 175 for a discussion of the uncannily autonomous book in Milton's *Areopagitica*.
64 See for example D. A. Novak, 'Sexuality in the Age of Technological Reproducibility', in J. Brister (ed.), *Oscar Wilde and Modern Culture: The Making of a Legend* (Chicago: University of Chicago Press, 2009), pp. 63–95, pp. 64–5.
65 O. Wilde, *Dorian Gray*, p. 253.
66 *Ibid.*, p. 289.
67 The self-consciousness of this moment is noted in J. Winchell, 'Wilde and Huysmans: Autonomy, Reference, and the Myth of Expiation' in R. Gagnier (ed.), *Critical Essays on Oscar Wilde* (New York: G. K. Hall, 1991), pp. 223–40, pp. 227–8.
68 See Miller, *Doubles*, pp. 256–7 for a brief analysis of the doubling motif

in this tale. See also R. Rogers, *A Psychoanalytical Study of the Double in Literature* (Detroit: Wayne State University Press, 1970), pp. 42–4.
69 H. R. Jauss, 'Literary History as a Challenge to Literary Theory', *New Literary History* 2.1. (1970), 7–37, p. 13.
70 J. Conrad, *Typhoon and other Tales* (Oxford: Oxford University Press, 2006), p. 179.
71 *Ibid.*, p. 179.
72 *Ibid.*, p. 181.
73 *Ibid.*, p. 184.
74 *Ibid.*, p. 185.
75 *Ibid.*, p. 186.
76 *Ibid.*, p. 188.
77 *Ibid.*, p. 208.
78 *Ibid.*, p. 194.
79 A helpful account of the tale's homoerotic subtext can be found in J. Phelan, *Narrative as Rhetoric: Technique, Audiences, Ethics, Ideology* (Columbus: Ohio State University Press, 1996), pp. 119–31.
80 Conrad, *Typhoon and other Tales*, p. 186.
81 *Ibid.*, p. 193.
82 *Ibid.*, p. 213.

3

Uncanny doubles: part two

Towards the end of Vladimir Nabokov's *Despair* (1934)[1] the narrator, Hermann, tries to give his story a title:

> What amazed me was the absence of a title on the first leaf: for assuredly I *had* at one time invented a title, something beginning with 'Memoirs of a –' of a what? I could not remember; and, anyway, 'Memoirs' seemed dreadfully dull and commonplace. What should I call my book then? 'The Double'? But Russian literature possessed one already.[2]

This move (and many other details in the novel) places *Despair* very self-consciously within the now well-established tradition of *Doppelgänger* literature.[3] In signalling his awareness of earlier precedents for *Despair* Nabokov inevitably draws attention to a 'redoubling' effect in his own work. The reference to 'Memoirs' as a possible title might recall Hogg's much earlier novel, particularly as Hermann is himself conspicuously sinful.[4] And there is also an unambiguous allusion to Fyodor Dostoevsky's 1846 novella *The Double*. It is significant that the allusion is made by the fictional character rather than just by Nabokov himself. Hermann's explicit invocation of the earlier novel invites the reader to wonder whether he, as well as Nabokov, has been influenced by the work. It is also half suggested that the authors of these earlier *Doppelgänger* texts are themselves in some uncanny way Hermann's doubles, that he is the author of all those earlier books as well as of his own bleak story, and that his dim memories of fixing on a title are in fact memories of earlier authorial incarnations. We can press further this doubling dynamic at work in Hermann's hesitation over a title; if we remember a similar moment from Andersen's short story 'The Shadow', quoted at the beginning of the previous chapter, a still more complex doubling process can be identified. In conjunction with the earlier Andersen quotation the allusion to Dostoevsky effects not simply a redoublement, but a doubled redoublement, as though in acknowledgement of the ever more complex lineage to which each new variation on the theme of the *Doppelgänger* can lay claim.

I have already suggested that the narrator of Conrad's 'The Secret Sharer' appears to have a good understanding of the *Doppelgänger* tradition. Hermann goes one step further and explicitly articulates his familiarity with the motif not just, as quoted above, in literature but also in film: 'on the screen I have seen a man meeting his double; or better to say an actor playing two parts'.[5] However, as I hope to demonstrate, Hermann's double, a man named Felix, has perhaps a still more sophisticated understanding of the significance of the literary double even than Hermann.

The story begins when Hermann comes across a sleeping tramp and notices in amazement that this man is his exact double. He persuades the tramp to dress in his clothes, supposedly to provide an alibi for a robbery which Hermann plans to carry out. But the real plan is more sinister, and Hermann kills the tramp so that (with the help of his wife) he can reap the benefits of a hefty life insurance policy. The novel's final twist comes when Hermann realises in horror that no one has been fooled by the trick, for there is in fact no special resemblance between him and Felix. It was a strange delusion, a more dramatic version of the self-deception displayed by Conrad's unnamed narrator. And, again like Conrad's character, Hermann is presented as a character with a special, even irrational, interest in the phenomenon of doubling. For example here he is drawn to the watery reflection of an already doubled landscape: 'A Y-stemmed couple of inseparable birches grew there (or a couple of couples, if you counted their reflections).'[6] (Exactly the same confusion between mirroring and simple repetition within a context of vegetation reflected in the water is displayed in the opening description of the Gulf of Siam in 'The Secret Sharer' of course.) Indeed Hermann is fascinated, not just by doubling but by redoubling, at one point self-consciously noting that: 'Here another literary device has crept in: the imitation of foreign novels, *themselves imitations.*'[7] (my italics)

Thus, he is fully and explicitly aware of his obsession, and is even conscious that he may be suffering from a delusion even though he doesn't quite grasp the precise nature of that delusion: 'I somehow found myself thinking that Felix could not come for the simple reason that he was a product of my imagination, which hankered after reflections, repetitions, masks.'[8] Hermann never offers a motive for this obsession but I think Nabokov does. Following in a tradition of homoerotic doubling, the implication seems to be that Hermann is a repressed homosexual. This interpretation emerges more forcefully on rereading the novel. If, like Hermann, we are deluded into thinking that Felix is his double then it won't seem especially odd that Hermann is offering a strange man money and arranging future encounters, or, more to the point, that Felix is taking up his various propositions as though they had a rational motive. Felix understands that Hermann thinks they are doubles and plays along with the idea but perhaps detects further hidden desires which a discourse of 'doubling' has so often encoded. The following exchange is suggestive. Hermann asks:

> 'What is the opinion you have formed of me? For you must have formed *some* kind of opinion, mustn't you?'
> 'Maybe you're an actor,' said Felix dubiously.
> 'If I understand you aright, friend, you mean that at our first meeting you thought: "Ah, he is probably one of those theatrical blokes, the dashing kind, with funny fancies and fine clothes; maybe a celebrity." Am I correct?'
> Felix fixed the toe of his shoe with which he was smoothing the gravel, and his face assumed a rather strained expression.
> 'I didn't think anything,' he said peevishly. 'I simply saw – well, that you were sort of curious about me, and so on.'[9]

Here it might seem that Felix and Hermann are talking at cross purposes and that Felix has an insight into the heart of his 'double' that Hermann himself lacks. Later Hermann describes how he and Felix share a hotel room, dwelling on an account of Felix undressing, noting how the other man touches his hand, and making a special point of estimating the length of the small space which separates their bed. He has a strange dream which implies both disgust and attraction towards the other sleeper:

> All around shadows floated; the bed next to mine was empty except for the broad burdock leaves which, owing to the damp, grow out of bedsteads. One could see, on those leaves, tell-tale stains of a slimy nature.[10]

Although ostensibly snail tracks, the association between the slimy trail and the other man's bed implies that the dream represents semen-stained sheets. Hermann is immersed in a *Doppelgänger* tradition which even includes a text he has written himself – he informs us that he once wrote a 'little story' (about doubles of course) 'in the Oscar Wilde style', a story which dwells at great length, incidentally, on the muscular appeal of a young sailor's torso.[11] It is possible that Hermann has read how reports of stained sheets were used to build the prosecution case against Wilde. Indeed Hermann comes very close to recognising a possible sexual basis for his interest in Felix when, on the next page, he almost abandons his murder plot, comparing himself to 'an adolescent [who], after yielding once again to a solitary and shameful vice' resolves to give into temptation no longer.[12] The vehicle and the tenor of this analogy are perhaps closer than Hermann guesses.

It cannot be established with certainty whether the various 'redoubling' effects I've identified in *Despair*, in particular the affinities with Conrad's earlier tale of a similarly delusional and homoerotic doubling, are chance echoes of earlier related fictions or conscious allusions on Nabokov's part. But one further redoublement in which *Despair* is implicated is surely no coincidence. Hermann's full name is in fact Hermann Hermann, and he is thus a precursor of Humbert Humbert, narrator of Nabokov's most famous novel, *Lolita* (1955). The already duplex name is obtrusively redoubled. Although the novel's other themes overshadow *Lolita*'s play with doubles, Humbert Humbert, like Hermann Hermann, is vexed by a 'double', his nemesis Clare Quilty. Their violent encounter in chapter 35 offers an exaggeratedly comical version of *Despair*'s homoerotic doubling: 'He was naked and goatish under his robe, and I felt suffocated as he rolled over me. I rolled over him. We rolled over me. They rolled over him. We rolled over us.'[13]

Daphne du Maurier also doubles her own doubles. Her 1957 novel of male doubles, *The Scapegoat*, could itself be described as the pallid, shadowy double of the earlier, highly celebrated *Rebecca* (1938).[14] It is an accomplished but not a charismatic text.[15] The doubling motif is far more clearly central to this later novel, whose narrator is a rather lonely, retiring academic, John, who teaches French history. While holidaying in Le Mans he encounters his exact physical double, Jean de Gué, who gets him drunk and steals his identity, leaving the bewildered John to take up his double's own position as head of a dysfunctional aristocratic family and proprietor of a failing glass works. His relationship with the irresponsible Jean parallels that between the second Mrs de Winter and Rebecca in several ways. Both 'interlopers' are retiring, gentle, solitary and slightly dull replacements for far more extravagant, flamboyant, selfish and sexually adventurous figures. Both feel unease, but also pleasure, in stepping into someone else's shoes, inhabiting an unfamiliar role. Of course there are also important differences. Whereas Jean and John are physically identical, Rebecca and the second Mrs de Winter aren't remotely alike, and whereas Rebecca is long dead, Jean is still very much alive. Although the changes from *Rebecca*, including the use of a male protagonist, are necessary in order to prevent *The Scapegoat* from being a recycled imitation of the better known novel, one of *The Scapegoat*'s most interesting features is the way it repeatedly offers odd echoes and reminders of *Rebecca*.

John's first glimpse of Jean de Gué's family home echoes the famous conclusion of *Rebecca*, the destruction of Manderley by fire. He sees the chateau 'looming ahead of me behind ivy-covered walls, the small windows in its two foremost towers aflame with the last dying whisper of the sun'.[16] Like Mrs de Winter, John finds himself lost in his new home, exploring unknown rooms. Just as Mrs de Winter comes upon Rebecca's old room in the West Wing, John stumbles into the room of Jean's sister Blanche. Both fumble about in the dark, feeling for the light switch and both are interrupted by sinister female servants, John by Charlotte; Mrs de Winter, far more famously, by Mrs Danvers:

> I shall never forget the expression on her face. Triumphant, gloating, excited in a strange unhealthy way. I felt very frightened.
> 'Is anything the matter, Madam?' she said.[17]

> 'Is there anything wrong, Monsieur le Comte?' she asked, and behind her small eyes I could see still greater curiosity. Her voice was intimate, confiding, as though possibly I had a secret that we might share.[18]

Indeed much of the narrative of *The Scapegoat* can be mapped onto *Rebecca* although sometimes only in a fragmented and disjointed way. In *Rebecca* Mrs de Winter experiences great embarrassment when a servant is blamed for the breakage of an ornament which she had broken herself. In *The Scapegoat* Jean's young daughter accidentally breaks a porcelain cat and dog. In each case the pieces are carefully retained in case they can be mended. This is a trivial incident, but the very inconsequentiality of the breakage in *The Scapegoat* perhaps makes the echo of *Rebecca* still more obtrusive, rather as the pointlessness of the resemblance between Lady Audley and her maid encourages the reader to interrogate it.

John gradually uncovers Jean's family secrets, discovering why, for example, Jean hasn't spoken to his sister Blanche for fifteen years – Jean had been responsible for the killing of her fiancé, Maurice Duval, by the French Resistance. Thus in both novels a revelation centres round a murder by shooting – the second Mrs de Winter famously discovers that Rebecca was shot by her husband rather than accidentally drowned – although in *The Scapegoat* one of the doubles is the murderer rather than the victim. Both John and Mrs de Winter only learn about the shootings late in the novel, and both do so shortly after making a dreadful but unintentional social gaffe. Mrs de Winter inadvertently makes her entrance at the Manderley fancy-dress ball, a major annual social event, wearing a dress identical to that worn by Rebecca at her own final appearance. The de Gué family have a similarly important position in local society and John is obliged to preside at another socially significant annual gathering, a shooting party. He cracks a joke about his own poor shooting skills and is greeted by appalled silence. It is only after this blunder that he learns how Jean masterminded the murder of Duval. In *Rebecca* gaffe and revelation are not quite so closely linked. However on the same evening that Mrs De Winter appears at the ball in her predecessor's costume, the boat containing Rebecca's body is discovered, precipitating Maxim's confession that he shot his wife after she taunted him that she was carrying another man's child.

Although Duval's death by shooting links him with Rebecca, her death while (apparently) pregnant links her with yet another character from *The Scapegoat*, Jean's wife Françoise, who falls to her death from a high window while seven months pregnant. But in a further twist it is perhaps the *second* Mrs de Winter whom the blonde and passive Françoise more closely resembles, and the circumstances leading to her death offer one of *The Scapegoat*'s strongest echoes of *Rebecca*. While the two women are together in Rebecca's old room looking out at the sea, Mrs Danvers tries to persuade Mrs de Winter to throw herself out of the window. She insists that no one wants her, that Maxim only cares for Rebecca's memory: 'You're not happy. Mr de Winter doesn't love you. There's not much for you to live for, is there? Why don't you jump now and have done with it?'[19] Once his – or rather Jean's – wife has jumped to her death, John learns with horror that the sinister servant Charlotte had played on Françoise's fears in a similar fashion, and to more lethal effect:

> I told her the truth, Monsieur le Comte. I said that when a father idolizes his daughter as Monsieur le Comte idolizes Marie-Noel, it is always difficult for the mother . . . I told her because I was sympathetic, Monsieur le Comte. I knew that Madame Jean was often lonely here.[20]

Françoise's dowry would only be released fully if she died or gave birth to a son, and she seems to have felt that the family wanted her out of the way. Her death, which occurs near the end of the novel, causes a crisis for the family who are anxious to avoid a verdict of suicide. The officials, rather like those in *Rebecca* who are keen to protect Maxim de Winter from scandal, are willing to accept that it was a terrible accident. Once the crisis has been smoothly resolved John, like Mrs de Winter, has a brief period of hope. Both 'secondary' figures feel they might finally be able to inhabit their roles with confidence. But both have their hopes dashed, Mrs de Winter by the fire; John by the return of Jean.

As well as being the close double of a single novel, *Rebecca*, *The Scapegoat* picks up on other aspects of the wider *Doppelgänger* tradition. As in *Despair*, there is a certain homoerotic charge in the first chance encounter between the lookalikes. The idea of homosexuality is imprinted in the reader's mind when Jean is trying to guess why John had planned a retreat to a French monastery: 'Perhaps you're a drunkard,' he said, 'or a homosexual.'[21] When the two men decide to dine together John experiences misgivings: 'I realized suddenly that I did not wish to be seen with him. I did not want waiters to look at us. I felt in some way furtive and ashamed.'[22] When John wakes up the next morning alone in a seedy hotel room like the one Felix and Hermann share in *Despair*, the same hint is made more strongly:

> 'I realized then that we must have exchanged clothes in a fit of drunken folly, and somehow the thought of it was distasteful, beastly, and I brushed it aside because I did not want to remember anything else that might have happened.'[23]

In addition to explicitly invoking homosexuality, both here and in the suggestion of a lesbian attraction between Rebecca and Mrs Danvers, du Maurier creates further more covert homoerotic, or gender-bending, possibilities for the reader who is able to map the second novel onto the first. The most obvious play with gender is the fact that paired women are replaced by paired men. But more important is the instability of the pairings created by the strange echoes of *Rebecca* in *The Scapegoat*. John is like Mrs de Winter, but so is the 'wife', Françoise, he inherits from his double, and yet she is also, in the manner of her death at least, like the very different Rebecca. Jean parallels both Maxim and Rebecca. Indeed it is perhaps Maxim whom Jean more closely resembles. This sexually ambiguous intertextual doubling may be seen as a reflection of du Maurier's perception of conflict within her own gender identity. She acknowledged a male 'double' within herself, which she referred to as the 'boy-in-the-box'.[24] The permeability between the sexes which is revealed by a comparison of her two *Doppelgänger* novels represents one way in which the 'boy' might escape from his box without attracting too much attention.

The end of the twentieth century was marked by a revival of the *Doppelgänger* to match that of the previous *fin de siècle*. Like their nineteenth-century counterparts, many of these modern explorations of the double – by writers such as Bret Easton Ellis, Chuck Palahniuk and Sarah Waters – caught the popular imagination and, in some cases, caused controversy. As well as doubling their characters, they double each other and, in many cases, the works of their nineteenth-century ancestors. One of the most interesting recent exponents of the *Doppelgänger* novel is the underrated British novelist Christopher Priest.[25] His best-known novel is perhaps *The Prestige* (1995), which was adapted into a successful film in 2006.[26] This is the tale of two rival magicians, both of whom possess different types of 'doubles'. Both magicians leave behind diaries in which they reveal how they performed slightly different versions of a spectacular trick in which each man was apparently transported instantaneously to a different location. One magician, Borden, is in reality a pair of identical twins. The explanation of the feat performed by the other magician, Angier, tips the book over into science fiction; he commissions from Nikola Tesla a machine which can duplicate people, transporting them some distance away while leaving behind a lifeless simulacrum. The main drawback of the device is the need to dispose of the 'prestige', or replicant, which is created each time the trick is performed. But the most charged 'doubling' relationship in the novel is perhaps that between the two rivals, Angier and Borden. Their lives strangely mirror one another, and the 'doubling' each undergoes is embedded in each man's memoir, both of which are in fact written by two hands rather than one. Borden's is written by both twins simultaneously. Angier's document is completed by an anomalous replicant – the only one of his many 'prestiges' who managed to develop consciousness and autonomy. To underline the parallels between the rival magicians each man's memoir ends with precisely the same sentence, 'I will go alone to the end', an assertion which is of course undermined through its repetition.[27]

Readers often express disappointment at the novel's ending, a wish for something more.[28] The problem is less with the central Victorian tale than with its frame, narrated by Andrew, a descendent of one of the two magicians. At the beginning of the novel he explains how he often feels he has a twin, with whom he is in secret communication. In a sense this feeling is confirmed when he finds out that, as a small child, he was thrown into Tesla's machine. It is the resulting simulacrum of his boyhood self, eventually discovered by Andrew in a vault, who is the implied source of the telepathic signals. But Angier himself was never disturbed by telepathic communications from his many inanimate doubles or 'prestiges'. So why is Andrew different?

Yet again we must travel outside the text to discover the answer to this question and track down Andrew's 'real' double. Like a magician himself, Priest makes us look in the wrong place by encouraging us to find all the solutions to the mystery within the covers of this book. Andrew's double, I would suggest, is not the inanimate child but the hero of an earlier novel by Priest, *The Affirmation* (1981). This unreliable narrator, Peter, wishes to create an alternative version of himself through fiction and writes an 'autobiography' set in the alternate world of Jethra. Within this inset fiction the 'Jethran' Peter wins a lottery which gives him the right to undergo a medical process called 'athanasia', which will make him immortal. But there is a catch – the process will also wipe out his memories. These must be given back to him, partly by his friends and partly by his own written account of himself. The same ontological anxieties are raised by this process as by Angier's duplication machine. Like so many of his protagonists – Peter of *The Affirmation*, Angier, Borden, Andrew – Priest is a self-duplicator.

The reader of Priest's novels is given further clues, beyond these similarities of theme, which help identify Andrew's real double as the narrator of *The Affirmation*. Both novels open with the narrator's girlfriend having just walked out on him and both are set in the north of England. In the opening of *The Affirmation* Peter carefully explains that his life has been disturbed by three simultaneous disasters: the loss of his job, his house and his girlfriend.[29] Andrew in *The Prestige* articulates precisely the same trio of woes. A particularly strong telepathic sensation overwhelms Andrew when he is sitting in a teashop in a Derbyshire village. Peter pays a similar visit to a Derbyshire teashop in *The Affirmation*. There is another intriguing link between the two novels although it involves Angier rather than Andrew. Borden reports at one point that Angier seems infirm: 'He moved stiffly, and several times favoured his left arm as if it were weaker than the other.'[30] This remark resonates uncannily with an apparently inconsequential detail from *The Prestige*'s 'double' *The Affirmation*. Its narrator, Peter, explains how he had an accident as a child: 'It was my left arm that was fractured. This I know beyond doubt, as one does not misremember such things, and to this day I am slightly weaker in that arm than in the other.'[31] He is therefore perturbed when he finds a photograph showing him with his *right* arm in a sling. The mystery is cleared up when he realises that the photograph was incorrectly printed from the negative. But, years later, this little incident focusing on mirror images finds its own mirror image in the description of Angier.

Telepathy, like other 'uncanny' phenomena, implies access to an unseen world or occult force. Here that unseen world is another *textual* world, another book in other words. Allusion and the uncanny, once again, go hand in hand. The hidden secret of *The Prestige* (its relationship with *The Affirmation*), like the punch line of a joke as defined by Arthur Koestler, effects a clash of matrices, the intrusion of a completely unexpected frame of reference.[32] The doubled books at the heart of the narrative, the memoirs of Borden and Angier respectively, echo the similarly doubled narrative of *The Affirmation*, with its parallel tales of Peter and his Jethran alter ego. When put together the two individual novels themselves becomes doubles, or rather doubled doubles.

We can trace Priest's interest in doubling beyond *The Prestige*, right up to his recent acclaimed novel *The Separation* (2002) which tells of identical twins Jack and Joe Sawyer, whose contrasting philosophies and personalities are reflected in two competing versions of twentieth-century history.[33] Roughly speaking, although this summary doesn't do justice to the shimmering and permeable complexity of Priest's doubled narrative, the reality in which Jack the RAF bomber pilot survives is the one we inhabit, in which the war didn't end until 1945. But in the world where it is Joe, the conscientious objector, who survives, the war ends in 1941, in response to the peace offer delivered by Rudolf Hess – or perhaps by Hess's double. Yet again the links between this novel and Priest's earlier treatments of related themes are not purely thematic. The novel opens in 1999 when Stuart Gratton, a historian, is delivered a manuscript by a woman he has never met before, a Mrs Angela Chipperton: 'There was a fleeting illusory sense that he had seen her before, that they had met somewhere.'[34] The *frisson* of *déjà vu* is felt equally strongly by those who have followed Priest's career. The setting, yet again, is Derbyshire. The opening move echoes that of *The Prestige* in which a mysterious woman also delivers a family memoir to the narrator. Even the feeling of uncanny connectivity is itself a repetition. Andrew, the narrator of *The Prestige*, has a similar experience when he senses the presence of his supposed 'twin'. Once we discover the real nature of the link between Stuart and Angela the connection with *The Prestige* becomes still more insistent. Angela is an intruder from an alternative universe; she is in fact Stuart's own alternative self. In this she closely resembles Andrew's inanimate prestige, not a twin, as he had supposed, but a duplication of himself. In both *The Prestige* and *The Separation*, therefore, the narrator senses a mysterious bond or *frisson* which may be accounted for either by the presence of a particular kind of *Doppelgänger*, a 'second self' within the fictional world of each individual novel, or else by the intrusion of an earlier textual world into that novel. *The Prestige* is haunted by *The Affirmation* and *The Separation*, in its turn, is haunted by *The Prestige*.

A further clue to vital links between these three novels is offered in a crucial scene in which Jack, the pilot brother, is injured but does not die. (In a later version of the same scene, in the second strand of the novel, Jack is killed at this point.) Like both Andrew and Angier before him he suffers an injury to the left, sinister side:

> 'My left arm was immovable because of the pain . . . I put my weight on my right elbow . . . I could favour the left side of my body, where most of the damage had been done . . . My left arm and hand were badly burned.'[35]

In fact Priest has returned so insistently to the theme of doubles that we can almost see his succession of interrelated novels as themselves a series of 'prestiges', inanimate and unchanging emblems of a series of moments in his life. In my own survey of *Doppelgänger* texts I've suggested that doubles uncannily reach out to their earlier counterparts in other books or even in the real world. In the case of Priest, still more uncannily, the central theme of his novels seems to have invaded his real life. To his irritation, a writer of comic books, Jim Owsley, adopted the pen name 'Christopher Priest' in the 1990s.[36] And – more cheerfully – while working on *The Prestige* and long after he first became preoccupied with doubles, Priest became the father of twins.[37]

Bret Easton Ellis is best known as the author of *American Psycho*, an apparently amoral tale of a handsome but psychopathic socialite which caused huge controversy when it was first published in 1991, exactly 100 years after *The Picture of Dorian Gray*. Like that of Priest, Easton Ellis's oeuvre is full of repetitions and duplications, although it is in *Glamorama* (1998) that the *Doppelgänger* motif is most clearly apparent.[38] The plot cannot easily be summarised. Although reality and fantasy both appear to be present, trying to separate the two neatly is no easier than dividing a Möbius strip. Tentatively, we might say that the protagonist, Victor, a vacuous wannabe actor, gets sucked into a bizarre conspiracy, travels to England where he is taken up by an improbable gang of models-turned-terrorists, and is eventually replaced by a *Doppelgänger* who (by contrast with the 'real' Victor) is hardworking and conformist.

Towards the end of the novel Victor fights the leader of the terrorist gang, a glamorous former model named Bobby Hughes. Their encounter takes place in a men's room: 'Bobby's standing at a sink, inspecting his face in a mirror. I'm screaming as I run toward him at full sprint, my fist raised, the gun in it.'[39] This is the first of a series of references to mirrors in the scene which, combined with various other clues and oddnesses, suggest that this fight, like some of those analysed in the previous chapter, is between antagonists who are also somehow doubles. An encounter between doubles is fraught with potential paradox and this perhaps explains the oddly directionless quality of the fight, which plays out as though both Victor and Bobby in turn were attacking nothing more substantial than their own reflections. Aiming at Bobby at close quarters, Victor manages only to hit the wall six times in succession. Although eventually Victor does succeed in stabbing Bobby to death – in so far as we can say that anything 'happens' in this textual hall of mirrors – the artificially prolonged contest implies a kind of impossibility at the heart of the two men's fight, even though it is eventually revealed that Bobby's failure to kill Victor is due to the fact his gun is jammed. Like the duel in *The Master of Ballantrae*, the fight flirts with the uncanny before offering a rational explanation:

> Bobby holds the gun at chest level, riding me, the barrel tilted toward my face.
> I try to scream, lashing my head back and forth.
> He pulls the trigger.
> I close my eyes.
> Nothing.
> He pulls it again.
> Nothing. For a second we're both still. [. . .]
> I pull the trigger, screaming while firing.
> Nothing.
> Bobby's gun is jammed, not firing, and I realize, too late, that somehow the safety on mine got switched on.[40]

But, although this could be seen as a classic encounter of doubles, there is in fact no suggestion that Bobby is Victor's double – Victor's eventual apparent double is a replicant whereas Bobby has an entirely separate identity. Yet again we can perhaps find an explanation for this anomaly outside the text, in a textual 'double' of *Glamorama*, Chuck Palahniuk's *Fight Club* (1996).[41] This novel also charts the relationship between a glamorous confident man, who turns out to be the leader of an anarchistic terrorist organisation, and an admiring protégé, who had formerly been preoccupied by style.[42] Here, just as in the later *Glamorama*, the narrator moves in with his new friend, gradually learns about these illegal activities and tries to put a stop to them. However in Palahniuk's novel it is eventually revealed that the glamorous Tyler Durden and the admiring narrator are the same person. This perhaps explains the otherwise apparently unearned and unexplained 'doubling' effect created between the parallel dyad of Bobby and Victor.

A further detail strengthens the case for a link between *Fight Club* and *Glamorama*. Victor is sent to England by a mysterious figure called Palakon, an unusual name which echoes that of *Fight Club*'s creator, Chuck Palahniuk. Interpreting Palakon as an avatar of Palahniuk accounts for Palakon's authorially omniscient control over the hapless Victor and is consistent with the way he propels Victor out of the life of surface inanity inhabited by all of Ellis's 'heroes' and into a situation so reminiscent of *Fight Club*. As well as acting as a bridge between two recent texts (*Glamorama* and *Fight Club*), Palakon, because he thus plays a role similar to that of Alan Campbell, could be said to suggest or create a link between the doubled texts of the previous *fin de siècle*, *Jekyll and Hyde* and *Dorian Gray*, and those of our own day.

Whereas Priest tends to duplicate himself and Bret Easton Ellis 'doubles' a novel by his contemporary Palahniuk, other recent writers have returned to the many powerful *Doppelgänger* texts of the nineteenth century for inspiration. In Louise Welsh's *The Bullet Trick* (2006), doubling and allusion haunt the margins of the novel in an uncannily uncertain way. The story's central character is called William Wilson, a slightly sleazy and not terribly successful magician. The novel contains more than one plot strand but it pivots around the 'bullet trick' of the title. While performing in Berlin, William Wilson is persuaded to participate in a 'faked' game of Russian roulette for a mysterious small group of rich voyeurs. He is assured that his Sally Bowles-like friend, a dancer called Sylvie, will never be in any danger, that the gun will contain only blanks; not surprisingly he suffers a breakdown when it turns out that the game was in deadly earnest, and that Sylvie has died at his hand.

The narrator's name seems intended to remind us of Poe's famous tale of a man haunted by his double, a tale which also ends with a fatal shooting, and we may well expect that Welsh's William Wilson will also at some point encounter his double. Louise Welsh herself supplied me with some helpful notes on her novel. She fully acknowledged the debt, the allusion, to Poe, yet also noted that: 'There are, I'm glad to say, a lot of William Wilsons in the Glasgow telephone directory.'[43] Here, yet again, we have an example of an allusion which aims for the same uncertain status we associate with the uncanny. Just as there might be a natural explanation for the events in, say, Hogg's *Memoirs and Confessions of a Justified Sinner*, so there might be a natural explanation for having the name William Wilson. A man could be named William Wilson in the normal course of events either by his parents or by his novelist creator even if they had never heard of Edgar Allan Poe. Thus the novel recasts the same puzzle as Poe's original tale in a new intertextual form. Is the relationship between two William Wilsons uncannily significant or purely coincidental? The answer would seem to depend on whether or not Welsh's William Wilson discovers that he has a double and thus cements his potential bond with Poe's character.

Doubles are teasingly present on the novel's peripheries. Two glamorous dancing girls are described almost as doubles and the book is full of mirrors and reflections. William Wilson himself is unusually interested in doubles and indulges in fantasies of self-duplication. He is particularly fascinated by the illustration on his *The Boy's Own Guide to Conjuring* which depicts a boy magician pulling a rabbit from a hat:

> On a table suspiciously swathed by a green cloth, reclines a copy of *The Boy's Own Guide to Conjuring*. The boy on its cover is pulling the same rabbit from the same hat and the same book rests face up showing the same image, though it is more of a smudge now.[44]

The playfully recessive cover reminds us that William Wilson is himself just a character from a book – and one who is based on another character in an earlier book to boot. But in Welsh's novel it seems at first glance that the only doubles her hero meets are the ones we all have access to:

> If I positioned the mirrors on my mother's dressing-table at a particular angle I could achieve the same effect, myself repeated over and over into infinity. It gave me a strange feeling to see all of these other Williams shadowing my actions.[45]

Yet in one way this William Wilson could be described as doubled. Like the ladies he appears to chop in half, William's narrative is split between his past and present selves, creating two stories which are interwoven together rather than presented in their natural chronological order. There is just a hint at a *Doppelgänger* encounter when he has a brush with a young junky in Glasgow: 'We faced each other across the lighter's glow and I wondered if I was looking at my future self, Old Scrooge meeting the ghost of Christmas future.'[46] He attacks the junky, in a scene of violence which echoes the gunshot and mirror of Poe's 'William Wilson', and pushes him onto the pavement:

> and he pitched backwards hitting his head against the cobbles with a gunshot crack that sounded across the street. I saw him lie still, felt a sickening realisation, then stepped towards him. My move was reflected across the road in the bright lights beyond the plate glass. In the mirror world of colour and warmth a girl stood up pointing towards me.[47]

However, within the context of this novel, the most significant echo here is of Sylvie's death, which William Wilson has already experienced but which has not yet been revealed to the reader. Although this shooting is of a female (and quite separate) character there are interesting points of contact between this violent act and the climactic scene of Poe's tale. In Poe, William Wilson shoots his double. Then he (and the reader) is convinced for a moment that he has in fact only shot himself, as he glimpses his bloody reflection in a mirror. Then there is yet a further reversal as he realizes he is indeed looking, not at a mirror, but at his double whom he has murdered.

The twists and turns of Welsh's plot are comparable although the dynamic is reversed. At first William Wilson is confident he runs no risk of being a murderer in shooting Sylvie but then he is forced to realise that he has killed her. In a final twist it transpires that he has been doubly tricked and that Sylvie's 'death' was cleverly staged. William Wilson had to be kept in the dark in order that his invisible ghoulish audience (just like the novel's readers) would be deceived by his genuine horror into believing that the game of Russian roulette hadn't been fixed. A shooting which began and ended in guilt for Poe's William Wilson begins and ends in conscious innocence for Welsh's hero. Welsh naturalises the *Doppelgänger* trope, reinventing it in order to comment on our uncertain relationship with ourselves, particularly on the gulf which separates us from both our earlier and our later incarnations who remain fascinatingly out of reach in a virtual hall of mirrors, close, even visible, yet untouchable.

The second half of the twentieth century witnessed a revival of interest in the Victorian period which has been reflected in the growth of 'neo-Victorian' novels, a trend which may be traced back to John Fowles's *The French Lieutenant's Woman* (1969) and whose best-known recent exponent is probably Sarah Waters. Her highly successful *Fingersmith* (2002) features female doubles and it may be no coincidence that this novel is one of the most explicitly allusive productions of the neo-Victorian genre. Its most important (and best-known) sources are *The Woman in White* and *Lady Audley's Secret*, although it contains echoes of many other sensation novels including Collins's *Legacy of Cain* and *No Name* as well as Sheridan Le Fanu's *The Rose and the Key*.[48] The novel's plot involves not one but two switches of identity between the heroines, Maud and Sue. First of all Sue, a working-class thief, is aghast to realise that she is to be confined in a lunatic asylum in the place of her victim-turned-persecutor, the aristocratic Maud. Then it is revealed that Sue and Maud were switched as babies, meaning that their exchange of identities is a return to the status quo rather than a genuine reversal. If doubling is important to the novel's plot, it is also central to its allusive texture. Part of the pleasure for literary readers lies in recognising that they, like Sue, have been misled.

In the very first chapter Waters starts to hint at *Fingersmith*'s debts to earlier texts when she describes how the handsome villain, Rivers, earns his living recycling tales, 'putting them slightly different each time, and pinning different titles on them, and so making one old story pass as twenty brand-new ones'.[49] We are perhaps more likely to interpret this as a possible coded reference to the novel's own imitative procedures if we notice the similarity between the name of the cunning plotter Rivers, and that of his creator, Sarah Waters. If Rivers is like the book's author, Maud is like the book itself. Her fetish for kid gloves means that she is leather bound like the volumes her uncle makes her work with. She herself is aware that she resembles a volume from her uncle's collection, and notes dryly: 'We are not meant for common usage, my fellow books and I. My uncle keeps us separate from the world.'[50] Her textual quality is also hinted at by Sue, who remarks that she knows what Maud's fate will be in the same way 'you might know the fate of a person in a story or a play'.[51] When we first encounter Maud we see her through the eyes of Sue. Initially she seems like a 'double' of Laura Fairlie; childish in appearance and apparently guileless, she seems doomed to share Laura's fate of being married for her money by a cynical adventurer and then being incarcerated in an asylum under false pretences. Her name apparently cements this link for both girls have surnames – Fairlie, Lilly – which suggest pallor and delicacy. But as soon as Maud is revealed to be a conspirator rather than a dupe she takes over the narrating voice, and we realise that in fact she 'doubles' a very different kind of heroine.

Maud informs us that her mother was insane and that she was born and brought up in a madhouse before being claimed by her uncle and eventually forced to act as his secretary and immerse herself in his collection of rare pornography. Her mother's condition and her own fear of growing mad serve to connect her, not with Laura, but with Lady Audley, as does the fact that she is only acting the part of an ingénue. (We may now notice that the name 'Audl(e)y' is buried in Maud Lilly's name.) She tells us about her dreary childhood as a copyist. Like Rivers she recycles old books and in erasing the pages, making them blank, she duplicates her own status as a cipher, a heroine who is dramatically rewritten halfway through the novel and who also seeks to rewrite Sue's role, transforming her from a streetwise trickster to a passive victim. Maud observes: 'She learns the ways of the house, not understanding that the habits and the fabrics that bind will, soon, bind her. Bind her, like morocco or like calf.'[52]

Once we recognise *Lady Audley's Secret* to be at least as vital a source as *The Woman in White* we can perhaps see how *Fingersmith* doesn't simply echo that novel but also uncovers an unexploited plot twist which Braddon never develops. As we saw in the previous chapter, Phoebe, Lady Audley's maid, seems destined to swap roles with her mistress. The central turn of *Fingersmith*, the theft of a maid's identity and her wrongful incarceration in a lunatic asylum, could have been Phoebe's fate. It is easy to imagine some further wrench of Braddon's plot in which Phoebe is forced to take Lady Audley's place in the asylum. Phoebe's knowledge of French, for example, is sufficiently unusual to seem placed in the novel for a definite purpose. It has no apparent relevance – but could have played some role had she indeed been forced to take her mistress's place in the asylum in French-speaking Belgium. It might have counted against any claim that she was really only a lady's maid, just as Sue's soft white hands seem to prove that she cannot possibly be a servant. If *Lady Audley's Secret* seems to probe a concealed subtext in *The Woman in White* then *Fingersmith*, in its turn, submits Braddon's novel to a similar process. Waters' novel also, rather like *Armadale*, offers a kind of synthesis between its two key intertexts. Sue is a naive trickster and Maud a kind of guilty innocent. They are neither as stainless as Laura nor as culpable as Lady Audley, and they finish the novel lovers as well as doubles.

Although it is not set in the Victorian period, Will Self's 2002 novel *Dorian: An Imitation* is even more explicitly bound to its nineteenth-century source material than Waters' novel.[53] Here the novel advertises its derived status for all to see. We may infer the presence of *Fight Club* in *Glamorama* and conjecture that Palakon is Palahniuk's double. There is no need for conjecture in the case of *Dorian* which replicates (albeit in updated form) the principal characters and events from Wilde's original novel, insistently 'outing' it in the process – the three main characters are all more or less gay. Self's Dorian is as depraved as Wilde's, and his callous nature is mostly clearly demonstrated in his deliberate infection of countless sexual partners with

HIV. He remains AIDS free, although his portrait is visibly ravaged by the disease. There are some nice touches in the novel's insistence on dragging Wilde's covert homoeroticism out into the open. Wotton's bachelor uncle becomes an openly homosexual older man, as though in response to Eve Kosofsky Sedgwick's analysis of the coded importance of 'uncle' figures.[54] Even Wilde's coyly anonymous key source is 'outed': 'He was reading *Against Nature* by Huysmans, the Penguin Classics edition with the Comte de Montesquiou on the cover.'[55]

I suggested in the previous chapter that Alan Campbell could be seen as an 'avatar' of one of *Dorian Gray*'s key precursors in the *Doppelgänger* tradition, *Jekyll and Hyde*. In *Dorian* we can detect a similar intrusion of its own precursor, *The Picture of Dorian Gray*, or rather of its creator, Oscar Wilde, into this later imitation. Sir Henry Wotton, Dorian's cynical and corrupt friend, was already in a sense Wilde's alter ego in the original novel, and his Wildean qualities are intensified by Self. As with most such updates of canonical novels we can say of *Dorian* that it seems to be set in a world exactly like our own except for one important absence – its source. If Dorian and Baz (Basil Hallward) lived in a world where *The Picture of Dorian Gray* could be bought in the local Waterstones and had as concrete an identity as the precisely observed edition of Huysmans, they might just notice something odd was happening. Wotton should be in the same position of ignorance so his tendency to quote from Wilde strikes a jarring note. He greets his dealer with the words 'Excuse me, my dear Bluejay, while I arise from this semirecumbent position'[56] echoing Lady Bracknell's injunction to Jack Worthing when she discovers him kneeling at the feet of Gwendolen.[57] Wotton echoes a still more famous line in the same play[58] when he remarks: 'For Baz to have died once would have been unfortunate; for him to die twice looks like carelessness.'[59] Also significant is the strange microclimate which protects Wotton's home. All seasons coexist in his garden:

> Outside the car, the impossibilist season that always embowered Chez Wotton was in full budding, flowering, fruiting and falling swing. Supernature's own couvade. Cherry and apple blossom drifted across the pavement, while everything in the gardens – from snowdrops to roses, to lilacs and delphiniums – was in bloom.[60]

In itself this suggests Wotton's uncanny status. In the context of Wilde it echoes the story of 'The Selfish Giant', in which the garden is unaffected by the seasonal changes outside its walls.

A further clue to Wotton's authorial status is given in an exchange between him and Dorian towards the opening of the novel. Dorian is appalled by his reckless driving:

> 'How d'you manage to get away with it?' he asked. 'You had no way of knowing if there was a car in the oncoming lane.'
> 'I have an aerial view, Dorian. I see the whole situation from above.'
> 'Are you serious?'
> 'Never more so.'
> 'But how? It's not possible.'[61]

But these little oddnesses are finally explained when we reach the book's epilogue. Here it is at first revealed that the narrative we have been reading is the work of Henry Wotton, who has now died from AIDS. The typescript has just been read by his wife Victoria and by Dorian himself. Dorian, it turns out, is a normally well preserved and comparatively blameless man, a keen supporter of Tony Blair who enjoys a nodding acquaintance with the Princess of Wales. Wotton's identity as the author of *Dorian* strengthens his association with Wilde. The 'real' and more wholesome Dorian takes the strange manuscript home and is increasingly tormented by the voice of Wotton's ghost. In the novel's coda it becomes apparent that Wotton/Wilde's narrative is seeping into the 'normal' life of Dorian and that the evil fiction is becoming a reality. Wotton's book, in other words, is playing a function similar to that of the original portrait, that of Dorian's sinister double. The status of Wilde's own original novel as a kind of double of Wilde, and one that would help destroy him as the portrait destroyed Dorian, was not fully apparent on its first publication. But now this additional extratextual doubling possibility has been incorporated into Self's new fiction, with its own doubled textual layers. Under the influence of the Wildean Wotton and his book, Dorian is unable to escape his fate. The endings of Will Self's Dorian and Will Self's *Dorian* are ultimately both overdetermined by the shade of a more powerful authorial presence, Oscar Wilde, and his novel-writing avatar, the rewritten Wotton. The Dorian of the inset fiction may have been destroyed by a portrait, but the 'real' Dorian, like the real Wilde, is destroyed by a text.

The novel's imitative status, flagged in Self's subtitle 'An Imitation', is reflected in the texture of Dorian's fictional world. Nine simultaneous videos of Dorian comprise the installation which replaces the conventional portrait. Video tape is prone to decay – and the decay of Dorian's image goes hand in hand with the decay of the medium itself – but is also easily reproduced:

> 'How long will these tapes last, Baz?' he asked.
> 'It's hard to say . . . Certainly years, if not decades, and by then they can be transferred to new tapes, and so on – for ever, I guess.'
> 'So these' – Dorian gestured – 'will remain young for ever while I grow old, then die?'
> 'Yeah, well,' Baz snorted derisively. 'You can't copy bodies – yet.'[62]

At the same time as the development of a postmodern aesthetic has further heightened the self-conscious reflexivity of the *Doppelgänger* tradition, technological advances, as Baz's final remark indicates, have given it a new idiom within which to work. Cloning technology, a staple of science fiction long before it became scientific fact, is characteristically used as a tool with which writers can explore the ethical and philosophical implications of the deliberate duplication of an individual. Like the double, however, the clone possesses the potential to create an uncanny charge when it signals its relationship not just with its clone siblings but, moving outside the confines of its own fictional world, with an array of clone texts.

David Mitchell's *Cloud Atlas* (2004), which comprises six nested short stories, is full of literary echoes, both of individual works and of broader generic traditions.[63] Many readers will find the chronologically penultimate section, 'An Orison of Sonmi', set in a bleakly dystopian future Korea, especially familiar, as it contains a disproportionate number of allusions to other works, most of them science fiction films or novels. For, rather like *The Picture of Dorian Gray*, *Cloud Atlas* is so embedded in a particular generic tradition as to seem derivative. Yet the obtrusive sense of *déjà lu* is part of the point. Sonmi is triply a clone. She is a clone within her own fiction, designed together with countless 'sisters' to live out her life as a slave of Papa Song Corp. She is also a reincarnation of *Cloud Atlas*'s four earlier protagonists, all of whom bear a comet birthmark on their shoulder. And finally she – and her story – is a 'clone' of countless earlier dystopian narratives. This final, more covert function, is nicely signalled by her full name – Sonmi-451. She is the latest of a sequence of clone sisters, and her text is the latest in a series of related texts, among them *Fahrenheit 451* (1953), Ray Bradbury's tale of a future America in which books are burned.

Throughout the episode we are insistently reminded of other

memorable texts. Sonmi at first takes against her work partner, Yoona-939, thinking her aloof and sullen[64] but eventually warms to Yoona who turns out to be a subversive rebel and a model for Sonmi herself to follow before her eventual destruction. The story here closely follows the opening of Margaret Atwood's *The Handmaid's Tale* in which Offred gradually realises that Ofglen, who at first seems primly conformist, is as hostile to the regime of Gilead as Offred herself.[65] Like Yoona, Ofglen is discovered and she commits suicide to escape arrest. Mitchell underscores this clear homage to Atwood by making Sonmi's interviewer drop a casual reference to 'the Pentecostal Revolutions of North America'.[66] A similarly sly move caps Mitchell's account of the revelatory experience of reading uncensored history books written by 'pre-skirmish thinkers'.[67] In case we hadn't noticed the similarities between Sonmi's experience and Bernard's exposure to Shakespeare in *Brave New World*, or Winston Smith's devouring of The Book in *1984*, Sonmi gives us a nudge. (The word 'Optimist' is an ironic reminder of the values upheld in Sonmi's society: 'The library refused many requests of course, but I succeeded with two Optimists translated from the Late English, Orwell and Huxley.'[68]) Sonmi is simultaneously a clone and a fully human individual just as Mitchell's novel is derived from countless others but articulates a memorably distinctive vision.

The climax of the episode is Sonmi's realisation that her sisters end their serving careers not in 'xultation' to a pampered life in Hawaii, but in death, and transformation into the 'soap', or doctored food, on which all the clones are fed. This clear allusion to Richard Fleischer's 1973 film *Soylent Green* is reinforced by a pointed reference to the same decaying ecosystems which force unwitting cannibalism on the overpopulated world of *Soylent Green*. And, typically, the protagonist of the previous episode of *Cloud Atlas* explicitly alludes to that film, quoting its famous line 'Soylent Green is people'.[69] The horrific recycling of her 'sisters' playfully echoes the episode's own, more overt, intra- and intertextual recycling dynamic. These repetitions and doublings reinforce one of Mitchell's central themes: that humanity is doomed to repeat the same patterns of greed, expansion and violence followed by destruction and decay.

The characteristic resonances of the *Doppelgänger* motif make it a particularly compelling marker of uncanny allusion. Traditionally, seeing one's double is associated with bad luck, even death. In literature this tradition is upheld and yet a double can also be an influence for good or an object of fascination. This strange compound of envy, fear, resentment, attraction and dependence might equally be said to characterise the relationship between texts and sources, writers and their influences. In each relationship we can identify a struggle for mastery which may be won either by the original, the 'source' or (as in Andersen's tale) by the shadow or double. Uncertainty is another hallmark of the *Doppelgänger* encounter, one which emerges with greatest clarity if (as so often happens) the doubles fight. Who is doing what to whom? Is the uncanny resemblance real or just the function of someone's self-deluding obsession with the idea of a *Doppelgänger*? Does the *Doppelgänger* even exist? These uncertainties over the nature (and even the existence) of textual *Doppelgängers* are similar to those which dog the critic who is trying to pin down the comparably uncertain phenomenon of allusion; that sense that two texts are somehow bound to one another. Although one doesn't want to become the critical equivalent of Hermann Hermann, seeing allusions everywhere in defiance of the evidence, it is important to remember (as Louise Welsh's reflections on the reuse of the name 'William Wilson' remind us) that an allusion can lose some of its uncanny charm if its allusivity is absolutely unequivocal. To take an example from this chapter, although my suggestion that there is a relationship between Palakon and Chuck Palahniuk would of course be strengthened if Palakon were actually called Palahniuk, my pleasure in the – possible – link would somehow be diminished if it were less teasing and uncertain.

Notes

1 The novel was first published in Russian in 1934 and then translated into English by the author in 1937.
2 V. Nabokov, *Despair* (New York: G. P. Putnam Son's, 1966), p. 211.
3 For a discussion of the *Doppelgänger* theme in *Despair* see J. W. Connolly, 'The Major Russian Novels', in J. W. Connolly (ed.), *The Cambridge Companion to Nabokov* (Cambridge: Cambridge University Press, 2005), pp. 135–50; G. E. Slethaug, *The Play of the Double in Postmodern American Fiction* (Carbondale: Southern Illinois University Press, 1993), pp. 33–57. Nabokov's interest in the double, and doubling, can be seen in many other novels, including *Lolita*, *Pale Fire* and *The Real Life of Sebastian Knight*. See J. W. Connolly, 'Nabokov's (re)visions of Dostoevsky' in J. W. Connolly (ed.), *Nabokov and his Fictions* (Cambridge: Cambridge University Press, 1999), pp. 141–57.

4 J. W. Connolly notes that in the original Russian the word used by Nabokov, *zapiski*, might invoke Gogol's *Diary of a Madman* (J. W. Connolly, 'The Function of Allusion in Nabokov's *Despair*', *Slavic and East European Journal*, 26.3 (1982), 302–13, p. 304.)
5 Nabokov, *Despair*, p. 25.
6 *Ibid.*, p. 43.
7 *Ibid.*, p. 55.
8 *Ibid.*, p. 80.
9 *Ibid.*, p. 87.
10 *Ibid.*, p. 107.
11 *Ibid.*, p. 118.
12 *Ibid.*, p. 107.
13 V. Nabokov, *Lolita* (London: Penguin, 1997), p. 297.
14 Similarly *Rebecca* can be interpreted as the uncanny double of *Jane Eyre*, with Mrs de Winter and Rebecca shadowing Jane and Bertha. Among the many parallels between the two novels is the role played by a catastrophic fire. See for example N. Abi-Ezzi, *The Double in the Fiction of R.L. Stevenson, Wilkie Collins and Daphne du Maurier* (Oxford: Peter Lang, 2003), pp. 264–9.
15 For discussions of this comparatively neglected novel see N. Abi-Ezzi, *The Double*, pp. 259–63; N. Auerbach, *Daphne du Maurier, Haunted Heiress* (Philadelphia: University of Pennsylvania Press, 2000), pp. 90–2; M. Forster, *Daphne du Maurier* (London: Arrow, 1994), pp. 283–90; A. Horner and S. Zlosnik, *Daphne du Maurier: Writing, Identity and the Gothic Imagination* (Basingstoke: Macmillan, 1998), pp. 145–58.
16 D. du Maurier, *The Scapegoat* (Philadelphia: University of Pennsylvania Press, 2000), p. 38.
17 D. du Maurier, *Rebecca* (London: Pan, 1975), p. 175.
18 du Maurier, *The Scapegoat*, p. 45.
19 du Maurier, *Rebecca*, p. 257.
20 du Maurier, *The Scapegoat*, p. 261.
21 *Ibid.*, p. 20.
22 *Ibid.*, p. 23.
23 *Ibid.*, p. 31.
24 See Forster, *Daphne du Maurier*, pp. 12–14.
25 For an excellent analysis of various doubling mechanisms in Priest's novels see P. Kincaid, *What It Is We Do When We Read Science Fiction* (London: Beccon Publications, 2008), pp. 89–137.
26 For a useful discussion of the novel's debts to other *Doppelgänger* texts, such as *Frankenstein*, see N. Ruddick, 'Reticence and Ostentation in Christopher Priest's Later Novels: *The Quiet Woman* and *The Prestige*', in A. M. Butler (ed.), *Christopher Priest: The Interaction* (London: The Science Fiction Foundation, 2005), pp. 9–96.

27 C. Priest, *The Prestige* (London: Touchstone, 1995), p. 134, p. 387.
28 See for example this discussion www.sfsignal.com/archives/2006/03/review-the-prestige-by-christopher-priest/, accessed 16 January 2011.
29 C. Priest, *The Affirmation* (London: Touchstone, 1996), pp. 2–3.
30 Priest, *The Prestige*, p. 106.
31 Priest, *The Affirmation*, p. 20.
32 A. Koestler, *The Act of Creation* (London: Hutchinson, 1976), p. 35.
33 See V. Stewart, 'The Other War: Christopher Priest's *The Separation*', in Butler (ed.), *Christopher Priest: The Interaction*, pp. 115–27 for an account of uncanny repetitions within the text.
34 C. Priest, *The Separation* (London: Gollancz, 2004), p. 5.
35 *Ibid.*, p. 53, p. 56.
36 www.ansible.co.uk/sfx/sfx123.html, accessed 3 August 2010.
37 www.infinityplus.co.uk/nonfiction/intcpriest.htm, accessed 3 August 2010.
38 For a discussion of doubling in the novel see H. S. Nielsen, 'Telling Doubles and Literal-minded Reading in Bret Easton Ellis's *Glamorama*', in A. Durand and N. Mandel (eds), *Novels of the Contemporary Extreme* (London: Continuum, 2006), pp. 20–30.
39 B. Easton Ellis, *Glamorama* (London: Picador, 2000), p. 432.
40 *Ibid.*, pp. 434–5.
41 For a comparison between the two novels see A. E. Blazer, '*Glamorama*, *Fight Club*, and the Terror of Narcissistic Abjection', in J. Prosser (ed.), *American Fiction of the 1990s: Reflections of History and Culture* (London and New York: Routledge, 2008), pp. 177–89.
42 K. Stirling suggests a further intertextual doubling possibility which has a particular resonance within this study. ('"Dr Jekyll and Mr Jackass": *Fight Club* as a Refraction of Hogg's *Justified Sinner* and Stevenson's *Dr Jekyll and Mr Hyde*', in C. Gutleben and S. Onega (eds), *Refracting the Canon in Contemporary British Literature and Film* (Amsterdam: Rodopi, 2004), pp. 83–94.) See also D. Cojocaru, 'Confessions of an American Psycho: James Hogg's and Bret Easton Ellis's Anti-Heroes' Journey from Vulnerability to Violence', *Contagion: Journal of Violence, Mimesis and Culture*, 15/16 (2008–9), 185–200.
43 Email correspondence with Louise Welsh received 2 February 2009.
44 L. Welsh, *The Bullet Trick* (Edinburgh: Canongate, 2006), p. 43.
45 *Ibid.*
46 *Ibid.*, p. 45.
47 *Ibid.*, pp. 46–7.
48 An indication of the degree to which Waters has immersed herself in the sensation fiction of the period is given in S. Waters, 'Sensational Fiction: Sarah Waters on the Echoes of "Sensation Novels" in *Fingersmith*', *The Guardian*, 17 June 2006 www.guardian.co.uk/books/2006/jun/17/fiction.sarahwaters, accessed 27 June 2010.

49 S. Waters, *Fingersmith* (London: Virago, 2002), p. 21.
50 *Ibid.*, p. 218.
51 *Ibid.*, p. 101.
52 *Ibid.*, pp. 250–1.
53 For an analysis of this novel see A. Smith, 'Death, Art, and Bodies: Queering the Queer Gothic in Will Self's *Dorian*' in W. Hughes and A. Smith (eds) *Queering the Gothic* (Manchester: Manchester University Press, 2009), pp. 177–92.
54 E. K. Sedgwick, *Tendencies* (London: Routledge, 1994), pp. 57–71.
55 W. Self, *Dorian* (London: Viking, 2002), pp. 54–5.
56 *Ibid.*, p. 106.
57 O. Wilde, *The Major Works* (Oxford: Oxford University Press, 2000), p. 492.
58 *Ibid.*, p. 494.
59 *Ibid.*, p. 106.
60 *Ibid.*, pp. 129–30.
61 *Ibid.*, p. 26.
62 *Ibid.*, p. 22.
63 Although the novel is too recent to have been the subject of much formal published research, *Cloud Atlas*, and its links with many other science fiction texts, has been discussed widely on the internet. The very many reviews it has attracted on Amazon, for example, identify some of its many sources. www.amazon.co.uk/Cloud-Atlas-David-Mitchell/dp/0340822775, accessed 28 June 2010.
64 D. Mitchell, *Cloud Atlas* (London: Sceptre, 2004), p. 190.
65 M. Atwood, *The Handmaid's Tale* (London: Everyman, 2006), p. 194.
66 Mitchell, *Cloud Atlas*, pp. 343–4.
67 *Ibid.*, p. 220.
68 *Ibid.*
69 *Ibid.*, p. 179.

4

Ruins

In Act 5 of *The Duchess of Malfi*, Antonio, the Duchess's husband, and his friend Delio, have an encounter with a mysterious echo in the ruins of an ancient abbey. This scene, though not itself notably allusive, can be read as a suggestive emblem of the capacity of ruins to function as uncanny allusion markers.[1] Antonio is still unaware that his wife, the Duchess of Malfi, together with their two children, has been murdered at the instigation of her scheming brothers, Ferdinand and the Cardinal. At this stage in the play Antonio still hopes to be reconciled with the Cardinal and reunited with his family. But the audience knows better and so, it seems, does the mysterious echo:

> Ant: It groan'd methought, and gave
> A very deadly accent.
> Echo: *Deadly accent.*
> Delio: I told you 'twas a pretty one: you may make it
> A huntsman, or a falconer, a musician,
> Or a thing of sorrow.
> Echo: *A thing of sorrow.*[2]

Ruins have traditionally been thought of as uncanny, haunted places.[3] As well as simply being the traces of the buildings in which people long since dead once lived, ruins have themselves often been figured as skeletons, corpses or ghosts. This association is implicit in the hint at anthropomorphism in Antonio's description of the courtyard as lying 'naked to the injuries of stormy weather' and more explicit in his suggestion that churches and cities, like men, suffer from death and disease: 'Churches and cities, which have diseases like to men, / Must have like death that we have.'[4] Earlier in the play the Duchess's waiting-woman, Cariola, makes a similar link when she compares her doomed mistress to 'some reverend monument / Whose ruins are even pitied'.[5]

The link between a crumbling building and a decaying corpse is strikingly described by Lord Byron, one of the most memorable poets of ruin, in *Childe Harold's Pilgrimage*:[6]

> Look on its broken arch, its ruin'd wall,
> Its chambers desolate and portals foul:
> Yes, this was once Ambition's airy hall,
> The dome of Thought, the palace of the Soul:
> Behold through each lack-lustre, eyeless hole.[7]

But it is not only the corpses of our ancestors which ruins have the power to evoke. In the same poem Byron famously describes himself as 'a ruin amidst ruins'[8] and the ruin's capacity to figure our own (decaying) body is also identified by Robert Ginsberg: 'We walk through the walls. We enter into the substance . . . Not the visage alone but the torso of the wall spreads about us. The former wall bears/bares its being in a space that we too occupy.'[9] The permeability of a building in decay enables the spectator to inhabit and even fuse with a ruin as well as simply to observe it. Thus in Pier Paolo Pasolini's 1967 film *Edipo Re*, for example, Oedipus's journey through a maze of ruined walls hints at a more metaphysical journey into his buried, subconscious fears and desires. Returning to *The Duchess of Malfi* we may note that Antonio is himself a kind of walking corpse, a ruin, at this point, overdetermined to death and deaf to the echo's many hints.[10]

This double identification whereby a ruin may denote both ourselves and our ancestors is mirrored in the textual ruin's ability to act as an uncanny allusion marker which becomes a bridge between texts from very different times. In the case of textual ruins, past, present and sometimes future are often layered on top of one another to create a palimpsest effect which may be intensified, modified or interrogated if one such ruin later becomes subject to imitation or allusion by another. Such temporal shifts are perhaps partly a function of the inherently anachronistic nature of ruins. Ginsberg notes that 'ruin incongruity is linked to anachronism, anomaly, ambiguity, irony, and uncanniness'[11] so it isn't perhaps surprising that further, more unexpected, anachronisms are embedded into so many textual ruins. Thus while Antonio feels that in walking through a ruin he is also stepping into 'some reverend history',[12] the scene also invokes incongruous 'memories' of a world which postdates Antonio because, for Webster's audiences, the spectacle of a ruined abbey would have been so strongly associated with the effects of the English Reformation on the landscape.

The kinds of double visions offered by ruins, sometimes a straightforward importation of the past into the present, sometimes something rather more complex, are similar to those associated both with allusion and with the uncanny. The power of an allusion depends upon a similar apprehension of the absent whole in the present trace or fragment, on the ability to hold two things in one's mind simultaneously and appreciate the gap or charge between them, the transforming effect of a new context. Doubleness, ambiguity, is also a hallmark of the uncanny. An unambiguously supernatural force is far less uncanny than one which just might have a natural explanation. Webster's echo is an excellent illustration of this characteristic of the uncanny. On the one hand it is a long-established local phenomenon which can be accounted for quite easily using purely rational and scientific methods. This is the view supported by Delio's coolly measured account. On the other hand Antonio thinks it sounds just like his wife, and this echo does in fact function very like a ghost, appearing just after the Duchess's death in order to warn her husband of danger. In the dialogue between Antonio and the echo, Webster is following the tradition (discussed in the introduction) whereby an echo, often the nymph Echo herself, is simultaneously a passive repeater and an agent with her own agenda. The poet cleverly ensures that the last few words have a slightly different meaning when repeated by the echo in isolation from the rest of the 'real' speaker's sentence, in some cases ingeniously truncating one of the words to intensify the effectiveness of the exchange. 'You'll find it impossible / To fly your fate' observes Antonio to Delio. '*O, fly your fate!*' responds the echo.[13] The response is clearly derived from Antonio – but is the echo conscious or unconscious of the precise effects she is creating? We may ask the same question of allusions of course.

The dynamic of echo has an affinity with ruin as well as with allusion. All three represent fragments of an original; all, partly through their incompleteness, act as a spur to further creativity and thought.[14] An indistinct echo allows the listener to extrapolate different possible utterances; crumbling masonry may be fashioned by the mind into a temple, a theatre or a palace; a fragment of an earlier text in a new work may, at least if the source is well known, send a reader to any number of relevant parts of the earlier work. Such puzzles and uncertainties can be pleasurable. Even Antonio is able to forget his perilous position for a moment and exclaim with an antiquarian enthusiasm perhaps more typical of later centuries: 'I do love these ancient ruins.'[15] This connoisseur's pleasure in ruins, the power they give the viewer to complete the picture, is suggested by Delio's words about the similarly incomplete and mysterious echo: 'You may make it / a huntsman, or a falconer, a musician / Or a thing of sorrow.' The aesthetic satisfaction generated by all three phenomena lies partly in the way they offer a pattern of sameness and difference, the same essential pattern of statement and refrain which lies behind so much of our enjoyment of architecture, music and poetry.

But the additional quality of mystery and incompleteness which is so clearly apparent in a ruin or an echo (the crafted, literary echo in any case) gives these phenomena a special bond with allusion. We have seen in *The Duchess of Malfi* that an echo, though only a fragment and a repetition, can change the meaning of its original and seem to possess a knowledge unknown to the originator. The same is true of an alluding text's relationship with its source. A ruin similarly, although ostensibly never more than a subset of its former self, can be more than the original, exerting a power over the spectator's imagination which it never did whole.

For the pleasure to be found in ruins is paradoxical. Part of the tantalising charm of a ruin is that we can never quite visualise its former state, but strain to do so and wish that the past splendour could be restored: here Byron, in *Childe Harold*, tries – and fails – to recapture the lost glory of Athens:

> Here let me trace
> The latent grandeur of thy dwelling place.
> It may not be; nor ev'n can Fancy's eye
> Restore what Time hath labour'd to deface.[16]

Yet a longing to behold the vanished buildings of Greece, Rome or Troy goes hand in hand with an acknowledgement that we might not care so much for the buildings in their pristine state. Rose Macaulay, writing about the ruins of Greek temples, once polished and polychrome, asks: 'Should we admire them so much, or should we feel a faint suggestion of garishness, even of bad taste, in those brilliant, accomplished, flawless places of worship set so opulently in the barren mountain land above seas the vivid blue of posters?'[17] Only in a later time, a modern setting, do such buildings reach their full, imperfect, perfection:

> there is a power
> And magic in the ruined battlement,
> For which the palace of the present hour
> Must yield its pomp, and wait till ages are its dower.
>
> Oh Time! The beautifier of the dead,
> Adorner of the ruin.[18]

A similar paradox inheres in the relationship between texts and sources explored in this chapter. The (perceived) superiority of the older text can only come about after its constant citation by later writers has given it the patina – and the mystery – of antiquity.[19] This paradox is reflected in the ambiguities and tensions which can be detected in so many evocations of the ruinous past. Often a later poet's apparent deference both to an earlier source and to the ruins of the past is belied by a barely concealed truculence. Rather similarly, on a purely physical and literal level, ruins evoke contradictory feelings. Many cultures have of course found a special beauty in ruins, even going so far as to destroy whole buildings, or to create 'ruins' from scratch, in their search for a picturesque effect. But feelings of awe – ruins have from time to time been viewed as the productions of gods or giants – can shade into dread. Even when not associated with the supernatural, ruins often accrue a sinister aura. As we shall see, they are thought to be inhabited by unpleasant or dangerous creatures, such as toads and snakes, and are associated with disease and death. Thus seen as locations of ill omen and ill health, ruins were often avoided by later generations, who chose instead to build new settlements at some remove from their ancestors' decaying dwellings. As he leaves the ruins and their echo behind him, Antonio declares, 'Come: I'll be out of this ague',[20] and ruins have certainly often been associated with illness, in particular fever.[21] Thus buildings, like texts, become less 'homely' the longer they survive, as their power to inspire both wonder and hostility becomes intensified.

Many have identified or implied a link between the fabric of a text and that of a building. In Andrew Marvell's *Upon Appleton House* a three-way pattern of correspondence between house, body and poem is ingeniously created. The poem opens with an example of the fusion between building and body discussed above:

> Within this sober Frame expect
> Work of no Forrain *Architect*;
> That unto Caves the Quarries drew,
> And Forrests did to Pastures hew;
> Who of his great Design in pain
> Did for a Model vault his Brain,
> Whose Columnes should so high be rais'd
> To arch the Brows that on them gaz'd.[22]

It then goes on to create a further parallel between the poet's eloquent 'lines' and the similarly simple but expressive lines of the house:

> *Humility* alone designs
> Those short but admirable Lines,
> By which, ungirt and unconstrain'd,
> Things greater are in less contain'd.[23]

Here the creation of a new text and a new house go hand in hand but buildings – and poems – are both equally amenable to being broken down and recycled. 'These fragments,' writes T. S. Eliot in *The Waste Land*, 'have I shored against my ruin.'[24] Quotations or allusions can be likened to ruined fragments, pillaged like marble from the Roman Forum to create fresh hybrids, such as those described by Rose Macaulay in *Pleasure of Ruins*. Here she explains how fragments from ancient ruins have often been redeployed in new constructions, sometimes to incongruous effect:

> Many [ruined abbeys and churches] were built up long since into manor houses or farm-houses or barns, so that one may see chancel arches and fragments of carved stone and Gothic windows in the most incongruous places, in a thousand farm buildings standing about the countryside, as in the seventeenth-century farm-house which has incorporated great fragments of Halesowen abbey, so that hay-waggons, cattle and horses are stabled within church walls set with cloister doorways, and lancet windows look down on munching carthorses.[25]

Such recycled ruins might be compared to allusions or quotations embedded in a later work, clues to the presence of a still earlier construct.

Ruins don't have to be thus redeployed in order to have a special affinity with allusions. Even when left alone they inevitably acquire a fresh context by which they are in some way transformed. As we've already seen, they owe much of their resonance to the gap which exists between their former grandeur and their present altered state. The viewer imports some sense of the long-vanished picture, original and whole, into the new scene. The ruins may be located in some deserted spot and have been partly obscured by vegetation. Or they may, on the other hand, be found in the middle of a bustling modern city, overwhelmed by more imposing modern buildings. Similarly an allusion depends for some of its charm on the way it acts as a link between past and present, as the intersection between an earlier text (which we must import into our reading for ourselves, just as we must use our imagination to imagine how the ruin originally looked) and a new context which may be indebted to the work to which it alludes but which also in its turn adds to that earlier work's richness and complexity.

It is hardly surprising, given the many perceived links between texts and buildings, that we often find archaeological metaphors within literary criticism, whether we are searching beneath the surface of a text to find its concealed sources or excavating it to discover buried meanings.[26] Frederic Jameson observes that we apprehend texts 'through sedimented layers of previous interpretations, or – if the text is brand-new – through the sedimented reading habits and categories developed by those inherited interpretative traditions'.[27] But when a text actually depicts a ruin such effects may be intensified, and the 'real' ruins within the fiction can function as uncanny allusion markers which hint at the buried presence of some still earlier text.

Indirectly or directly many such descriptions of ruins in Western literature hark back to a passage from Book 8 of Virgil's *Aeneid*. This programmatic passage for any consideration of ruins in literature is in fact an anti- or ante-ruin, for it describes the beginning rather than the end of a great civilisation. Evander, a Greek leader now settled in Italy, shows his new ally, Aeneas, around the future site of Rome:

> hinc ad Tarpeiam sedem et Capitolia ducit
> aurea nunc, olim silvestribus horrida dumis.[28]
>
> (From here he leads him to the Tarpeian house, and the Capitol –
> golden now, then bristling with woodland thickets.)

If not originally, then certainly in the light of later texts and later history, this passage accrues temporal ambiguities. We might at first assume that *nunc*, 'now', refers to the action of the poem rather than to Virgil's own time. The contrasting *olim*, here translated 'then', does not absolutely resolve the situation. Although its primary meaning is 'once', suggesting the past, it can also mean 'at a future time'.[29] The line allows a progression from splendour to decay to lurk behind the ostensibly more triumphalist vision. Thus to the obvious contrast between Rome's primitive beginnings and future splendour, we can add a third picture, of a future, decaying Rome. Admittedly the contrast between a prosperous present and a desolate future is weak and fugitive in comparison with the default, optimistic interpretation, supported both by normal word usage and the poem's context. Yet a few lines later the reader is offered a second invitation to peer into the future:

> Talibus inter se dictis ad tecta subibant
> pauperis Euandri, passimque armenta videbant
> Romanoque foro et lautis mugire Carinis.[30]
>
> (So talking to each other, they came to the house of humble Evander, and saw cattle all about, lowing in the Roman Forum and in the fashionable Carinae.)

The Roman reader was required to travel back from the Augustan 'present' to Rome's pastoral past, bringing Evander's cattle forward in time to become an incongruous virtual presence in the busy urban centre of Virgil's own day. But these lines also seem to invite an apocalyptic reading. If we interpret the scene as a vision of the future we don't have to layer past and present on top of one another to create a hybrid montage. As a vision of Rome's possible future the picture of cows lowing in the Forum is simply and literally true. In *Archaeologies of English Renaissance Literature*, Philip Schwyzer makes the following observation about a group of English Renaissance treatments of ruin, including Shakespeare's Sonnet 73:

> Each is an experiment in double vision, exploring how different objects may occupy a single space, and how a reader or viewer may hold conflicting impressions in mind at the same time. Each moreover conveys an experience of instability, in which fixed images of the Reformation dissolve into their opposites.[31]

The same quality of 'double vision' inheres in Virgil's vision of the Forum.

At the same time as he shows Aeneas the site of the Capitol, Evander points out the ruined walls of two earlier great cities, founded by Janus and Saturn.[32] Two-headed Janus, god of the threshold, is an appropriate presence within a passage which simultaneously looks forward to the future and back to the past. Ruins are themselves Janus-headed. This triple vision, which brings past, present and future together in one place, recalls a parallel moment from Book 6 of the *Aeneid*, Aeneas's encounter with both his ancestors and his unborn descendents in the underworld. As well as placing dead, living and future men together in a single point of space and time, Virgil further conflates the generations by presenting Aeneas's descendents as reincarnations of the dead.[33]

As we have seen, ruins are in many ways ambiguous, both as material presences and as textual markers. They can be seen both as picturesquely elegiac and as ominously apocalyptic. And, rather as *olim* can signal a movement backwards or forwards in time, although they signal decay and loss they can paradoxically resemble fresh constructions, unfinished rather than dilapidated.[34] Thus in Virgil's *Aeneid* the ruins of Troy – which act as the catalyst for Aeneas's quest – are mirrored both in the foundations of Carthage and in the site of future Rome as well as, more logically, in the remains of the ancient cities founded by Janus and Saturn.

For later writers, this passage proved an irresistible allusion trigger, activating a range of responses from men and women who flourished after Virgil's veiled prediction had been fulfilled. Rome's second childhood strangely resembled its infancy. After its destruction by invaders in the fifth century CE, the Forum did indeed become both a ruin and a cow field – the 'Campo Vaccino' – where cattle grazed among the ruins.[35] And even before Rome's fall we can find self-consciously post-Virgilian literary ruins which seem to enact a sense of loss and decay. Less than a century after the *Aeneid* was written, the poet Lucan produced his violently energetic account of the Civil War between Caesar and Pompey, the *Pharsalia*. Caesar, the poem's charismatic though destructive protagonist, goes on what can only be described as a sightseeing tour of the ruins of Troy.[36] A particularly striking feature of this episode is its obtrusive textuality. The fabric of the poem and the ruined landscape become one. [37]

The initial impulse for Caesar's journey was his search for Pompey:

cuius vestigia frustra
terris sparsa legens fama duce tendit in undas
Threiciasque legit fauces et amore notatum.[38]

(In vain he followed Pompey's scattered traces over the land, and then report guided him to the sea. He sailed along the Thracian straits and the waters made famous by the lovers)

The polyptoton here, whereby two different parts of the same verb *lego* are used in the same position in subsequent lines, catches the eye and indeed the ear, especially given the echo of *terris sparsa* in *Threicasque*. This rhetorical device draws attention to *lego*, which may be translated here first as 'following' (952) and then as 'coasted along' (953), but which has a further important meaning: to read. *Notatum* similarly has connotations of marking or writing, and Caesar seems to travel into a world of texts and signs rather than a simple physical landscape.

> circumit exustae nomen memorabile Troiae
> magnaque Phoebei quaerit vestigia muri.[39]
>
> (He walked around the memorable name of burnt out Troy, and searched for the mighty remains of the wall that Apollo raised. (my translation))

The Loeb edition offers the translation: 'He walked round the burnt city of Troy, now only a famous name.' This version occludes the oddly textual quality of Lucan's landscape. Like the protagonist of Philip K. Dick's science fiction novel *Time out of Joint* (1959), for whom objects slip away to be replaced with pieces of paper with their names on, Caesar inhabits a world which is made up of words rather than things. This reification of the name, of the signifier, encourages us to look more closely at these ruined walls.

> iam siluae steriles et putres robore trunci
> assaraci pressere domos et templa deorum
> iam lassa radice tenent, ac tota teguntur
> Pergama dumetis: etiam periere ruinae.[40]
>
> (Now barren woods and rotting tree-trunks grow over the palace of Assaracus, and their worn-out roots clutch the temples of the gods, and Pergama is covered over with thorn-brakes: the very ruins have been destroyed.)

As Philip Hardie notes, these barren woods and rotting tree trunks enact a decline from Virgil's bucolic anti-ruins and 'the very ruins have been destroyed' might operate intertextually to signal this decline.[41] The reference to the *silvae*, encroaching and sterile, adds a self-deprecating reflexivity to this vision of a ruined ruin, for the word was also used as a generic title for collections of occasional poems, including the *Silvae* of Lucan's contemporary, the poet Statius. The image of the ruined ruin might thus shadow the trajectory from the Golden to the Silver Age of Roman literature.

Caesar continues his journey into the legendary and textual past. In the space of a few lines he ticks off Hesione's rock, Anchises' marriage-chamber, Oenone's peak, and the spot where Paris bestowed the apple upon Aphrodite. 'Nullum est sine nomine saxum', 'no stone is without a name',[42] writes Lucan, again suggesting that the name is physically present in the scene. The words also might recall Virgil's own description of the fall of Troy, experienced at first hand by Aeneas of course. The decapitated trunk of Priam, unlike Lucan's inanimate stones, lacks a name, is 'sine nomine corpus'.[43] This corrective echo of Virgil might counter hints at Lucan's belated desuetude. While the landscape is barer and older than it was in Aeneas's time, it has a compensating textual and cultural richness not yet realised at the point of Troy's destruction, something like the 'aura' which, Walter Benjamin suggests, inheres in revered cultural artefacts.[44] Troy's full value is only achieved at the cost of distance and time, a process of aestheticisation already begun within the fiction of the *Aeneid*, for the recent conflict is depicted on the walls of Dido's palace. Thus to be secondary, like Lucan, is not necessarily to be inferior. Only in retrospect can a city ruined by war acquire beauty and cultural value.

This ambiguity is glanced at in an eighteenth-century translation of Lucan's poem by Nicholas Rowe. Rowe translates Lucan's well-known 'etiam periere ruinae'[45] as 'even the ruined ruins are decayed'.[46] This might be said to enact a further movement of belatedness, whereby a 'modern' poet, and a translator to boot, feels inferior to a classic predecessor. But the change from 'even the ruins are ruined' to 'even the ruined ruins are decayed' may suggest a further degree of disintegration but also represents an overtopping or trumping of Lucan's original paradox. A comparable effect is created by William Empson's echo of Tennyson in 'Missing Dates'. The line 'The woods decay, the woods decay and fall' from 'Tithonus' seems, as John Hollander notes, to have metamorphosed into 'The waste remains, the waste remains and kills' in Empson's poem.[47]

Eventually the prophecy of future ruin which may be excavated from the *Aeneid* was, at least partially, fulfilled. In *Rome in the*

Dark Ages, Peter Llewellyn describes how the city's infrastructure collapsed, as Rome's political and cultural importance dwindled: 'The low-lying centre near the river was becoming unhealthy as the complex organisation that under the emperors had maintained the banks and drainage disappeared; on the outskirts of the city the aqueducts, broken in the wars and sketchily repaired, dripped and formed stagnant, fever-bearing swamps.'[48] The twelfth-century *Ligurinus* of Günther offers a particularly lurid account of a swampy and pestilential Rome:

> sqalida torpet humus, corruptis stagna lacusque
> inficiuntur aquis, pigrisque paludibus atrae
> exhalant nebulae . . .
> adde quod antiquis horrens inculta ruinis
> parte sui maiore vacat generisque nocentis
> plurima monstriferis animancia Roma cavernis
> occulit. Hic virides colubri nigrique bufones,
> hic sua pennati posuerunt lustra dracones.[49]

> (The choked earth is sterile and the standing pools are tainted by filthy streams. Black vapours steam from sluggish swamps . . . Wild Rome is filled with ancient ruins. The greater part of the city is deserted. Many kinds of monstrous beasts lurk in its shades. Here are green toads and black serpents, and here winged dragons make their lair.) (my translation)

Even after Rome had again become an important and prosperous city, the Forum remained in ruins. Writing in 1430, Poggio Bracciolini described its fall, linking (like both Byron and Webster's Antonio) the ruins of decaying buildings with human remains:

> The forum of the Roman people, where they assembled to enact their laws and elect their magistrates, is now enclosed for the cultivation of pot-herbs, or thrown open for the reception of swine and buffalos. The public and private edifices that were founded for eternity, lie prostrate, naked and broken, like the limb of a mighty giant.[50]

Roman ruins weren't only to be found in Rome of course. Roughly 1,300 years ago the anonymous author of the Anglo-Saxon poem 'The Ruin' described with wonder the achievements of the departed conquerors. He is filled with awe when he contemplates the scale of the ancient ruins (probably those of Roman Bath) and the luxuries enjoyed by the Romans.

> The city buildings fell apart, the works
> Of giants crumble. Tumbled are the towers
> Ruined the roofs, and broken the barred gate,
> Frost in the plaster, all the ceilings gape,
> . . . the dead departed master-builders,
> Until a hundred generations now
> Of people have passed by . . .
>
> Stone buildings stood, and the hot stream cast forth
> Wide sprays of water, which a wall enclosed
> In its bright compass, where convenient
> Stood hot baths ready for them at the centre.
> Hot streams poured forth over the clear grey stone,
> To the round pool and down into the baths.[51]

Although the poem's detail suggests an eye-witness report there are hints at a more universal and metaphorical application, and commentators have identified possible echoes of Biblical catastrophes such as the Tower of Babel or the ruined empires foretold in the Book of Revelation.[52] Thus like Book 8 of the *Aeneid* the poem can be read simultaneously as a record of the past and a vision of the future.

The poem's possible association between past and future, between the fall of Rome and the end of civilisation as a whole, prefigures many similar effects of montage in later literature. Indeed the fate of the poem's only surviving manuscript (in the Exeter Book) contributes to this sense of history's cycles being endlessly repeated, for the poem's lament for the fragmented ruins is itself ruined and fragmented by fire damage. This reflexive enactment of ruin is clearly not the poet's intention, even though it is congruent with his sense of his own age as one of decline, as well as with that persistent affinity, already identified, between textuality and the built environment.

It is unclear whether the narrator of 'The Ruin' regrets the passing of the Romans or thinks they were over-reachers whose fate should be read as a warning. Ruins have a similarly equivocal charge in Edmund Spenser's sonnet sequence *Ruines of Rome*, which is secondary both to Rome (and many of its poets) and to Joachim du Bellay, for it is a reasonably close translation of the French poet's earlier *Antiquités de Rome*.[53] Throughout the sequence Spenser appears to communicate a sense of the poet's own diffidence and inferiority in the face of Rome's majestic ruins. For example in Sonnet 25 Spenser figures himself as a kind of poetic architect, but one whose powers are insufficient. Punning on the double meanings (from building and from writing) of 'lofty' and 'compyle',[54] he wishes he was infused with the spirit of Virgil so that he could 'build with levell of my lofty style, / That which no hands can evermore compyle.'[55] However statements of decline are countered by intimations of a greater confidence both in his own powers and in the potential of the new civilisation to which he belongs.[56] For example Sonnet 13, which at first seems self-deprecating, can be read as a veiled challenge.

> Nor the swift furie of the flames aspiring,
> Nor the deep wounds of victours raging blade,
> Nor ruthlesse spoyle of soldiers blood-desiring,
> The which so oft thee (Rome) their conquest made;
>   Ne stroke on stroke of fortune variable,
>   Ne rust of age hating continuance,
> Nor wrath of Gods, nor spight of men unstable,
> Nor thou oppos'd against thine owne puissance;
>   Nor th'horrible uprore of windes high blowing,
>   Nor swelling streames of that God snakie-paced,
> Which hath so often with his overflowing
> Thee drenched, have thy pride so much abaced;
>   But that this nothing, which they have thee left,
>   Makes the world wonder, what they from thee reft.

On an initial reading the narrator seems forced into humble prostration even by the most ruined fragments of Rome. But if we are alert to the poem's intertextual resonances then its message may seem more assertive. It echoes a similar account of time's ravages in a particularly celebrated Latin poem, Horace's 'Ode 3.30'. In Horace's poem, explicit parallels are drawn between buildings and texts, and this may signal for the reader similar, but more tacit, parallels in Spenser:[57]

> Exegi monumentum aere perennius
> regalique situ pyramidum altius,
> quod non imber edax, non Aquilo inpotens
> possit diruere aut innumerabilis
> annorum series et fuga temporum.
> Non omnis moriar multaque pars mei
> vitabit Libitinam; usque ego postera
> crescam laude recens, dum Capitolium
> scandet cum tacita uirgine pontifex.[58]

(I have finished a monument more lasting than bronze and loftier than the Pyramids' royal pile, one that no wasting rain, no furious north wind can destroy, or the countless chain of years and the ages' flight. I shall not altogether die, but a mighty part of me shall escape the death-goddess. On and on shall I grow, ever fresh with the glory of after time. So long as the Pontiff climbs the Capitol with the silent Vestal.)

The parallel is created as much by the rhetorical repetition of the negative 'nor'/*non* constructions as by the similarities between the threatening forces. Because Horace's comparison between his works and a 'monumentum aere perennius', a monument more lasting than bronze, is so well known, Spenser's imitation of the poem, in the context of actual buildings and monuments, invites the reader to consider the relevance of the poem to Rome's textual, as well as its physical, remains. In particular we may be drawn to map the ruins Spenser depicts onto Horace's ode itself.

The familiarity of the Horace may make Spenser's conclusion surprising, in that change rather than persistence is finally revealed to us. An apparent promise of triumphal endurance suddenly changes into a still admiring, but more bleak, vision. Our mental picture of Rome's glory suddenly collapses into ruin. This sudden fall is simultaneous with the poem's final turn; its turn away from Horace. Because Horace's poem fuses his poetry with the idea of an enduring building it is fitting that Spenser's reminder that Rome's buildings have vanished should go hand in hand with his dismantling of the Horatian source. Ostensibly the tone is still one of awe. Even the ancients' 'nothing' is astonishing. But, particularly because of the contrast with Horace's self-confident sense of his immunity to time, an odd effect of bathos is produced. Some observations of Leonard Barkan's are suggestive in this context:

> It is in the nature of imitation, influence, and inspiration that they may seek to efface their origins, or even that they may unconsciously seek readily effaceable origins. That is certainly what Petrarch, Ariosto, and du Bellay were doing when they constructed their poetics on an emptied out field of classical art and architecture . . . I remain with a certain consciousness that the modern culture which appropriates the classical past in part seeks to make something out of nothing. That 'nothing' may in the end be less about artistic quality than about historical distance and all the inevitable erasures that come with fragmentation, loss of context, and illegibility.[59]

Returning to Spenser's Sonnet 13, the final couplet, by exaggerating partial absence (ruin) into complete absence (nothing), seems to offer a *reductio ad absurdum* of the commonplace that Roman ruins are a measure of its greatness.[60]

This implicitly more confident, if not combative, treatment of Rome is paralleled in Sonnet 30. Here Spenser describes the destruction of Rome by barbarians and the subsequent fate of its remains:

> Like as the seeded field greene grasse first showed,
> Then from greene grasse into a stalke doth spring,
> And from a stalke into an eare forth-growes,
> Which eare the frutefull graine doth shortly bring;
> And as in season due the husband mowes
> The waving lockes of those faire yeallow heares,
> Which bound in sheaves, and layd in comely rowes,
> Upon the naked fields in stackes he reares:
> So grew the Romane Empire by degree,
> Till that Barbarian hands it quite did spill,
> And left of it but these olde markes to see,
> Of which all passers by doo somewhat pill:
> As they which gleane, the reliques use to gather,
> Which th'husbandeman behind him chanst to scater.

As Thomas Greene notes (with reference to du Bellay's original sequence) the sequence's own pillaging of some of the most celebrated Latin poetic texts in *The Ruins of Rome* seems implicated here.[61] But, like Sonnet 13, this poem is less self-deprecating than it at first seems to be. The beginning of the sonnet reminds us that corn is grown from seed, and thus the possibility of a burgeoning new culture to equal that of Rome may be hinted at in the initially pathetic image of the gleaner. (After the fall of Rome new buildings arose from its ruins, either using masonry plundered from sites such as the Forum, or, still more drastically, by burning the marble to produce powdered lime, an ingredient of mortar.[62]) Another hint at new life springing from the ruins is perhaps indicated by a slight slippage within the sonnet. The force and referent of 'so' in line 9 is uncertain. It is not clear whether Rome 'grew' like the cornfield or like the pile of sheaves. If the former, the barbarians themselves become the husbandman, and, as in Virgil's double vision of the bucolic once and future forum, ruin and revival are elided.[63]

Much of the significance of John Dyer's *Ruins of Rome* (1740) is, like Spenser's imitation of Horace, only fully revealed once it is read in the light of its key intertexts. On first reading it appears to be an optimistic (and slightly smug) reflection on the decay of Rome and the contrasting power and authority of Britain. Dyer invokes Virgil's account of Aeneas's visit to the site of Rome in order to articulate the city's return to its roots as pastoral decay replaces pastoral primitivism.

> And the rough reliques of Carinæ's street,
> Where now the shepherd to his nibbling sheep
> Sits piping with his oaten reed; as erst
> There pip'd the shepherd to his nibbling sheep,
> When th' humble roof Anchises' son explor'd
> Of good Evander, wealth-despising king,
> Amid the thickets: so revolves the scene;
> So Time ordains, who rolls the things of pride
> From dust again to dust.[64]

Despite the emphasis on a cyclical view of history, the final lines of the passage quoted below suggest that Dyer thinks that his own empire, unlike that of Rome, is destined for immortality:

> May others more delight in tuneful airs;
> In masque and dance excel: to sculptur'd stone
> Give with superior skill the living look;
> More pompous piles erect, or pencil soft
> With warmer touch the visionary board:
> But thou, thy nobler Britons teach to rule;
> To check the ravage of tyrannic sway;
> To quell the proud; to spread the joys of peace,
> And various blessings of ingenious trade.
> Be these our arts; and ever may we guard,
> Ever defend thee with undaunted heart.[65]

But if we recognise the source of these lines it becomes clear that Dyer is not, after all, quite so confident, for they also derive from the *Aeneid* where they are spoken by the shade of Anchises to his son Aeneas.[66] As Dyer has just presented us with a picture of Rome in ruins, his co-option of Anchises' account of a triumphant Rome within a British context seems less of a statement of nationalistic self-confidence, more of a warning. Anne Janowitz's account of Dyer's supposed Whiggish optimism seems misplaced:

> Dyer enlists poetry in an effort to forge an image of an autonomous nation aware of itself historically, and so able to defend itself from history's depredations. This confidence is the analytical ground of 'Whig history,' with both its poise and its posturing. Again we sense

the necessity of a prior, Roman ruin, to the present nation-making enterprise.[67]

Later she claims, of the very lines which follow Virgil's so closely, 'the poet is able to construct a poetic boundary between the ruins and himself, between the past and present, while preserving the analogy between Rome and Britain'.[68] It might be said that the complete opposite is in fact the case, that Dyer collapses the distinction between past and present in these lines. In this poem, to use Dyer's own words, 'Fanes roll'd on fanes, and tombs on buried tombs.'[69] Here, and in 'Yet once again, my Muse / Yet once again'[70] – stutters of repetition seem to flag the ironic cyclicality of history. Whereas recognition of Spenser's Horatian source turns a self-deprecating poem into an assertive one, an awareness of Dyer's imitation of Virgil transforms a triumphalist vision of England into a much more guarded and limited – though probably sincere – expression of patriotism. We may be reminded of the way Virgil hints at Rome's own future decay in his ambiguous description of cattle lowing in the Forum.

The way Dyer's poem changes its meaning, becomes, to use an archaeological metaphor, more layered and thus more nuanced when read in the light of his Virgilian source, is an important indication of the ways textual ruins speak to one another. One of the recurring themes of this study is the fact that literary texts, though individually interesting and valuable, gain still more textual energy when viewed as part of a larger, complexly interdependent, literary tradition. Walter Benjamin's observation on memory casts a suggestive light on this phenomenon. 'And the man who merely makes an inventory of his findings, while failing to establish the exact location of where in today's ground the ancient treasures have been stored up, cheats himself of his prize.'[71] Now literature, like an archaeological dig, can be sliced two ways. For the full narrative of a site to be gauged it is important to analyse the relationship between traces and artefacts on a single level, representing a particular historical period, and also the relationship between the different levels themselves, charting patterns of growth, stagnation and decay. It is the former model, the study of the horizontal rather than the vertical plane, which more closely resembles most recent literary critical practice. But we can learn something different from a text if we are alert to its own memories, and listen to its dialogue with its precursors.

With the advent of Romanticism, ruins were seen by many as

suggestively picturesque, and some were even constructed artificially. Yet this attraction to ruins often went hand in hand with a cultural lack of confidence, a sense of literary entropy, replacing supposed Enlightenment optimism.[72] In the early nineteenth century there was a craze for depictions (both visual and literary) of a decaying world. Notable examples are Joseph Gandy's painting *The Bank of England in Ruins* (1830) and Horace Smith's companion poem to Percy Shelley's 'Ozymandias', 'On a Stupendous Leg of Granite' (1818). Although both are set in the future, both hark back, explicitly and self-consciously, to the classical past. The Gandy painting at first glance seems to be a depiction of a classical ruin but is in fact a projection of a future England in which the modern neoclassical architecture of the painter's own day will be in a state of picturesque but ominous decay. Smith's poem envisages a chillingly primitive Englishman of the future who stops to gaze at the ruins of London just as the narrator of 'The Ruin' reflects on ruined Roman remains:

> when through the wilderness
> Where London stood, holding the wolf in chase,
> He meets some fragment huge, and stops to guess
> What wonderful, but unrecorded, race
> Once dwelt in that annihilated place.[73]

These imaginative projections of their own decay demonstrate an odd blend of humility and complacency, an awareness of their civilisation's mortality combined with a sense that their culture may one day be as resonant as that of Greece or Rome.[74] The precise techniques may be different from those used by the earlier writers discussed in this chapter but the ambivalent attitude towards ruins is much the same.

Despite the Romantic preoccupation with such ruins of the future, visions of a decaying London or Paris, Rome was still a key inspiration for ruin literature. In Mary Shelley's 'The Reanimated Roman' (1819), the story's supernatural premise allows a Roman to be confronted with his city's future decay. Shelley describes how the miraculously revived Valerius, a relict of Republican Rome, surveys with horror the remains of the Forum:

> My heart beat with fear and indignation as I approached the Forum by ways unknown to me. And the spell broke as I beheld the shattered columns and ruined temples of the Campo Vaccino – by that disgraceful name must now be designated the Roman Forum. I gazed round,

but nothing there is as it was – I saw ruins of temples built after my time.⁷⁵

This passage imitates and fulfils Virgil's buried prophecy of the future which, like the echo which haunts the abbey in *The Duchess of Malfi*, knows more than its original. Valerius enjoys hearing the poetry of Virgil read to him by Isabel, a Scottish lady whom he befriends – he died too early to have known Virgil's works in his first life. For Valerius, we may imagine, the description of Rome's site in the *Aeneid* would have seemed an eerie prophecy of its early nineteenth-century state. But Valerius' fondness for Isabel, a barbarian from Ultima Thule by his first life standards, strikes a note of hope, a reminder that ruins can be rebuilt. The splendours of the classical world haven't been destroyed. They have simply migrated westward again, continuing the trajectory initiated by Aeneas when he sailed from Troy to Italy.

Mary Shelley returned to the Forum in her novel of plague and extinction, *The Last Man* (1826).⁷⁶ The novel is particularly interesting in its (almost gratuitous) importation of the classical world into an ostensibly futuristic text. It charts the eventual extinction of mankind from a cholera-like illness and is presented as an ancient manuscript, a sibylline prophecy foretelling events destined to happen in the twenty-first century, discovered by chance during a visit to Naples:

> What appeared to us more astonishing, was that these writings were expressed in various languages: some unknown to my companion, ancient Chaldee, and Egyptian hieroglyphics, old as the Pyramids. Stranger still, some were in modern dialects, English and Italian.⁷⁷

As well as adding an uncanny illusion of verisimilitude, this device (like Book 8 of the *Aeneid*) associates Rome's semi-mythical past with its future decay, recasting history as a process which is not simply cyclical but uncannily circular. Because the manuscript is written in English it seems to have travelled through time as a physical object, somehow leaving Rome's final hour to return to its dawn, for it is in Rome that the last man of the title, Lionel Verney, composes his account of the plague. Yet again we can detect a dynamic of circularity and repetition at work in the literature of apocalypse. Whereas Virgil encouraged his Roman readers to imagine a forum filled with mooing cows, Verney has to make an imaginative effort to fill the same space with people. His own generation is as absent as Virgil's and the image of a Forum inhabited by peasants, once an emblem of decline, is now itself an object for elegiac contemplation:

> I strove, I resolved, to force myself to see the Plebeian multitude and lofty Patrician forms congregated around; and, as the Diorama of ages passed across my subdued fancy, they were replaced by the modern Roman; the Pope, in his white stole, distributing benedictions to the kneeling worshippers; the friar in his cowl; the dark-eyed girl, veiled by her mezzera; the noisy, sun-burnt rustic, leading his herd of buffaloes and oxen to the Campo Vaccino . . . sheep were grazing untended on the Palatine, and a buffalo stalked down the Sacred Way that led to the Capitol.[78]

Rome now resembles Eliot's Waste Land, equally barren either of picturesquely ancient or sleazily modern life:

> The nymphs are departed.
> Sweet Thames, run softly, till I end my song.
> The river bears no empty bottles, sandwich papers,
> Silk handkerchiefs, cardboard boxes, cigarette ends
> Or other testimony of summer nights. The nymphs are departed.[79]

Eliot, and modernists more generally, are conspicuous for their reliance on fragments from the past. Yet although the dynamic of ruin and fragmentation is so crucial to their aesthetic, they don't generally offer those sustained accounts of imagined or actual ruins which have the power to act as uncanny allusion markers. However one brief, memorable vision of ruin which comes at the end of *The Waste Land* exemplifies the double, triple or in this case multiple vision which characterises the literary ruins with which this chapter is concerned. Here Eliot explicitly taps into the cyclical ruin tradition, invoking ruined cities from the distant past and (in the case of Vienna and London) a projected future, all of which are somehow, mysteriously identical to one another.

> What is the city over the mountains
> Cracks and reforms and burst in the violet air
> Falling towers
> Jerusalem Athens Alexandria
> Vienna London
> Unreal.[80]

Such temporal conflations are particularly prominent in science fiction, a genre much preoccupied with the ruins of the future although, as we shall see, often with a Janus-like eye to the ruins of the past. In J. G. Ballard's 1962 novel *The Drowned World*, civilisation is being destroyed by rising temperatures and sea levels which have transformed London into a primeval swamp. In this surreal vision of the future, vegetation has improbably regressed to an earlier state. The survivors attempt, rather lamely, to account for this most improbable instance of biological devolution: 'Well, one could simply say that in response to the rises in temperature, humidity and radiation levels the flora and fauna of this planet are beginning to assume once again the forms they displayed the last time such conditions were present – roughly speaking, the Triassic period.'[81]

Ballard's vision of ruin – which thus affects the natural as well as the built environment – is matched by a parallel move of *textual* regression as the novel also moves backwards towards its literary forebears, most strikingly Joseph Conrad's *Heart of Darkness*.[82] In this novel, Conrad's narrator Marlow describes his journey in similarly, though less dramatically, regressive terms: 'Going up that river was like travelling back to the earliest beginnings of the world, when vegetation rioted on the earth and the big trees were kings.'[83] Marlow also famously compares the lot of the European colonial with that of a Roman soldier exiled in primitive, swampy Britain. In Ballard we have returned full circle to a Britain where the protagonist, Kerans, is described as 'surveying the winding creeks and hanging jungles like an old-time African explorer',[84] a Britain which is primitive and swampy once again – and which contains numerous echoes of *Heart of Darkness*. The bizarre Strangman, who presides over a crew of black sailors who ferry him about the swamps, is a Kurtz-like figure. His appropriation of another solitary survivor, Beatrice, as a kind of consort, recalls Conrad's description of Kurtz's African mistress:

> She sat numbly beside him in her blue evening dress, her hair studded with three or four of the tiaras Strangman had looted from the old jewellery vaults, her breasts smothered under a mass of glittering chains and crescents like a mad queen in a horror drama.[85]

> innumerable necklaces of glass beads on her neck; bizarre things, charms, gifts of witch-men, that hung about her, glittered and trembled at every step. She must have had the value of several elephant tusks upon her.[86]

Memory operates within the fiction of the text, but also outside the pages of the book in the mind of the reader. Bodkin asks Kerans:

'But I'm really thinking of something else. Is it only the external landscape which is altering? How often recently most of us have had the feeling of déjà vu, of having seen all this before, in fact of remembering these swamps and lagoons all too well.'[87] On one level this invokes Ballard's notion of a kind of atavistic and unconscious memory of humanity's swampy dawn. On another it invokes the reader's literary memories of *Heart of Darkness*.

Earlier texts can similarly be identified in the ruined England of John Christopher's *Tripods* trilogy (1967–68). These novels can themselves be seen as a kind of 'ruin' of H. G. Wells's *The War of the Worlds*, showing us what might have happened if Wells's aliens had not succumbed to the bacteria of Earth. Here the young hero, Will, is a rebel in a future society which is ruled by the Tripods, alien invaders who have subjugated the earth by enforcing a system of 'capping'. Once they are 14, children have a metallic membrane attached to their skull which makes them compliant and unquestioning. But Will is saved from this fate by the encouragement of an old man, one of the few who have managed to avoid being capped. Will asks the old man:

> 'Do you know how long it has been?'
> 'That the Tripods have ruled? More than a hundred years. But to the Capped, it is the same as ten thousand.'[88]

The same exaggerated sense of the passing of time since civilisation's collapse was revealed by the author of 'The Ruin' who claimed that a hundred generations had lived since the Roman buildings first crumbled. Even though Christopher may not have known 'The Ruin', it does seem as though he is deliberately trying to invoke the Dark Ages, encouraging the reader to view his novel's setting as a kind of palimpsest whereby his imagined future uncannily echoes a much earlier period rather as 'The Ruin' itself seems, equally uncannily, to anticipate an apocalyptic future. The nearest city to Will is Winchester, a city strongly associated with the pre-industrial past as the capital of Wessex. A particular effect is created by Christopher's choice of Winchester, and this may be contrasted with Wells's own strategy of using the most banally suburban settings – the Martians land in Woking – in order to heighten the horror of his story. Other neo-Medieval elements include society's return to a feudal system, and the re-adoption of tournaments. What characterises this neo-Medievalism is its illogic, comparable to the illogic of backwards evolution in *The Drowned World* or the still more striking evolutionary reverses suffered by humans in *Planet of the Apes*.[89] Thus rather than just presenting a return to the use of horses and tallow candles in the absence of cars and electric lights – a natural, indeed inevitable, regression – the text depicts the recuperation of Medieval motifs or language for no good reason. If we identify this neo-Medievalism not as simple regression but as a re-enactment of a historical and archetypal fall from civilisation to barbarism we can detect the ruins of Rome haunting Christopher's modern post-apocalyptic text.

A further ruin haunts the text, Shelley's 'Ozymandias' (1818), an enigmatic and memorable exploration of transience and decay which needs no further exposition on its own account here. Significantly it is the name assumed by the old man who helps Will plan his bid for freedom. As one of the very few adults who have escaped the cap Ozymandias (who quotes from the poem and seems to have bestowed the name upon himself) represents a rare fragment from humanity's past, a little trace of an earlier and more prosperous period of earth's civilisation, even though Will can make no more of the allusion than Smith's hunter could of the ruins of London. The precise signal communicated by this choice of name is ambiguous. It might be interpreted as a reflection on the downfall of humanity, once as proud as Ozymandias and now destroyed just as finally. Or, particularly in the context of veiled allusions to the parallel fall of proud Rome, the name could be a beacon of hope, reminding us that ruins can herald a new chapter rather than the conclusion of humanity's history. A succession of ruins can be paradoxically less bleak than an isolated example.

If Christopher invites us to excavate earlier 'ruins' texts beneath the surface of the *Tripods*, Ronald Wright's more recent foray into the future, *A Scientific Romance* (1997), is very clearly built upon the foundations of earlier visions of apocalypse.[90] Its central conceit is also directly derived from H. G. Wells, but from *The Time Machine* (1895) rather than *The War of the Worlds*. The hero, David Lambert, claims to have discovered Wells' real time machine and travels into a far future where humanity has been nearly destroyed by (among other evils) BSE and global warming. The ruins, rather like Priest's ghostly 'prestige', work on two levels, one of which is only available if we have read some of the novel's major sources. Literally, within the fiction of the story, they are the projected remains of our own world. But Wright also invites us to see them as textual ruins, beneath which we can discover traces of earlier versions of England's decay. The fragments David Lambert finds are unambiguously 'ruined ruins'. That is, they are explicitly and negatively contrasted with earlier literary apocalypses. Lambert himself articulates the novel's reliance on literary predecessors, recalling the books he has read and noting ironically: 'With such fragments I am shored against these ruins.'[91] In the following passage he invokes Mary Shelley's *The Last Man*, quoting the words of the novel's narrator, Lionel Verney:

> On the outskirts of Hertford yesterday, I passed a spot where the river's cutting through a rubbish tip – a scree of glass, rust, and polythene like bits of loo paper . . . 'If the earth should again be peopled,' – Verney could boast – 'we, the lost race, would, in the relics left behind, present no contemptible exhibition to the newcomers.' All very well in 1826, but who could say that now? Our final century has left more of a mess than our previous million years'.[92]

Lambert has already dryly noted that 'one suspects that the future isn't what it used to be' and seems to wish that the apocalypse might have struck while England was still in a position to produce some prettily picturesque ruins.[93] He compares the future of his millennial England with that described by M. P. Shiel a hundred years earlier in his 1901 novel *The Purple Cloud*[94] and also invites comparisons with Richard Jefferies's similarly bucolic *After London* (1885) – the debt to Jefferies's novel is flagged by the fact that Wright gives the second section of his novel the same title.[95]

The future world of Jefferies's late-Victorian apocalypse, *After London*, like that of the Tripods, is neo-Medieval in style and depicts a return to a past which, if not simply nostalgic, is not completely pessimistic either. Jefferies didn't care for London, so its reversion to a pestilent swamp isn't particularly horrifying. Even if the reader has a preference for a more advanced civilisation, the novel offers grounds for hope through its invocation of the earlier fall of Rome. If Jefferies's hero, Felix, is living through a second Dark Age there is always the chance of a new Renaissance. This cyclicality, this sense not just of ruin but of ruined ruin, is nicely suggested by one of Felix's precious relics, an account of Roman history written for Victorian children: 'The abridgment of Roman history had been scorched by a forest fire, and the charred edges of the leaves had dropped away in semi-circular holes.'[96] The same kind of felicitous reflexivity which ruined, also through fire, the Anglo-Saxon poem

'The Ruin', has here truncated a history which was already abridged. This link between Rome and our own civilisation is strengthened by Jefferies's descriptions of future London:

> For this marvellous city, of which such legends are related, was after all only of brick, and when the ivy grew over and trees and shrubs sprang up, and, lastly, the waters underneath burst in, this huge metropolis was soon overthrown. At this day all those parts which were built upon low ground are marshes and swamps . . . Trees and bushes covered them; ivy and nettles concealed the crumbling masses of brick . . . It is a vast stagnant swamp, which no man dare enter, since death would be his inevitable fate.[97]

Such apparent tacit allusions to the many accounts of swampy Rome allow Jefferies's reader some hope. Wright's *A Scientific Romance*, on the other hand, seems to exclude hope almost entirely. Wright's terrifying, compelling portrait of England's banally inexorable decline, its history excavated from the ruins by his time-travelling hero, outdoes Jefferies, recreating that novel's quest narrative in a markedly bleaker vision of apocalypse.

Yet another conflation of Rome's fall and some future apocalypse is hinted at in *Titus* (2000), Julie Taymor's imaginative film version of *Titus Andronicus*. The film opens with young Lucius playing with toy Roman soldiers, modern soldiers and robots, spurting them all with ketchup, before a massive blast of light at the window throws him in terror to the ground. Although what follows suggests that only conventional weapons have been used, the rather heavy-handed irony of the situation is characteristic of 1980s nuclear war narratives, as is the mismatch between an everyday setting in the prosperous West and its immediate total destruction. The film goes on to juxtapose elements from different periods of history with surreal illogic, retaining a good deal of Roman paraphernalia, but combining it with images and music from both the time of Mussolini and the present day.[98] The martial scenes in particular, where motorbikes incongruously appear beside primitive weapons and armour, combine the different elements in order to create a post-apocalyptic atmosphere reminiscent of the cult Australian film *Mad Max* (1979), set in a near future world where order has broken down following global disaster. Thus *Titus* is able to highlight the play's portrait of a society in decay and of a Rome which can only cling on to its identity and deter the savages at the gate by becoming equally bloodthirsty, eventually joining forces with the barbaric outsiders. The film's anachronistic blend of old and new creates a complex of possibilities comparable to those suggested in *Aeneid* 8. We can see the juxtapositions as a surreal and impossible construct, a collage of different eras brought together by the filmmaker's imagination, or as a broadly realistic vision of a possible future in which time has as it were gone backwards, where technological advances are still present but buried under an encroaching primitivism like Lucan's ruins of Troy choked by sterile thickets.

In *Becoming Posthumous* (2002), Jeremy Tambling claims that 'updating seems to me a way of occluding historical difference, of denying the historical character of the piece'.[99] I would counter that, at least in some instances, updating actually draws attention to historical difference and if it does in any way deny the original's historical specificity it does so in order to bring out more fully its *transhistorical* significance. A good example is Pope's 'The First Epistle of the Second Book of Horace Imitated', discussed in the introduction. Because Pope's ancients lived many hundreds of years after Horace's 'moderns', the point of the satire emerges, for the reader familiar with the original, with a newly unanswerable force. Taymor's update is similarly telling. Her apparently anachronistic importation of the present (and the future) into her film could be seen as an attempt to reproduce the play's own curious anachronisms (such as references to duelling and to Elizabethan weapons), which are to some degree occluded for the modern reader for whom Elizabethan England and the later Roman Empire are both ancient history.

One of the most striking anachronisms in the play is this unexpected and apparently motiveless introduction of a ruin:

> Renowmed Lucius, from our troops I stray'd
> To gaze upon a ruinous monastery,
> And as I earnestly did fix mine eye
> Upon the wasted building[100]

This ruinous abbey seems to represent both a temporal and a geographical anomaly for, like the ruined abbey in *The Duchess of Malfi*, it would have put its original audience in mind of the depredations which resulted from the English Reformation.[101] The character (simply called Second Goth) is living through the last days of the Roman Empire yet seems to be offered an uncanny glimpse of the (partial) fall of Rome's next incarnation as the seat of Christianity. It is as though the soldier has wandered, not just away from his troops, but out of his time and his text. The potentially uncanny charge of the lines is made more pointed by the emphasis on the Goth's prolonged, fascinated gaze. If *Titus Andronicus* looks forward to Rome's future, it also nods backwards, Janus-headed, to its past, for its mutilated heroine Lavinia shares a name with the second wife of Rome's supposed founder, Aeneas. This effect of palimpsest (comparable to the many others we have seen in this chapter) is reproduced by Taymor in her own use of future Romes. As well as replicating, and indeed exaggerating, the uncanny temporal shifts of Shakespeare's original play, Taymor invites the viewer to identify parallel shifts *between* the works. In other words a new dimension to the palimpsest is created intertextually, offering a still more complex and inexorably cyclical pattern of peaks and troughs.

In 'Civilisation and its Discontents', Sigmund Freud described Rome's virtual layers in an evocative and much quoted passage:

> Let us, by a flight of the imagination, suppose that Rome is not a human habitation but a psychical entity with a similarly long and copious past – an entity, that is to say, in which nothing that has come into existence will have passed away and all the earlier phases of development exist alongside the later ones.[102]

Catharine Edwards links this passage with the way individual texts, such as the *Aeneid*, offer us a double or triple vision of Rome, allowing us to glimpse different phases of its development simultaneously.[103] But this isn't the whole story. Freud's description also captures something of the still more complex vision of Rome derived from reading accounts of ruins in the light of their textual predecessors which, like the ruined foundations of a city, 'exist alongside the later ones' and are in some way part of their fabric. Thus just as Shakespeare mapped the decline of his own age onto the decline of Rome, Taymor added a further layer, introducing a more modern discourse of decay into the frame, invoking and reinforcing Shakespeare's own hints at historical relativism. The addition of further peaks and troughs of civilisation into the mixture strengthens the sense of cyclicality. Taymor's half hints at a reruined post-apocalyptic Rome recall Macaulay's fancy of some future 'radio-active, plague-struck' Rome which might yet in some distant time spark its own 'new era of ruin-pleasure'.[104]

Not all recent ruins are built on so many strata. Sometimes, like the sham ruins of the eighteenth century, they spring up like mushrooms, apparently out of nowhere. Even such new ruins can, however, still have a special allusive charge. Two interesting 'new' ruins can, for example, be identified in two works of twentieth-century science fiction, the film *Forbidden Planet*[105] and Robert Silverberg's 1968 novel, *The Man in the Maze*. In both narratives a human explorer has been exiled on a distant planet which contains the remains of an alien race whose mysterious technology is far superior to anything produced on Earth. In *Forbidden Planet* the scientist Morbius labours to discover the secrets of the long dead Krell whose machines are buried beneath the surface of the planet, only to be eventually destroyed by the powers he unleashes.[106] In *The Man in the Maze*, Muller has to grapple with the lethal maze whose many snares were fashioned years ago by another vanished superior species. Both of these apparently futuristic stories are in fact modelled on much earlier texts. *Forbidden Planet* is an updated retelling of *The Tempest* whereas *The Man in the Maze* is a version of the legend of Philoctetes.[107] And in both cases the presence of a wondrous but long extinct alien species is particularly intrusive because it has no real basis in the source text. If these ruins are in fact fresh inventions, how can they function as allusion markers? Perhaps because they represent, not any narrative element from the source, but the source itself. The mysterious ruins in both these science fiction adaptations could be said to be the visible signs of their originals, the brooding presence of an ancient canonical work haunting a product of modern popular culture.

Notes

1 For a very useful discussion of ruins in the play see M. Neill, 'Monuments and Ruins as Symbols in *The Duchess of Malfi*', in J. Redmond (ed.), *Drama and Symbolism* (Cambridge: Cambridge University Press, 1982), pp. 71–87.
2 J. Webster, *Three Plays*, ed. J. R. Brown (London: Penguin, 1972), 5.3.19–23. Some of the discussions in this chapter appeared (in an earlier form) in '"Plato's Stepchildren": SF and the Classics', in L. Hardwick and C. Stray (eds), *A Companion to Classical Receptions* (Oxford: Blackwell, 2008), pp. 415–27.
3 Many have analysed the importance of ruins within literary, artistic, architectural and other cultural contexts. One of the best-known and most accessible discussions of ruins is R. Macaulay's *Pleasure of Ruins* (London: Thames & Hudson, 1966). A more recent study, rather similar in scope, is C. Woodward's engaging *In Ruins* (London: Chatto & Windus, 2001). An account of ruins' cultural and aesthetic significance

is offered by R. Ginsberg in *The Aesthetics of Ruins* (Amsterdam and New York: Rodopi, 2004).
4   5.3.18–19.
5   Webster, *The Duchess of Malfi*, 4.2.33–4. Compare also Bosola's dying words: 'O, I am gone! - / We are only like dead walls, or vaulted graves, / That ruin'd, yield no echo.' (*Ibid.*, 5.5.96–8)
6   A. Janowitz discusses Byron's preoccupation with ruins in *England's Ruins: Poetic Purpose and the National Landscape* (Oxford : Basil Blackwell, 1990), pp. 40–53.
7   G. Byron, *The Complete Poetical Works*, ed. J. J. McGann (Oxford: Clarendon Press, 1980), 7 vols, vol. 2, p. 46.
8   *Ibid.*, p. 132.
9   Ginsberg, *The Aesthetics of Ruins*, p. 10. Woodward offers a further useful analysis of the perceived correspondences between ruins and bodies. Woodward, *In Ruins*, pp. 88–107.
10 Compare another intimation of mortality in the farewell scene between Antonio and the Duchess:

> Duch. Let me look upon you once more; for that speech
> Came from a dying father: your kiss is colder
> Than that I have seen an holy anchorite
> Give to a dead man's skull. (3.5.87–90)

11 Ginsberg, *The Aesthetics of Ruins*, p. 51.
12 Webster, *The Duchess of Malfi*, 5.3.11.
13 *Ibid.*, 5.3.34–5.
14 'The form converts us from passivity. Smashing the dullness that envelopes us, it opens us to the free possibility of form . . . Form flushes us from the unresponsive shelter into the sensitized field. The ruin is an artist in bringing us out into response.' (Ginsberg, *The Aesthetics of Ruins*, p. 18.)
15 Webster, *The Duchess of Malfi*, 5.3.9.
16 Byron, *Complete Poetical Works*, p. 47.
17 Macaulay, *Pleasure of Ruins*, p. 333.
18 Byron, *Complete Poetical Works*, p. 167.
19 See for example Macaulay, *Pleasure of Ruins*, p. 199 on the superior charm of ruins.
20 Webster, *The Duchess of Malfi*, 5.3.47.
21 A well-known and comparatively recent example is Henry James's 1878 story 'Daisy Miller'. The heroine succumbs to fever after an imprudent nighttime walk in the Colosseum.
22 A. Marvell, *The Complete English Poems*, ed. E. Story Donno (London: Allen Lane, 1972), p. 75.
23 *Ibid.*, p. 76.

24 T. S. Eliot, *Collected Poems 1909-62* (London: Faber & Faber, 2002), p. 69.
25 Macaulay, *Pleasure of Ruins*, p. 335.
26 Philip Schwyzer offers an excellent account of the 'buried affinity' between archaeology and literary criticism in *Archaeologies of English Renaissance Literature* (Oxford: Oxford University Press, 2007), pp. 4–10.
27 F. Jameson, *The Political Unconscious: Narrative as a Socially Symbolic Act* (Ithaca, N.Y.: Cornell University Press, 1981), p. 9.
28 Virgil, *Aeneid*, trans. H. Rushton Fairclough (Cambridge, Mass.: Harvard University Press, 2000), 8.347–8.
29 Compare C. Edwards, *Writing Rome: Textual Approaches to the City* (Cambridge: Cambridge University Press, 1996), pp. 31–2. The ambiguity of *olim* is discussed by J. E. G. Zetzel in '*Romane memento*: Justice and Judgement in *Aeneid* 6', *Transactions and Proceedings of the American Philological Association*, 119 (1989), 263–8.
30 Virgil, *Aeneid*, 8.359–61.
31 Schwyzer, *Archaeologies of English Renaissance Literature*, p. 75.
32 Virgil, *Aeneid*, 8.357–8.
33 *Ibid.*, 6.724–51.
34 See Macaulay, *Pleasure of Ruins*, p. 16.
35 See Edwards, *Writing Rome*, p. 13.
36 Diana Spencer analyses this episode in 'Lucan's Follies: Memory and Ruin in a Civil-War Landscape', *Greece and Rome*, 52.1 (2005), 46–69.
37 And the *Pharsalia* would itself remain, ruin-like, unfinished and incomplete. See Edwards, *Writing Rome*, pp. 6–8 and *passim* on the relationship between Rome's monuments and her texts.
38 Lucan, *Pharsalia*, trans. J. D. Duff (Cambridge, Mass.: Harvard University Press, 1969), 9.952–4.
39 *Ibid.*, 964–5.
40 *Ibid.*, 966–9.
41 P. Hardie, 'Augustan Poets and the Mutability of Rome' in A. Powell (ed.), *Roman Poetry and Propaganda in the Age of Augustus* (Bristol: Bristol Classical Press, 1992), pp. 59–82.
42 Lucan, *Pharsalia*, 9.973.
43 Virgil, *Aeneid*, 2.558.
44 W. Benjamin, *The Work of Art in the Age of Mechanical Reproduction*, trans. J. A. Underwood (London: Penguin, 2008).
45 Lucan, *Pharsalia*, 9.969.
46 Lucan, *Pharsalia*, eds S. A. Brown and C. Martindale, trans. Nicholas Rowe (London: Everyman, 1997), 9.1637.
47 J. Hollander, *The Figure of Echo: A Mode of Allusion in Milton and After* (Berkeley: University of California Press, 1981), pp. 95–6.

48 P. Llewellyn, *Rome in the Dark Ages* (London: Faber & Faber, 1971), p. 194.
49 Günther, *Ligurinus*, ed. E. Assmann (Hannover: Hahn, 1987), p. 274.
50 Quoted in Maculay, *Pleasure of Ruins*, p. 176.
51 R. Hamer, *Choice of Anglo-Saxon Verse* (London: Faber & Faber, 1970), pp. 27–9.
52 See M. Alexander, *Old English Literature* (London: Macmillan, 1983), p. 14.
53 Much of my analysis of Spenser might equally well be applied to Du Bellay, and my own focus on Spenser is due in part to the greater accessibility of his poems to English speaking readers. Du Bellay's use of ruins is discussed in I. G. Daemmrich, 'The Ruins Motif as Artistic Device in French Literature, Part 1', in *The Journal of Aesthetics and Art Criticism*, 30.4 (1972), 449–57. A particularly suggestive reading of Du Bellay, and of Renaissance responses to Rome's ruins more generally, can be found in T. M. Greene, 'Resurrecting Rome: the Double Task of the Humanist Imagination', in P. Ramsay (ed.), *Rome in the Renaissance: The City and the Myth* (Binghampton, N.Y.: Center for Medieval and Early Renaissance Studies, 1982), pp. 41–54. An analysis of Spenser's response to Du Bellay is offered by L. Barkan in 'Ruins and Visions; Spenser, Pictures, Rome', in J. K. Morrison and M. Greenfield (eds), *Edmund Spenser: Essays on Culture and Allegory* (Aldershot: Ashgate, 2000), pp. 9–36. See also A. Janowitz, *England's Ruins*, pp. 20–7.
54 For a further Roman parallel see Propertius 4.1 which conflates poetry and architecture using similar puns: 'Moenia namque pio coner disponere versu: / ei mihi, quod nostro est parvus in ore sonus!'; 'For I would fain lay out those walls in duteous verse: ah me, that a voice so feeble sits upon my lips', 57–8. 'Roma, fave, tibi surgit opus'; 'Rome, smile on me, my work rises for you' (67). Propertius, *Elegies*, trans. G. P. Goold (Cambridge, Mass.: Harvard University Press, 2000).
55 E. Spenser, *Shorter Poems*, eds. W. A. Oram, *et alia* (New Haven and London: Yale University Press, 1989), p. 400.
56 For a discussion of similar contradictory impulses in Spenser's model, Du Bellay, see G.W. Pigman III, 'Du Bellay's Ambivalence Towards Rome in the *Antiquitez*', in *Rome in the Renaissance: The City and the Myth* (New York: Medieval and Renaissance Texts and Studies, 1982), pp. 321–32.
57 Another well-known poem which recalls Horace's 'Ode' is Shakespeare's Sonnet 55.
58 Horace, *Odes and Epodes*, trans. C. E. Bennett (Cambridge, Mass.: Harvard University Press, 1999), p. 279.
59 L. Barkan, *Unearthing the Past: Archaeology and Aesthetics in the*

Making of Renaissance Culture (New Haven and London: Yale University Press, 1999), p. xxxi.
60 A twelfth-century example of this motif, penned by Hildebert of Lavardin, is cited by Barkan: 'Nothing, Rome, is equal to you; even when you are nearly all in ruins, you teach us how great you would be if your fragments were whole.' (*Ibid.*, p. 123.)
61 Greene, 'Resurrecting Rome', p. 45.
62 See Woodward, *In Ruins*, pp. 7–8 and Macaulay, *Pleasure of Ruins*, p. 177 for accounts of this practice.
63 On the gleaner as Renaissance man see T. M. Greene, *The Light in Troy* (New Haven: Yale University Press, 1982), p. 241.
64 J. Dyer, *Poems 1761* (Menston: Scolar Press, 1971), p. 35.
65 *Ibid.*, pp. 29-30.
66 Virgil, *Aeneid*, 6. 847–53.
67 Janowitz, *England's Ruins*, p. 30.
68 *Ibid.*, p. 33.
69 *Ibid.*, p. 20. It is also worth noting that the poem is so suffused with echoes of Milton's Paradise that it becomes hard to see a return to 'primitivism' as necessarily regressive.
70 *Ibid.*, p. 20.
71 W. Benjamin, 'Excavation and Memory' in *Selected Writings*, ed. M. W. Jennings (Cambridge, Mass.: Harvard University Press, 1999), vol. 2, p. 576. See also J. Wallace, *Digging the Dirt: The Archaeological Imagination* (London: Duckworth, 2004).
72 A great deal has been written about ruins in this period. See for example L. Goldstein, *Ruins and Empire: The Evolution of a Theme in Augustan and Romantic Literature* (Pittsburgh: University of Pittsburgh Press, 1977); J. J. McGann, 'Rome and its Romantic Significance', in A. Patterson (ed.), *Roman Images* (Baltimore: Johns Hopkins University Press, 1984), pp. 83–104.
73 H. Smith, *The Poetical Works* (London: Henry Colburn, 1846), p. 234. Another typical vision of London in decay is offered by Shelley in the letter prefixed to *Peter Bell the Third* in which 'St. Pauls and Westminster Abbey shall stand, shapeless and nameless ruins, in the midst of an unpeopled marsh; when the piers of Waterloo Bridge shall become the nuclei of islets of reeds and osiers'. This passage, together with other Romantic glimpses of the future, is discussed by J. Wolfreys in *Writing London: The Trace of the Urban Text from Blake to Dickens* (Basingstoke: Macmillan, 1998), pp. 61–84.
74 This ambiguity is discussed by Schwyzer, *Archaeologies of English Renaissance Literature*, p. 174.
75 M. Shelley, *Collected Tales and Stories* (Baltimore: Johns Hopkins University Press, 1976), p. 335.

76 Useful discussions of this novel include M. Bradshaw, 'Mary Shelley's Last Man (The End of the World as we know it)', in D. Littlewood and P. Stockwell (eds), *Impossibility Fiction* (Amsterdam: Rodopi, 1996), pp. 163–75.
77 M. Shelley, *The Last Man* (Peterborough, Ontario: Broadview, 1996), p. 7.
78 *Ibid.*, p. 360.
79 Eliot, *Collected Poems*, p. 60.
80 *Ibid.*, p. 67.
81 J.G. Ballard, *The Drowned World* (London: Harper Perennial, 2006), p. 42.
82 J.G. Ballard claimed not to have read *Heart of Darkness* before writing *The Drowned World*. Patrick A. McCarthy responds sceptically to Ballard's disclaimer, yet also suggests a number of mediating texts which may help explain Conrad's presence in the novel. ('Allusions in Ballard's *The Drowned World*', *Science Fiction Studies*, 24.2 (1997), 302–10).
83 J. Conrad, *Heart of Darkness* (Oxford: Oxford University Press, 2002), p. 136.
84 Ballard, *The Drowned World*, p. 12.
85 *Ibid.*, p. 131.
86 Conrad, *Heart of Darkness*, pp. 100–1.
87 Ballard, *The Drowned World*, p. 42.
88 J. Christopher, *The White Mountains* (New York: Simon Pulse, 2003), p. 38.
89 Dir. F. J. Schaffner, 1968.
90 See Gayla McGlamery, 'The Three Tropographies of Ronald Wright's *A Scientific Romance*', *Canadian Literature*, 185 (2005), 92–109.
91 R. Wright, *A Scientific Romance* (London: Transworld, 1997), p. 205.
92 *Ibid.*, pp. 185–6.
93 *Ibid.*, p. 83.
94 *Ibid.*, p. 111.
95 For a discussion of *After London* see Woodward, *In Ruins*, pp. 74–6
96 R. Jefferies, *After London* (Oxford: Oxford University Press, 1980), p. 47.
97 *Ibid.*, pp. 36–7.
98 On Taymor's use of colliding eras see for example T. Cartelli, 'Taymor's *Titus* in Time and Space: Surrogation and Interpolation', *Renaissance Drama* 34 (2005), 163–84.
99 J. Tambling, *Becoming Posthumous: Life and Death in Literary and Cultural Studies* (Edinburgh: Edinburgh University Press, 2002), p. 13.
100 W. Shakespeare, *The Riverside Shakespeare*, ed. H. Baker *et al* (Boston and New York: Houghton Mifflin Company, 1987), 5.1.19–22.

101 See Schwyzer, *Archaeologies of English Renaissance Literature*, pp. 99–101 for a useful discussion of ruins in the play.
102 S. Freud, *Civilisation and its Discontents*, trans. James Strachey (New York: W. W. Norton, 1961), p. 18.
103 Edwards, *Writing Rome*, p. 27.
104 Macaulay, *Pleasure of Ruins*, p. 203.
105 Dir. Fred M. Wilcox (1956).
106 See M. K. Booker, *Alternate Americas: Science Fiction Film and American Culture* (Westport: Greenwood, 2006), pp. 43–57; A. T. Vaughan and V. M. Vaughan, *Shakespeare's Caliban: A Cultural History* (Cambridge: Cambridge University Press, 1991), pp. 204–6.
107 The links are discussed by J. Dean in 'The Sick Hero Reborn: Two Versions of the Philoctetes Myth', *Comparative Literature Studies*, 17.3 (1980), 334–40.

5

Reanimation: Orpheus and Pygmalion

In *Areopagitica* Milton offers a memorable account of a book's capacity for a 'life' independent of its author:

> For books are not absolutely dead things, but do contain a potency of life in them to be as active as that soul was whose progeny they are; nay, they do preserve as in a vial the purest efficacy and extraction of that living intellect that bred them.[1]

There is something just a little uncanny about Milton's evocation of the book as an artifact which might develop a quasi-autonomous existence. Books are 'not absolutely dead things', but neither are they unambiguously alive. This equivocal, hybrid state, to the modern if not to the seventeenth-century ear, might suggest some uncanny variant of the 'undead', a vampire or a zombie, or perhaps a manufactured simulacrum of humanity such as a golem or robot. A book may find new life in its readers, possessing them as the French critic Georges Poulet suggests:

> I am someone who happens to have as objects of his own thought, thoughts which are part of a book I am reading, and which are therefore the cogitations of another. They are the thoughts of another, and yet it is I who am their subject. The situation is even more astonishing than the one noted above. I am thinking the thoughts of another.[2]

Poulet goes on to frame this process in still more uncanny terms, casting the book as a kind of revenant, a potential usurper of the reader's own consciousness:

> If the work thinks itself in me, does this mean that, during a complete loss of consciousness on my part, another thinking entity invades me taking advantage of my unconsciousness in order to think itself without my being able to think?[3]

He answers his own question in the negative but goes on to assert: 'He and I, we start having a common consciousness.'[4]

This uncanny sense of accessing the mind of a writer long since dead has an extra resonance in the context of film, a medium whose discovery enabled the dead to move and speak as though alive. Superstition, the belief in ghosts, had finally become a reality.

> Cinema has always been in league with the sorcerer's art. Magic, animism and the occult haunt its inception and history. In raising the dead and conjuring seeming materiality out of immaterial light and shadow, filmmaking resembles necromancy.[5]

The 'spectral' medium of cinema thus has a particular affinity with reanimation. In his 1960 film, *The Testament of Orpheus*, writer and director Jean Cocteau asserts, as though unconsciously echoing Milton's account of the book as revenant, that 'a film is a petrifying source of thought. It brings dead acts to life. It makes it possible to give apparent reality to the unreal'.

So far I have mentioned only the spectral quality of simple repetition, of the process which takes place when an old book or film is taken up one more time. But writers, as well as readers and viewers, are responsible for giving old stories a new lease of life, and it is this kind of textual 'reanimation' which is most relevant to this chapter. A book may be renewed through transmission, infecting further texts which demonstrate its influence through allusion or imitation. Reanimation has a very clear reflexive force. Any retelling of *Frankenstein*, it could be argued, mimics the novel's original dynamic when it brings the original back to life, usually deforming Shelley's original conception in the process. *Dracula* (though not Dracula) has managed to reproduce itself endlessly, continually being renewed by the injection of fresh blood into the vampire tradition. Yet although one may, as I have just done, elide the process of reanimation within a story with the text's own revival in a subsequent literary tradition, reanimation does not necessarily flag or mimic allusion in every reworking of a text such as *Frankenstein*. Only some literary reanimations are invested with a special reflexive charge, functioning as uncanny allusion markers. Raphael Lyne has identified a particularly compelling example of a corpse's miraculous reanimation which seems to invite the reader to reflect on the simultaneous revival of a source text. This is Prospero's speech beginning 'Ye elves of hills, brooks, standing lakes, and groves' which is so closely modelled on

Medea's address to the gods in Book 7 of the *Metamorphoses* that it might be termed a translation or quotation.[6] Shakespeare's close imitation of Ovid itself enacts a kind of literary necromancy. Thus when Prospero in the course of this same speech declares 'Graves at my command / Have wak'd their sleepers',[7] he both echoes Medea's original claim and obliquely alludes to Shakespeare's own role as a reanimator of Ovid.[8]

In this chapter I will explore further the association between the literary tradition of the uncannily animated – or reanimated – human and the text which has been brought back to life by an imitator or translator. Although the most famous such human is male (Frankenstein's monster) my own focus will be limited to female corpses and statues. Perhaps the most memorable examples in each category, corpse bride and living statue, are Eurydice and Galatea,[9] in particular the versions offered us by Ovid in his *Metamorphoses*. Although Ovid did not create either tale he was almost certainly the first to associate them together; he does this by making Orpheus himself the narrator of Pygmalion's story. Over the course of the two narratives' complex afterlives, the mythic traditions seem themselves to acquire the kind of independent 'life' which Milton ascribes to individual books in *Areopagitica*. Like an analysand undergoing treatment and slowly bringing buried fears and desires up from the unconscious to the surface of the conscious mind, the myths seem afflicted by a compulsion to repeat which works to reveal more and more openly certain buried impulses or anxieties which dog their afterlives, impulses which may or may not have originally inspired these memorable stories but which they certainly later tapped into.[10] This compulsion to repeat inheres in the original narrative. Eurydice dies twice, and her story is then echoed in that of Pygmalion – indeed the tale of the sculptor can be seen as a kind of early 'reanimation' of Orpheus's own story. The story of Pygmalion is then itself reanimated, for Orpheus goes on to tell another tale of a woman's love for her own creator, that of incestuous Myrrha and her father Cinyras.[11]

One of the impulses which appears to drive the entwined myths' rich afterlives is an apparent preoccupation with homosexual desire. There is more than one possible explanation for the prominence of this theme. One factor might be the fact that Eurydice and Galatea, revenant and statue, both call the category of 'woman' into question in their different ways, suggesting 'queer' alternatives to heteronormativity. But the continuing association between these tales and homoeroticism cannot be fully explained with reference to details in Ovid's original poem. It is also in part a cumulative process which is reinforced by repetition in a series of texts which seem to enact or re-enact an anxious and compulsive return to that which has been suppressed. The internal repetitions in Ovid, and the persistent repetitions in these myths' afterlives, have the capacity to enhance the uncanny effect for the reader. Freud discusses the unsettling quality of repetition in certain conditions:

> The factor of the repetition of the same thing will perhaps not appeal to everyone as a source of uncanny feeling. From what I have observed, this phenomenon does undoubtedly, subject to certain conditions, arouse an uncanny feeling, which, furthermore, recalls the sense of helplessness experienced in some dream-states.[12]

Half-memories of having encountered something like this before, in the mind of, to take just one possible example, the reader of 'The Sandman' who knows *Vertigo* well, may, particularly if they cannot be pinned down, create that 'uncanny feeling' Freud describes.

It is not always possible to establish how far, if at all, each example discussed in this chapter was directly influenced by earlier instances. Helen Cooper's account of a literary 'meme' is useful here as it creates a fiction of autonomy, if not full consciousness, not simply for individual books (as described in *Areopagitica*), but for potent literary motifs as well. Cooper defines a literary meme as 'an idea that behaves like a gene in its ability to replicate faithfully and abundantly, but also on occasion to adjust, mutate, and therefore survive in different forms and cultures'.[13] Another relevant critical context is Abraham and Torok's discussion of haunting within the context of a family line. Their words might also be applied to a *textual* line of descent, in which pressures from the past leave an imprint on future generations:

> The buried speech of the parent becomes (a) dead (gap), without a burial place, in the child. This unknown phantom comes back from the unconscious to haunt and leads to phobias, madness, and obsessions. Its effect can persist through several generations and determine the fate of an entire family line.[14]

Orpheus's account of a sculptor who brings an ivory woman to life, a story he tells after his failed attempt to bring back Eurydice from the dead, can be read as a wish-fulfilment narrative, as a transformed retelling of his own more melancholy experience. The modern reader may find it suggestive to think of Orpheus as a patient on the psychiatrist's couch recounting his dream. An analyst, we may fancifully imagine, might well wish to probe the reasons for making Galatea an *ivory* statue. Ivory is not a convenient medium for a life-sized statue; marble would have been a more obvious choice. Perhaps, because it is a type of bone, the dead trace of a once living creature, ivory reveals Orpheus's own preoccupation with reanimation rather than the Pygmalion story's ostensible focus on animation. So after her second brief life, Eurydice in a sense is reborn one further time as Pygmalion's ivory maid. It is a chiastic reversal as well as a rebirth. A gaze is followed by death in the first story whereas the statue comes to life and then turns her own gaze on her lover:

> dataque oscula virgo
> sensit, et erubuit timidumque ad lumina lumen
> attolens partier cum caelo vidit amantem.[15]

> (The maiden felt the kisses, blushed and, lifting up her timid eyes up to the light, she saw the sky and her lover at the same time.)

This implied bond between the two women, the sense that elements are being repeated, may lie behind some of the changes made to the Pygmalion story in Ted Hughes's translation, the fourteenth episode of *Tales from Ovid*. In Hughes's account of the myth control seems to be wrested away from Pygmalion; the creation of the statue is initiated by the spirit of Galatea herself who comes to him in a dream:

> Though this dream
> Was not so much the dream of a perfect woman
> As of a spectre, sick of unbeing,
> That had taken possession of his body
> To find herself a life.
>
> She moved into his hands,
> She took possession of his fingers
> And began to sculpt a perfect woman.[16]

Rather surprisingly Hughes chose not to translate the memorable episode of Orpheus and Eurydice, yet perhaps it is more of an absent presence than a complete absence in the *Tales*. Hughes's Galatea is a 'spectre'; in other words she has already had one life and is anxious to find a new one. As a ghost she seems closer to

Eurydice than to Pygmalion's statue. It is as though Pygmalion's status as a kind of avatar of Orpheus in the latter's wish-fulfilment narrative has come closer to the surface in Hughes's translation. Yet, even though his Pygmalion eventually falls in love with the ivory maid, Hughes's initial description of the ghostly Galatea hardly seems auspicious. She brings to the surface an anxiety, even a horror of women which haunts both Ovid's tales even though they deal, at least ostensibly, with heterosexual passion. If we maintain an awareness of Orpheus as narrator in Hughes (although there is no internal prompt to do so) we might note further ways in which the translation allows his traumatic experience with Eurydice to colour the tale of Pygmalion.[17] As in Ovid, we hear how Pygmalion developed an aversion to women after witnessing the dreadful behaviour of the Propoetides:[18]

> He adored woman, but he saw
> The wickedness of these particular women
> Transform, as by some occult connection,
> Every woman's uterus to a spider.
> Her face, voice, gestures, hair became its web.
> Her perfume was a floating horror. Her glance
> Left a spider-bite. He couldn't control it.[19]

The references to spiders are unovidian. The last line and a half of the above quotation are particularly suggestive. We have a fatal glance, the bite from a poisonous creature, and a final rather ambiguous statement: 'He couldn't control it.' In Hughes's version the traumatised Orphic narrator seems to be allowing his unconscious anxieties to float to the surface. Eurydice was killed by a venomous bite, although from a snake rather than a spider. Here the poisonous bite is only a metaphorical one, stemming from a woman's glance. Again we may wonder if Orpheus is remembering his experience with Eurydice, where a glance proved fatal, even though he is transferring his own destructive powers to women, hiding and yet revealing his anxieties through inversion. This possibility is reinforced by that slightly cryptic 'he couldn't control it'. Within the immediate context of the poem it would seem that Pygmalion's inability to withstand the destructive charm of a woman's gaze is being described. But we might also speculate whether Orpheus is replaying his guilt at being unable to stop himself looking back at Eurydice. By strengthening both the Eurydicean subtext and Pygmalion's misogyny, Hughes's translation may invite the reader to return to Book 10 of the *Metamorphoses* and interrogate it further.

After his double loss Orpheus, like Pygmalion, renounces the love of women. However while the sculptor finds solace in his art, Orpheus chooses a rather different alternative:

> ille etiam Thracum populis fuit auctor amorem
> in teneros transferre mares citraque iuventam
> aetatis breve ver et primos carpere flores.[20]
>
> (He set the example for the people of Thrace of giving his love to tender boys, and enjoying the springtime and first flower of their youth.)

The fact that Orpheus switches his attentions to boys may be interpreted in more than one way. The simplest explanation is that, having lost his ideal woman, Orpheus favours lovers who do not invite direct comparisons with his adored wife. But the mythical narrative also invites less purely literal readings. Orpheus's journey to the underworld, to a place which is buried and inaccessible, might figure the 'return of the repressed'. The journey can be read symbolically as a mechanism which reveals his homosexual desires.

Given that the repressed, in Freudian terms, tends to become manifest in some distorted or even inverted fashion, the story of Eurydice could represent a man's secret wish for his wife to die, leaving him free to pursue other desires. In other words the story of Eurydice, in which a wife is lost, as well as that of Pygmalion, in which a wife is found, contains an element of wish-fulfilment. Ovid certainly offers the reader some grounds for wondering whether Orpheus really wanted his wife back after all. Commentators have noticed a coolness, almost a reluctance, in his plea for her return.[21] His comparative lack of emotion makes his fatal backward glance seem more the fulfilment of a suppressed wish than a tragic second loss. Such an interpretation might seem anachronistic in the context of classical culture's arguably quite different sexual paradigms (in the *Metamorphoses* the desires of the gods move unanxiously and unselfconsciously from girls to boys and back again) but could help explain aspects of the myth's reception by much later writers.

In similar fashion, Pygmalion's statue, created in response to the deficiencies of women, might be interpreted as a veiled account of a man who rejected women in order to choose men, rather as it can be seen as an oddly distorted version of events in Orpheus's own life.

And a persistent feature of the story's reception is an engagement with the statue's power as a constructed woman to signal queer identities of various kinds and to highlight the fluidity and contingency of gender roles. Men and female statues are both 'not women.' (Dead wives, such as Eurydice, are also 'not women' of course.) They can both be used or perceived as substitutes for women – whether they are defective or superior, convincing or unconvincing, is a matter to be decided both by the context and the reader's personal taste. The rest of this chapter will thus explore two separate yet related characteristics of the revenant wife and the animated female statue: their association with a buried queer subtext and their capacity to act as allusion markers pointing to a buried source. In the earlier texts uncanny allusion markers are less in evidence but they set up the patterns to which later works will return with a more reflexively allusive charge. These two ostensibly different kinds of signals (of queerness and of allusivity) often work hand in hand. The identification of the buried source may illuminate a homosexual subtext. We may feel more secure about identifying a text as queer on the basis of comparatively subtle hints if we can demonstrate that the text is part of a linked sequence, all using the same 'code' to, as it were, communicate with each other. It is significant that in many animated statue narratives the statue is not created but found, unearthed rather like Eurydice, reflecting both its status as a pre-existing trope and its association with buried and suppressed tendencies. In the case of Eurydice's afterlife it is the 'double loss' which becomes a marker of repetition. The sense of repeated, inevitable (and perhaps wished for) loss acquires a particular charge the more her story is repeated.

Curious repetitions are to the fore in an early reworking of the Eurydice story, the anonymous thirteenth- or fourteenth-century poem *Sir Orfeo*. The original dynamic of repetition in Ovid's story, Eurydice's double death, is retained, yet recast as a more positive double narrative whereby we get not one, but two, emotional reunions and Orfeo is allowed to keep his rescued wife Heurodis. The second reunion is that between Orfeo and his faithful steward. If the second death of Ovid's Eurydice can in any way be seen as a wish-fulfilment narrative which reflects homosexual desire, then here the narrative has been transformed into a more open gratification of a yearning for a bond which, if not homosexual, is certainly strongly homosocial.[22] The poem's patterns encourage the reader to associate the reunion between man and wife with the reunion between king and steward.

The rescue of Heurodis involves Orfeo, disguised as a common minstrel, craving admittance from the porter at the gate of fairyland, being taken to the fairy king and queen and delighting the audience with his music. Once she has been restored to him he returns home, but remains disguised and, once again, begs for help, this time from his steward. Yet again, he plays before a courtly and appreciative audience who fail to guess his real identity and there is a marked sense of *déjà vu* as Orpheus once again picks up his harp:

> [Orfeo] tok his harp so miri of soun
> & tempreþ his harp as he wele can,
> And blissful notes he þer gan . . .
>
> He toke his harp & tempred schille.
> Þe blissefulest notes he harped þere
> That euer ani man y-herd wiþ ere[23]

He tells the steward that the harp's real owner is dead. The loyal steward responds:

> Now me is wo!
> Þat was mi lord, Sir Orfeo!
> Allas! wreche, what schal y do
> Þat have swiche a lord y-lore?[24]

Earlier in the poem, once his wife had been lost to the fairies, we learned that Orfeo 'oft swoned opon the stone'.[25] The steward also 'fell aswon to grounde'[26] before joyfully realising that his master in fact stands before him. The two losses – and the two moments of joyful reunion – thus mirror one another, with Orfeo reenacting both his own role and, as an apparent 'revenant', that of Eurydice. The importance of the bond between the two men is reinforced when Orfeo declares that he will make him his heir, bypassing any need for Heurodis to provide him with children.

Sir Orfeo thus generates its own internal economy of allusive reflexivity. The moment when the steward recognises Sir Orfeo is matched by our own recognition that we are reading a replay of the first reunion. And the (apparent) reanimation of the king mirrors his wife's more literal return from the fairy netherworld. The poem's repetitions both mirror and distort the repetitions in the Ovidian source. There are other odd echoes of earlier versions of the story. Heurodis does not die in this version. Instead she falls into the power of the fairies when she falls asleep under an 'impe-tree'. The fairies warn her that she will be torn to pieces unless she returns the next day and accompanies them to fairyland:

> And ʒif þou makest ous y-let,
> Whar þou be, þou worst y-fet,
> & to-tore þine limes al,
> That noþing help þe no schal.[27]

This threatened *sparagmos* seems like a distorted echo of Orpheus's own eventual fate in the story's sequel, his violent death at the hands of the Maenads. A still clearer echo of his 'own' fate comes when Orfeo claims that he saw the body of Orfeo 'to-torn smale'[28] beside his harp. The steward bewails the fact 'Þat him was so hard grace y-ʒarked / & so vile deþ y-marked'.[29] The emphasis on the unavoidable dictates of fate in these lines strengthens the likelihood that the reader who knows the original myth will connect Orfeo's 'death' with Orpheus's death. *Sir Orfeo* itself can thus be read as a fragmented and oddly reassembled, as well as a reanimated, version of Ovid. Bodily mutilation and textual fragmentation go hand in hand in many later responses to both this story and that of Pygmalion.

Before exploring the post-Ovidian progress of the Pygmalion narrative, I want to return briefly to the *Metamorphoses* itself. Another Ovidian tale, much less widely imitated than those of Orpheus and Pygmalion, acts as a further queer 'lever' encouraging the reader to prise open the lid of the Orpheus/Pygmalion pairing to uncover its homoerotic subtext. This is the story which immediately precedes that of Orpheus, that of Iphis and Ianthe. Orpheus's narrative of Pygmalion's frustrated passion for the statue is often taken out of its original context in the *Metamorphoses*, but if it is read shortly after the parallel tale of Iphis's own impossible longing for Ianthe it may engender an uncanny sense of *déjà vu* in the reader. Telethusa, the mother of Iphis, was told by her husband that their baby must be put to death if it is a girl. But she is reassured by a vision of Io (as Isis), promising her that all will be well, and exhorting her not to hesitate to save her child. So Telethusa boldly pretends that her daughter is a boy, and rejoices when her husband names her Iphis, as this is a name which is given to both boys and girls. Iphis falls in love with Ianthe but dreads their wedding day when her true identity will inevitably become known. However Isis manifests herself once again and the girl metamorphoses into a boy in the nick of time. As well as being contiguous with the story of Orpheus – Hymen travels straight from this marriage to attend the less auspicious wedding of Orpheus and Eurydice – the tale offers clear parallels with that of Pygmalion. In both cases an impossible and inappropriate love is enabled by the miraculous intervention of a benevolent goddess who effects a transformation which removes the barrier to marriage. Iphis, following his sex change, is yet another type of 'not woman'. Because the story of Pygmalion is so well known and that of Iphis so obscure, the modern reader will tend to overlook the way in which the statue's animation is also a replay, a reanimation, of the miracle which enables Iphis to marry. But the position of Iphis's story in the poem helps explain why later responses to Pygmalion often foreground gender instability.

Interestingly, the afterlives of the two stories (Pygmalion and Iphis) have served to further entwine the tales together. Iphis's best-known literary descendent is Lyly's *Gallathea* in which the love between Phillida and Gallathea (both disguised as boys in order to avoid being virgin sacrifices to Neptune) is made lawful when one girl (we never find out which) is metamorphosed into a man.[30] Venus explicitly invokes the Ovidian precedent, taking the credit for Isis' miracle: 'What is to love or the mistress of love unpossible? Was it not Venus that did the like to Iphis and Ianthes? How say ye, are ye agreed, one to be a boy presently?'[31] Lyly presumably named his heroine after one of myth's more obscure Galateas, the mother of Leucippus, a boy whose story is essentially the same as that of Iphis although in his case the miracle-working goddess was Leto. When some much later writer, perhaps Jean-Jacques Rousseau in his 1770 play *Pygmalion*, first gave the name Galatea to Pygmalion's statue it is possible that he did so without reference either to Lyly's play or to the (rather recondite) story of Leucippus.[32] But even if the entanglement between Iphis and Pygmalion, via the name Galatea, came about by chance, it has had the effect of encouraging readers, writers and critics to note the parallels between the two stories. Phillipa Berry, for example, overlooking the late christening of the statue, assumes the name Gallathea was chosen by Lyly in order to invoke the story of Pygmalion.[33] Even though this apparent onomastic clue turns out to be a red herring, it is certainly possible to identify other Elizabethan writers who associate the statue as inappropriate love object with impossible or unwelcome same-sex desire.[34]

In order to establish this pattern I will analyse its presence in texts which do not seem to use the idea of (re)animation as an uncanny allusion marker, but which are an important part of the background to later texts, particularly those where a homoerotic subtext is perhaps only recognisable in the light of its earlier intertexts. The principal cue for such an interpretation seems to have been the sculptor's initial lack of sexual interest in 'normal' women, particularly when associated with the additional nudge to the reader provided by the tastes of the tale's narrator, Orpheus. Only a slight reinflection is needed to recast Pygmalion's indifference and disapproval as a sexual preference for men. This is how John Marston's description of the sculptor in 'The Metamorphosis of Pygmalion's Image' (1598) for example, when taken out of context, is likely to strike the reader:[35]

> *Pigmalion*, whose hie loue-hating minde
> Disdain'd to yeeld seruile affection,
> Or amorous sute to any woman-kinde
> *Knowing their wants and mens perfection.* (my italics)[36]

John Rainolds warns readers to 'beware of beautifull boyes transformed into women by putting on their raiment, their feature, looks and facions. For men may be ravished with loue of stones, of dead stuffe, framed by cunning grauers to beautifull womens likenes; as, in poets fables appeareth by Pygmalion'.[37] The bond between the convincing representation of a female by a male and the convincing representation of a woman in art is articulated particularly explicitly in a satire, 'Ingling Pyander' published in 1599 by T. M. (sometimes identified as Thomas Middleton). Here a lovely but deceptive vision of beauty is described:

> Yet Troynovant that all-admirèd town,
> Where thousands still do travel up and down,
> Of beauty's counterfeits affords not one
> So like a lovely smiling paragon
> As Is Pyander in a nymph's attire,
> Whose rolling eye sets gazers' hearts on fire,
> Whose cherry lip, black brow and smiles procure
> Lust-burning buzzards to the tempting lure.[38]

But this gorgeous nymph, as the narrator discovers to his disgust, is in fact a transvestite:

> Trust not a painted puppet as I haue done,
> Who far more doted then Pygmalion.

The streets are full of juggling parasites
With the true shape of virgins' counterfeits.[39]

A comparable moment can be identified in Sidney's *Old Arcadia*. Musidorus is helping his friend Pyrocles disguise himself as an Amazon. He adduces one myth which very readily lends itself to a homoerotic reading, that of Narcissus. Then he makes a slightly more unexpected allusion to Pygmalion:

> Sweet cousin, since you are framed of such a loving mettle, I pray you, take heed of looking yourself in a glass lest Narcissus's fortune fall unto you. For my part, I promise you, if I were not fully resolved never to submit my heart to these fancies, I were like enough, while I dressed you, to become a young Pygmalion.[40]

Musidorus makes a woman out of a man. Pygmalion makes a woman out of stone. Both are attracted to their own creations. There is perhaps a further reason why Musidorus – or rather Sidney – jumps from Narcissus to Pygmalion. After explaining that Narcissus imagines his reflection to be real, Ovid describes the effect of his self-infatuation on the youth:

> adstupet ipse sibi vultuque inmotus eodem
> haeret, ut e pario formatum marmore signum.[41]

> (He looks in speechless wonder at himself and hangs there motionless in the same expression, like a statue carved from Parian marble.)

Both the youth and his reflection resemble a statue, and the marble thus wittily connotes both stupefaction and apparent hardhearted indifference. A few lines later Ovid plays with the conventions of blazon when, as though glancing back to the statue simile, he refers to Narcissus's *eburnea colla*, his ivory neck.[42] The association between Narcissus and a statue is yet another lever, like the story of Iphis, encouraging the reader of Ovid to associate same-sex desire with statuphilia. In the *Metamorphoses*, as well as in its afterlife, we can identify a compulsion to repeat.

Later in the *Arcadia*, we find yet another telling reference to Pygmalion. 'Cleophila' reveals that he is really Pyrocles, much to Philoclea's delight:

> The joy which wrought into Pygmalion's mind while he found his beloved image wax little and little both softer and warmer in his folded arms, till at length it accomplished his gladness with a perfect woman's

shape, still beautified with the former perfections, was even such as, by each degree of Cleophila's words, stealing entered into Philoclea's soul.[43]

The story has been cross-gendered, with Philoclea cast as the sculptor. Still more significantly, one kind of miracle (animation) has been replaced by another, an Iphis-like sex change. In fact, based on the *Arcadia*'s two references to the myth, a reader who did not know the story of Pygmalion might well imagine that it was about a man who fell hopelessly in love with one of his own sex, and whose beloved was transformed into a woman by divine intervention.

Although it is does not allude directly to Pygmalion, Shakespeare's Sonnet 20 also associates a female statue (of sorts) with the object of homoerotic desire. The sculptor, once again, is a woman, Nature, and so, at first, is her statue – making him/her male is her final touch. The conceit of Nature as sculptor is strengthened by the vocabulary of art ('painted') as well as by the suggestion that the 'statue' is more static than ordinary women. The unchanging heart, the eyes which are bright yet still, might signify either modesty or inanimation:

> A woman's face with Nature's own hand painted
> Hast thou, the master-mistress of my passion;
> A woman's gentle heart but not acquainted
> With shifting change as is false women's fashion;
> An eye more bright than theirs, less false in rolling,
> Gilding the object whereupon it gazeth.[44]

This was not the last time Shakespeare would tease his reader with a living statue. Establishing a correspondence between the Pygmalion story and same-sex desire in Elizabethan poetry may affect how we respond to the period's most famous version of Pygmalion, *The Winter's Tale*, a play whose heroine incorporates elements of both Eurydice and Galatea. Here, as in many later responses to the mythic cluster, stutters of internal repetition and duplication reflect the text's complex intertexual dynamic whereby classical sources are being replayed in a new context.

I have suggested that Orpheus's ostensible longing for Eurydice to return from the dead seems shadowed by the possibility of the opposite longing, for a wife to die. Leontes of course makes that desire quite explicit; he is preparing to sentence his wife to death just before she collapses and appears to die. Even his final reunion with Hermione, an ostensibly joyful event, is presented with a degree of equivocation. Thus, rather like Hughes's translation, the play could be said to bring the buried anxieties and tensions of the original myth a good deal closer to the surface.

Hermione is a conduit for a charged relationship between two men, although in Shakespeare's play this relationship is characterised by intense jealousy. J. I. M. Stewart first propounded a Freudian, homosexual explanation for Leontes's bizarrely sudden and ill-founded distrust of his virtuous wife Hermione in 1949.[45] He adduced Freud's theory that delusional, paranoid jealousy such as that experienced by Leontes stems from a repressed impulse to be unfaithful with someone of the same sex. Specifically, in the case of Leontes, a repressed desire for Polixines may be indicated. Their childhood friendship is thus lovingly recalled by Polixines:[46]

> We were as twinn'd lambs, that did frisk i' th' sun,
> And bleat the one at th'other. What we chang'd,
> Was innocence for innocence; we knew not
> The doctrine of ill-doing, nor dream'd
> That any did.[47]

Stewart does not I think pursue his argument as far as it can go. Leontes's discourse of parity and of twinning, quoted above, bleeds into his description of Hermione's own supposed intimacy with Polixines. He claims that they are 'making practic'd smiles / As in a looking-glass'.[48] This detail doesn't really make sense in this context. Why would two supposedly illicit lovers behave like artificial courtiers? They would be more likely to hide than affect smiles. Perhaps, to extend Stewart's own Freudian reading, the idea of a looking glass is the visible sign of Leontes's own (largely repressed) sense of attraction to his boyhood double. Leontes again seems to betray himself when he accuses Hermione and asserts that 'your actions are my dreams'.[49] Ostensibly he means 'my suspicions, dreams, about you are true, justified.' But the words could also be interpreted: 'what you do (i.e. sleep with Polixines) I've only dreamed of doing'.

Another odd insight into the two kings' boyhood relationship is suggested by Leontes's response to the young Florizel in Act 5:

> Your father's image is so hit in you,
> (His very air) that I should call you brother,
> As I did him, and speak of something wildly
> By us perform'd before.[50]

'Wildly' hangs uncertainly in the sentence, and may qualify either Leontes's speech or his earlier actions, and in either case suggests a sense of transgression. As in Ovid's version of the Eurydice narrative, and particularly in *Sir Orfeo*, the reunion with a revenant wife is associated with the establishment or re-establishment of strong ties with men. This is consistent with Freud's characterisation of the *Unheimliche* as the reappearance of events or thoughts which have been repressed since childhood. Here Florizel is a copy of Polixines, duplicating him as strikingly as the 'statue' duplicates Hermione, and suggesting a symbolic parity between Leontes's reunion with Polixines via his son and his reunion with his wife via what seems to be only a copy, a statue. The two 'reunions' (with Hermione, and with Polixines through Florizel), as well as both hinging on a dynamic of miraculous reproduction, reproduce each other, much as Orfeo's reunion with his steward oddly echoes that with his wife. This heightened play with mirroring and twinning draws attention to possible buried symbolic parities between Hermione and Polixines. The phrase 'perform'd before' may also have a reflexive, metatheatrical charge. The topics of reanimation and doubling, both of which resonate here, may remind us that myths are being reanimated and doubled by the playwright as well as characters within the fiction of the play.[51] The play imitates and thus revives the stories of Galatea and Eurydice.[52] The uncanniness of the play's climax, the restoration of Hermione, depends, like all uncanny moments, on the uncertainty it generates. But in this instance it is the play's complex allusivity which helps drive this uncertainty, as the play's competing intertexts suggest different explanations for her miraculous revival.

Leontes is shamed by his inferiority to a pattern wife for whose death he is responsible and reveals some equivocation in his feelings about her despite (or because of) her virtue. The peerless Hermione, as described by Paulina, seems already somewhat artificial, unmatched even by a fantasy hybrid of impossible perfection, whose (hypothetical) manufacture strangely recalls that of another descendent of Galatea, Frankenstein's monster:

> If, one by one, you wedded all the world,
> Or, from the all that are, took something good
> To make a perfect woman, she you kill'd
> Would be unparallel'd.[53]

Again the evocation of a fragmented Hermione has a possible textual charge, given her various (re)animated literary ancestors. His response to Paulina is interesting in its almost curt acknowledgement of Hermione's virtues and his much more energetic irritation at Paulina's persecution of him:

> 'I think so. Kill'd?
> She I kill'd? I did so; but thou strik'st me
> Sorely, to say I did: it is as bitter
> Upon thy tongue as in my thought. Now, good now,
> Say so but seldom.'[54]

Leontes seems to have mixed feelings about his 'dead' wife, and his vision of her as a revenant, quoted below, may betray guilt but little love or longing: the phrase 'No more such wives' must be interpreted 'there is no other wife so good as Hermione' but also perhaps suggests 'I'm not going through that again':

> No more such wives, therefore no wife. One worse,
> And better us'd, would make her sainted spirit
> Again possess her corpse, and on this stage
> (Where we offenders now) appear soul-vex'd,
> And begin, 'Why to me-?'[55]

The phrase 'on this stage' is obtrusively metatheatrical, and the reference to a resentful revenant reminds us of the stories, as well as the wife, who is being revived. The words 'her sainted spirit again possess her corpse' might suggest not just a reanimation but almost a *re*reanimation, a sense that this is one of an endless series of wifely revivals, and that Leontes himself, who finds it so easy to imagine what his revived wife might say, has gone through this before. Indeed we have already heard a vivid account of an earlier reanimation of the 'dead' Hermione. This is Antigonus's dream which describes the appearance of Hermione as a ghost. The audience has been encouraged to assume that Hermione is really dead and will be inclined, like Antigonus, to interpret this as a genuine portent. She correctly prophesies his imminent death and bestows the name of Perdita on her daughter. It is an unsettling passage because, although the words of 'Hermione' are moving, her demeanour is uncanny:

> To me comes a creature,
> Sometimes her head on one side, some another . . .
> And (gasping to begin some speech) her eyes

Became two spouts: the fury spent, anon
Did this break from her . . .
And so, with shrieks
She melted into air.[56]

The verb 'spout' in Shakespeare is often associated with pouring blood, once with eyes spouting blood, never (apart from here) with tears. The atmosphere of trauma and violence which suffuses the speech might even suggest that it is indeed blood which is pouring from Hermione's eyes. Certainly Paulina's own later description of a woman composed of miscellaneous body parts anticipates a new emphasis on fragmentation and dismemberment in later responses to the Pygmalion/Orpheus myth; both statues and dead bodies are more susceptible to fragmentation than is a living human, and hands and eyes are the parts of the statue or corpse which seem most vulnerable. If we accept that homosexuality is associated with at least one strand of the two myths' reception, then we might connect this emphasis on the severed hand or eye with castration anxiety.[57] In the texts I will turn to next, broken hands feature prominently. Such fragments, akin to the ruins described in the previous chapter, can also function as markers of uncanny allusion, pointing to further buried materials which must be found for the whole picture to be seen, and reflecting the way a tradition may disintegrate – or proliferate.

The severed hand is one of Freud's key markers of the uncanny although he is careful to point out that not all severed hands are uncanny. Such hands are most disturbing when they seem to develop autonomous life, separate from their former owner. This is a common motif in horror literature and film.[58] But perhaps a more genuinely uncanny hand is the one described by Keats in this fragment:

This living hand, now warm and capable
Of earnest grasping, would, if it were cold
And in the icy silence of the tomb,
So haunt thy days and chill thy dreaming nights
That thou would wish thine own heart dry of blood
So in my veins red life might stream again,
And thou be conscience-calmed. See here it is —
I hold it towards you.[59]

Although we assume that Keats imagines that even his dead hand will remain fixed to his corpse, there is a suggestion of dismemberment in the 'living hand'. The phrase suggests at least a faint possibility that, rather like Milton's books, the hand has acquired a life, and thoughts, of its own.[60] The invitation to link body and text is extended by Keats as the last line and half effects a near elision between the hand and the textual fragment.

Hands reach out to both men and readers in three related tales which build on the tradition of an animated stone or bronze Venus, all variations on the theme of a statue who comes to rob a young man of his mortal bride. The earliest extant version can be found in William of Malmesbury's twelfth-century *Chronicle of the Kings of England*.[61] A young Roman places a ring on a bronze Venus's finger, which curls up, preventing him retrieving it. Later he is disturbed in bed by a shadowy presence who claims to be Venus, and stops him from sleeping with his wife. He consults a priest called Palumbus who tells him to deliver a letter to the leader of a mysterious procession which he will see if he waits one night at a crossroads. This ruse wins him back his ring and his wife, but brings down the wrath of the leader, presumably Jupiter, on Palumbus, who cuts off his limbs as part of a penance for 'unheard of crimes'. This invocation of unnamed sins, combined with dismemberment, will resonate in several later responses to the tale.

The parallels between statuphilia and homosexuality are central to all three later responses to the legend. Here a dynamic of repetition, excavation and reanimation inheres within each tale but also, more crucially, between the tales. In the first two stories, both written in the nineteenth century, the ostensible focus is on a man's misguided passion for a beautiful antique statue, but in each case a further homosexual subtext can be identified; a subtext which becomes more obvious if we read them as a pair. In the third, more modern, story homosexuality is an overt rather than a covert presence, and this change is reflected in the depiction of the statue herself.

Prosper Mérimée's 'The Venus of Ille' (1837) is narrated by a dispassionate outsider, a middle-aged man of leisure who is travelling in France and pays a visit to an old friend whose son, Alphonse, is about to make an advantageous marriage. The narrator's host, Monsieur de Peyrehorade, is a keen amateur of antiquities who has recently discovered a copper statue of Venus in his grounds. The statue is presented explicitly as an alternative to women. Peyrehorade exclaims to the narrator: 'Mais vous êtes un homme grave et vous ne regardez plus les femmes. J'ai mieux que cela à vous montrer. Je vous ferai voir quelque chose!' ('Anyway, you're a serious kind of a chap, you don't have much of an eye for women any more. I've got better things than that to show you. I've got something really good for you to see!).[62]

The groom, despite his youth, seems scarcely more interested in women than the middle-aged narrator – certainly he seems pretty indifferent to his bride. (There are some telling hints that he is anxious about his potency on the wedding night.) Although she is young and beautiful he values her dowry more than her person. The pivotal moment comes when the groom carelessly places the ring destined for his bride on the finger of the copper Venus. Uncannily, although the statue otherwise seems to remain inanimate, 'le doigt de la Vénus est retiré, reployé' ('the statue's finger moved away, curved in').[63] He is doomed to be her bridegroom and dies in her powerful metallic embrace. We hear how the terrified wife became aware of an icy figure joining her in bed and fainted when she realised this was the statue. When she regains consciousness her husband is lying dead in the arms of the Venus.

Various indicators invite a queer reading of 'The Venus of Ille' and the initial prompt centres around this same hand, which at first appears to us as a fragment, detached from the rest of the body which is still buried under the ground. The hand, when it first emerges, is assumed to be male – it resembles 'la main d'un mort' ('the hand of a dead man'),[64] rather than a woman. Moreover the statue itself is six foot tall. These details might encourage us to look again at the story's setting. Why Ille? As a town in the Languedoc-Roussillon area of southern France, Ille seems as likely a place as any other to unearth an antique statue. But it is perhaps suggestive that *ille* is the Latin for 'he', yet another clue that this Venus is ambiguously gendered. Although Mérimée's Venus in fact keeps both her hands and her eyes, the reader is made to visualise the possibility that both might be separated from her body. The hand (as we have seen) first appears as a fragment, reflecting the story's own fragmented and incomplete nature, the fact that we have to dig to find its sources and subtext. The eyes are identified as the source of much of the Venus's uncanny power: 'Elle vous fixe avec ses grands yeux blancs . . . On dirait qu'elle vous dévisage' ('She fixes her big white eyes on you . . . You feel like she's staring straight at you').[65] An urchin expresses a wish to take them from her: 'Si j'avais mon ciseau à froid . . . je lui ferais bientôt sauter ses grands yeux blancs, comme je tirerais une amande de sa coquille' ('If I had my cold chisel . . . I'd soon make her big white eyes pop out, the same way I prise an almond out of its shell').[66]

Also significant is the construction of a kind of double narrative in the tale. The young groom is naturally rather lethargic but is roused by his desire to prove himself in tennis; his enthusiasm for the sport is prominent in the tale. Alphonse's favourite partner, Jean Coll, is injured when the newly excavated statue falls on his leg. As a local guide explains to the narrator: 'C'est que M. Alphonse de Peyrehorade en a été triste, car c'est Coll qui faisait sa partie. Voilà qui était beau à voir comme ils se renvoyaient les balles. Paf! Paf! Jamais elles ne touchaient terre' ('Monsieur Alphonse de Peyrehorade was really down in the mouth about it, as it was Coll who used to play with him. A fine sight it was, too, when they returned the balls to each other. Thwock! Thwock! Those balls never even touched the ground').[67] When his neighbours are beaten by a party of wandering Spaniards, Alphonse is spurred to compete with the strangers. His own opponent's physique is described in some detail: 'C'était un homme d'une quarantaine d'années, sec et nerveux, haut de six pieds, et sa peau olivâtre avait une teinte presque aussi foncée que le bronze de Vénus' ('He was a man in his forties, wiry and muscular, six feet tall; his olive-hued skin was almost as dark-toned as the bronze of the statue of Venus').[68] Immediately before commencing play Alphonse's good looks and vigour are emphasised – as is his complete indifference to his wife: 'Alors je le trouvai vraiment beau. Il était passioneé . . . Et sa fiancée? Ma foi, si cela eût été nécessaire, il aurait, je crois, fait ajourner le mariage' ('At that point I found him really handsome. He was filled with passion . . . and his fiancée? . . . Well, I swear that, if it had been necessary, he'd have doubtless postponed the wedding').[69] It is before beginning play that Alphonse puts the ring on the statue's finger. This coincidence and the odd correspondences between the Spanish player and the Venus (their height and colouring) suggest a symbolic act of infidelity.[70] Such a hint at a symbolic connection is consistent with the Venus's injury to Alphonse's tennis partner (an injury to the intended bride, her rival, would seem more logical) and also with the statue's position at the edge of the tennis court – its slightly incongruous location is emphasised by the narrator. When Alphonse beats the Spaniard, his opponent threatens to pay him back. Therefore the narrator suspects that he is behind Alphonse's mysterious death.

Thus we have two alternative explanations – the competitive

violence of the defeated Spaniard, or the erotic violence of the goddess. The tennis element appears almost inconsequential in a tale which is otherwise so economical and it seems to demand some kind of further explanation.[71] If we allow the central narrative of the Venus and the odd tennis subplot to become elided then we are presented with the narrative of a man stolen away from his bride by a male lover.

Fragmentation becomes more prominent in the next two tales. 'The Venus of Ille' had a profound impact on the young Henry James who commented on its peculiar power and translated it into English. Although the translation was not accepted for publication and is now lost, the tale's impact can be traced in one of James's original short stories, 'The Last of the Valerii', published in 1874. This also features a female statue, a Juno this time, with an ambiguously gendered hand, and the story as a whole is susceptible to a rather similar queering. Reading 'The Last of the Valerii' in the light of the earlier tale highlights those elements that they have in common and emphasises the importance of these for James. The mirroring effect between them draws out details in each, individually perhaps inconsequential, which invite a search for hidden secrets.[72]

'The Last of the Valerii', like 'The Venus of Ille', has an unnamed, older male narrator who is a witness to the affairs of a young heterosexual couple (in this case newly married) and to the aftermath of a wonderful statue's excavation. It is narrated by an American whose young goddaughter, Martha, marries an Italian count, Marco Valerio. The Count is fascinated though also haunted by the presence of antique statues even before he finds the Juno. His fascinated horror is focused on their eyes: 'I can't bear to look the statues in the face. I seem to see other strange eyes in the empty sockets, and I hardly know what they say to me. I call the poor old statues ghosts.'[73] It is appropriate that the narrator should see the statues as spectres as the story itself is so clearly itself a revenant behind which another text can be detected staring out.

James copied Mérimée's choice of a middle-aged, unmarried man as witness to the events. This correspondence between the tales is a good example of a detail which becomes more significant through repetition and reanimation. Identifying which elements are compulsively repeated helps us identify the true significance of the story for all its authors. The unearthing of the statue within James's story parallels his own 'unearthing' of Mérimée. And if we, in our turn, unearth the link we will appreciate the way the occluded queer subtexts of the tales reinforce and illuminate one another. Once the Count beholds the Juno, discovered during the course of an archaeological excavation of his grounds, his relationship with Martha goes sour. The narrator anxiously charts the couple's growing estrangement, which, we are led to believe, arises from Valerio's atavistic return to the pagan beliefs of his ancestors (embodied in the Juno). Finally Martha solves the problem by ordering that the statue be reburied, leaving the Count apparently cured. Although 'The Last of the Valerii' can certainly be read as a dramatised clash between modern Italy and her primitive Roman past, like 'The Venus of Ille' it also invites a 'queer' reading, a submerged narrative of a marriage threatened by the husband's homosexuality.[74]

Like Mérimée's tale, 'The Last of the Valerii' has a kind of double narrative which offers us two choices, two explanations. A strange fault line runs through the godfather's narrative, making it difficult for the reader to piece together the whole story – and, particularly, to reconstitute the narrator's original impressions. The effect is comparable to the double explanation for Alphonse's death provided by Mérimée, for the choice for James's readers, though more subtly presented, is also between homosexuality and statuphilia as the solution to a mystery, those two competing barriers to marriage which Ovid explored in the parallel tales of Pygmalion and Iphis. Both Mérimée and James take the different themes of Ovid's two stories and present them, not as two distinct narratives, but as alternative explanations of the same story.

In hindsight, as the godfather writes, he knows perfectly well that the Juno is responsible for the Count's alienation from Martha. The entire tale is narrated from this perspective – from its first discovery he chooses to make us aware of the Juno as a portentous and rather threatening figure. However initially, at the time when the events actually took place, the godfather was in the dark as to the cause of the Count's strange behaviour. Yet because we always have the benefit of the narrator's hindsight, we don't immediately realise that he hasn't guessed that paganism is at the root of his goddaughter's marriage problems. In fact it is only after rereading the story that the potential significance and possible nature of the narrator's interim suspicions is made clear. The godfather's uneasy sense that Martha 'was the least bit oddly mated'[75] and his description of her puzzlement when Valerio falls under the Juno's spell, for example, reflect impressions that predate his discovery of the Juno's impact on the Count:

> She sat at times with her eyes fixed on him with a kind of imploring curiosity, as if for the present she were too much surprised to be angry. What passed between them in private, I had, of course, no warrant to inquire. Nothing, I suspected – and that was the misery! . . . But from his wife he kept his face inexorably averted; and when she approached him with some melancholy attempt at fondness, he received it with an ill-concealed shudder.[76]

It is hinted that Valerio, like Mérimée's bridegroom, has problems with potency, problems which are more clearly linked to aversion than they were in the earlier tale. An important clue to what might have gone through the narrator's mind at this point can be found in his description of the Count's fascination with another statue, that of Hermes, which had always stood in his grounds. The godfather finds the Count sitting in his garden at night gazing at it. For the reader the statue is most likely to figure paganism and act as a surrogate for the Juno.[77] But it is possible that the godfather reads the signals quite differently. The Count's description of the Hermes suggests a figure both effeminate and sensual 'pouting his great lips';[78] he explains that he used to think the statue frightening but finds that now it 'suggests the most delightful images':

> 'The Hermes, for a wonder, had kept his nose; and when I reflected that my dear Countess was being neglected for this senseless pagan block, I secretly promised myself to come the next day with a hammer and deal him such a lusty blow as would make him too ridiculous for a sentimental tête-à-tête.'[79]

This reflection seems rather jocular and inconsequential and it is easy for the reader to skim over its surface implication – that the Hermes is in some way a sexual rival to the Countess. Because the Juno is so portentously and mysteriously potent within the story, we may overlook the way the Hermes apparently wrong-foots the narrator. But if we remember that the godfather does not yet realise the impact the Juno has had on the Count, his reaction to the Hermes incident provides us with a further clue that homosexuality is suspected: 'Meanwhile, however, the Count's infatuation was no laughing matter, and I expressed my sincerest conviction when I said, after a pause, that I should recommend him to see either a priest or a physician.'[80] We will probably assume that the godfather's feelings of disgust mixed with pity, and his advice that the Count consult either a priest or a doctor, are prompted by fears that he is becoming a pagan. Yet in fact when the Count finally does articulate his pagan impulses, the godfather's first impulse is one of amused relief:

> I seemed to touch the source of his trouble, and my relief was great, for my discovery made me feel like bursting into laughter . . . In my gratitude, I was ready to thank any gods he pleased . . . A sturdy young Latin I had called poor Marco, and he was sturdier, indeed, than I had dreamed him! Discretion was now out of place.[81]

Although anxiety about Martha's 'dignity' might easily be ascribed to suspicion that the Count was having an affair with a woman, the emphasis on his 'sturdiness' (rather than, say, his 'worthiness') perhaps implies a pleased relief at discovering, after all, that he is conventionallly masculine. Rather similarly the Count's response to the interest his Juno excites resembles that of a man anxious to put a stop to gossip of a more personal kind. He denies the very existence of his statue:

> 'But you have something, surely. The rumour is running through Rome.'
>
> 'The rumour be damned!' cried the Count, savagely. 'I've *nothing* – do you understand? Be so good as to say so to your friends!'[82]

And one almost wonders whether a more personal disappointment is encoded in the brief description of the antiquarian's professional chagrin: 'The answer was explicit, and the poor archaeologist departed, tossing his flaxen mane.'[83]

The hand of the Venus in Mérimée at first emerges as an apparent fragment but is in fact still attached to the body. In James's story the hand is actually broken off, perhaps reflecting the apparent emasculation of the Count. Again, it is the first visible sign of the statue, brought to the narrator by the excavator, 'an earth-stained fragment of marble'.[84] The Count keeps the hand in a silver box. Like the hand in 'The Venus of Ille' the Juno's hand seems to become suggestively androgynous if not absolutely masculine once separated from its body. When an inquisitive visitor enquires about this the Count explains:

> 'It is the hand of a beautiful creature,' he said, 'whom I once greatly admired.'

'Ah – a Roman?' said the gentleman, with a smirk.
'A Greek,' said the Count, with a frown.[85]

The Count's correction is emphasised because it comes at the very end of the tale and is significant in the context of the homosexual resonances of classicism, particularly Hellenism, at this period. The phrase 'beautiful creature' would of course normally denote a woman but the context makes this assumption less certain. Although we earlier learnt that the Juno was 'wrought, as a whole, in the large and simple manner of the great Greek period',[86] it may be significant that the distinction is made so emphatically, particularly as the name Juno is unequivocally Roman. If, at any level, the shift from Roman to Greek is a shift in far more than location, then it may be compared with a similar correction in Tom Stoppard's *The Invention of Love*. A. E. Housman is under discussion:

> Chamberlain: He's a Latin prof.
> Jerome: But of the Greek persuasion, would you say George?[87]

Thus James's tale ends, where Mérimée's began, with an uncanny hand of indeterminate gender which seems to reach back to its predecessor.

The final tale within this series, another twentieth-century response to the 'stone Venus' tradition, Anthony Burgess's novella *The Eve of Saint Venus*, takes up the pattern by opening with the fury of a connoisseur, Sir Benjamin Drayton, when he realises the housemaid has broken the finger off his stone Venus. Sir Benjamin's love of antiquities is part of a more general yearning for a past which he cannot access:

> The past is dead, and all that was good is buried with it. And here's this thick horrible door of the present with its tantalising keyhole. You can press your eye or ear to it, but you can't turn either into a key. The past goes on inside, that perpetual party, becoming wilder and wilder, but there's no admittance.[88]

In fact the Venus is a fake, rather than a genuine Greek or Roman, and she is part of a rather motley collection of 'classical' statues presented to Sir Benjamin by his maverick brother. Perhaps her modernity, her status as an imitation, and her place as part of a collection rather than as a unique find, reflects Burgess's awareness that the 'statue bride' tradition is getting a bit cluttered – Sir Benjamin's wife makes a suggestive reference to her husband's fondness for 'that perpetually expanding club he calls the past'.[89]

But, although Burgess is stacking his story on top of a growing pile of similar narratives, he introduces an important twist. It is open lesbianism rather than covert male homosexuality which threatens a marriage in this story. Burgess's explicit emphasis on homosexuality retrospectively strengthens the more buried hints offered by the two earlier tales. Writing in the middle of the twentieth century, Burgess has no need to conceal this topic. Just as the statue in his story does not have to be unearthed from the ground, so the sexuality she (in part) represents is also apparent on the text's surface, and does not have to be excavated. The journalist Julia Webb represents a sexual temptation to the prospective bride, Diana Drayton, an aspiring artist: 'You'll have a chance to work unhindered by babies and shopping and a man breathing down your neck . . . I'll be more than a husband or a friend.'[90] Immediately after Julia's intervention, we hear of Ambrose the bridegroom's strange encounter with the Venus. Following the traditional pattern of such stories, he has been tempted to place the wedding ring on one of her fingers only to see it curl up, making it impossible for him to reclaim the ring. In the context of the scene we have just witnessed between Diana and Julia the Venus seems as much like a threat, or rival to, Ambrose himself as a rival for Diana. Ambrose wants to break the finger off, and it is perhaps a sign of this story's late position in the 'stone Venus' tradition that we experience a double sense of *déjà vu*, recalling the similar predicament of Mérimée's Alphonse and the broken hand of James's Juno, but also the opening of Burgess's own story which begins with the Venus losing one of her fingers. It is as though, true to its Ovidian roots, the story is being told twice in some way, and this metafictional atmosphere is strengthened by Sir Benjamin's response to being told of the moving statue: 'I've read about such things. In the past these things were always happening . . . those effigies . . . epitomise the past.'[91] And as Ambrose's friend Crowther-Mason observes: 'The past . . . is never discarded. The past is made richer by the unfolding present. The gods are still alive, aspects of the breathtaking, growing, moving, widening, unifying pattern.'[92] Burgess not only revives the earlier tales, he reanimates them by shining a clearer light on their buried subtexts.

Venus's precise significance remains uncertain in the story. Although the goddess does seem to view Ambrose as her husband, she also seems in some way to represent a lesbian lure, replacing the male homosexual temptation represented by such statues in earlier versions of the narrative. Julia's eventual acceptance that Diana will marry coincides with the mysterious return of Ambrose's wedding ring by a dove. Their parallel gracious gestures suggest that these two forceful females are somehow linked. Sir Benjamin's final musings, prompted by the shocking sight of all his statues destroyed by lightning, perhaps also function as a reflection on the way in which the 'stone Venus' story has been deflected from its original trajectory by Burgess:

> He himself could only turn to the past, but he heard that it was already possible to change the past, bringing the past continually up to date, a perpetual jackal fawning on the present, a malleable witness with no qualms about perjury.'[93]

We can take up this invitation to change the past and observe that, on reflection, the murder of the bridegroom in Mérimée's tale doesn't really seem very lover-like. Burgess's story enables the creation of a new (mis)reading of 'The Venus of Ille', in which the copper Venus wanted to get Alphonse out of the way in order to gain easier access to the bride (whom she had joined in bed before the bridegroom arrived on the scene).

Cocteau's Orphic trilogy also glances at the stone Venus meme, particularly in the opening film, *The Blood of the Poet* (1930). In the first of the film's strangely fragmented episodes, called 'The Wounded Hand or the Scars of the Poet', an artist paints a face and rubs off its mouth with his hand. This mouth appears to move and speak on the hand, engaging the artist in (auto)erotic caresses. Then the artist wipes the mouth on to a female statue, both of whose arms have been broken off, in an extreme version of the fragmentation we've seen in other depictions of the stone Venus. Although he goes on to break the statue into still smaller fragments, she returns, at first disguised as a beautiful living woman, reverting to her true statue form only after presiding over the violent deaths of two young men. This is the first of the Orphic trilogy, and in the movement from this film to the central and best-known film of the three, *Orphée* itself,[94] we can trace a reversal of the original Ovidian dynamic. Eurydice seems to haunt Ovid's later story of Pygmalion, but in Cocteau's mythography Orphée is haunted by the Pygmalion narrative which shadowed the earlier *The Blood of the Poet*, and which features the destruction rather than the creation of a beautiful statue. The sets of *Orphée* are full of classical statues; when he is being attacked by the mob, Orphée complains that they are throwing 'stones to make a bust of me' and in the same scene he asks: 'What does the marble think as a masterpiece is hewn?' This reversal of Ovid's narrative is mirrored in the film's cinematography. Exploiting that 'spectral' quality of film I mentioned at the beginning of the chapter, Cocteau reanimates his characters by playing the film backwards, the simplest way of presenting their return from death to life. And he reanimates Ovid by playing him backwards too.

E. T. A. Hoffmann's 'The Sandman' (1816–17) and Hitchcock's 1958 film *Vertigo* together comprise another significant conjoined pair of responses to the paired myths of Orpheus and Pygmalion.[95] Like 'The Venus of Ille' and 'The Last of the Valerii', 'The Sandman' is the tale of a man torn between a real and an artificial woman.[96] Like so many other texts which draw on the Pygmalion/Orpheus connection it presents us with a man whose preference for an artificially perfect woman is associated both with possible repressed homosexuality and with castration anxiety.[97] Although written before the tales of Mérimée and James, 'The Sandman' is bound up with Pygmalion's twentieth-century reception and has proved a significant vector for the tradition's continuing potency. For many modern readers the story's inherent uncanny charge and strange internal echoes will be enhanced by an additional sense of *déjà vu*, for they will have already read a detailed account of its plot in Freud's influential essay on the uncanny. For film-lovers a further vertiginous sense of repetition may be engendered by the tale as it strikingly prefigures Hitchcock's *Vertigo*, discussed below.

The Sandman of the title is a mysterious and threatening figure, Dr Coppelius, who becomes associated in the mind of the story's protagonist Nathaniel with the mythical sandman who sprinkles sand in the eyes of naughty children who won't go to sleep. When Nathaniel is caught looking on at the secret alchemical experiments performed by his father and Coppelius, the latter threatens to attack his eyes. Coppelius, in a dreamily autoallusive move typical within this tradition, appears later in the story under the name of Coppola, a maker of lenses and (more disturbingly) the manufacturer of the enchanting eyes of the beautiful automaton, Olympia. Nathaniel is tricked into thinking Olympia a real woman and becomes infatuated with her although he is in fact already engaged to another girl, Clara. Clara is a forceful and highly articulate woman who is amused by Nathaniel's morbid fear of the Sandman and carefully explains how his fancies are produced from his subconscious mind. Olympia, on the other hand, can only say, 'Ah'. If Clara (as we shall see) is a version of Eurydice, Olympia is clearly a Galatea. Although Clara's lively intelligence might seem to connote reality in contrast to the dumbness of Olympia, this is not how the situation strikes Nathaniel. He is oblivious to the doll's obvious artificiality but accuses his fiancée of being an automaton because she is so cool and sceptical.[98] This perhaps suggests the confusing status of 'woman' as a category within a discourse of reality and its counterfeits. It is easier to be a 'real' woman, passive, silent and obliging, if you are a doll or a statue. (This is a theme which is brought out very strongly in Hitchcock's apparent response to 'The Sandman' in *Vertigo*.) Thus we can add a fourth type of 'not woman' to the categories of statue, corpse and man: the real woman who resists stereotyped feminine behaviour.

Nathaniel seems estranged from Clara even before he first beholds Olympia, and his odd preference for writing to her brother Lothario rather than to her directly is emphasised by the text. Nathaniel's preference for Olympia and his bond with Lothario both signal an attraction to 'not women'. Eventually he discovers the truth about Olympia when her eyes (in a horrible moment symbolic of castration for Freud) fall out on to the floor. This might be said to reproduce, in Freudian terms, a man's horror and fear at discovering that a woman has no penis and has thus in his eyes been castrated.

Although at first all goes well after the horrid revelation of Olympia's artificiality, and he seems happily reunited with Clara, later Nathaniel falls prey to a further fit of madness and tries to throw her off a tower:

> Leaping up high in the air and laughing horribly at the same time, he began to shout in a piercing voice, 'Spin round, wooden doll! Spin round, wooden doll!' With the strength of a giant he laid hold upon Clara and tried to hurl her over, but in an agony of despair she clutched fast hold of the railing that went round the gallery.[99]

The episode reads like a distorted and violent reenactment of Orpheus's second loss of Eurydice. Having been offered a second chance at happiness, Nathaniel, like Orpheus, seems determined to lose her again. Like *The Winter's Tale*, this story picks up on the bare hint in Ovid that Orpheus was not, after all, so very anxious to keep Eurydice alive. The ease with which a moment of tragic horror – Orpheus's genuine anguish at the loss of Eurydice – can be transformed into a crime scene is suggested by paintings of Orpheus and Eurydice. The viewer who did not know the myth might well think that the artists Watts and Kratzenstein, for example, were depicting a murder. Christian Gottlieb Kratzenstein's 1806 'Orpheus and Eurydice' could be a depiction of a man who has just pushed a woman to her death, whereas George Frederic Watts's more brooding and dreamlike 'Orpheus and Eurydice' (1869) looks as much like a strangulation as a final embrace.

Hitchcock's masterpiece *Vertigo* (1958) – almost certainly influenced by 'The Sandman', for Hitchcock owned several copies of Hoffmann's tales[100] – is a further example of the tendency for the narratives of Pygmalion and Eurydice to merge together.[101] The central character is a single middle-aged man, Scottie, who had once been engaged to a woman called Midge, still a close friend. Although the scenario of *Vertigo* cannot be precisely mapped on to 'The Sandman', Midge's shrewd intelligence aligns her strongly with Clara, as does her lack of allure. In the course of his work as a detective, Scottie has been left injured by an accident which has given him a profound fear of heights. The accident was particularly horrific because a fellow police officer fell to his death while (successfully) preventing Scottie meeting the same fate. The initial chase scene has been 'queered' by Theodore Price who figures his pursuit of the young male criminal as an erotic chase.[102] But if we are aware of the Orpheus subtext it is more tempting to 'queer' his encounter with his doomed colleague. The horror, the sense of guilt and responsibility, align Scottie's situation with that of Orpheus after losing Eurydice for the second time.

A more obvious Eurydice figure in the film is 'Madeleine Elster', although, as the quotation marks suggest, she is also a Galatea, a fabrication. 'Madeleine' is a beautiful but apparently deranged blonde whom Scottie investigates in his role as a private detective, commissioned by the woman's husband, an old college friend named Gavin Elster, who claims to be worried that his wife thinks she is being haunted by the shade of her great grandmother, the beautiful Carlotta, who committed suicide. When Madeleine climbs up a bell tower Scottie is prevented by vertigo from following her and watches in horror as she falls to her death.

His fear of heights, the vertigo which drives the film's complex plot, has been interpreted as a symbolic horror of femininity. According to Theodore Price both Scottie's limp and his tendency to fainting spells are signs of effeminacy, although it is also possible to see his physical helplessness as a sign of childlike dependence on a mother figure.[103] But, like Clara, Midge can be seen as a threatening as well as a nurturing figure, an intelligent and resourceful woman with a successful career as a designer. As Robert Samuels points out, there is an ironic reversal in their positions. Because of the injuries he acquired at the beginning of the film Scottie must wear a corset and thus in a sense be feminised. Midge, on the other hand, as a designer of bras, shares in the control over the female form more usually associated with men.[104]

Like Orpheus as 'author' of Pygmalion, Scottie fantasises about a possible substitute for his lost love but one sculpted out of flesh and blood rather than marble. Here again, the urge to create a perfect woman can be seen as a symptom of hostile or fearful feelings about women rather than simple desire. Judy, the girl he picks up and chooses to mould to Madeleine's form, is resentful of his control and of his refusal to accept her as a feisty brunette rather than a cool blonde. The film's twist comes when it is revealed that Judy is in fact 'Madeleine', that she never really died, but had instead been complicit in a plot hatched by Gavin Elster to murder the real Madeleine, a plot whose success depended on a cruel exploitation of Scottie's vertigo which they knew would prevent him reaching the top of the bell tower. Angered by Judy's treachery, Stewart takes her to the tower from which she originally 'fell'. Here the distraught Judy, startled with terror when a nun appears at the top of the stairs, falls to her death. Scottie, like Orpheus, has lost his love a second time.

This tower is insistently associated with repetition in the film. As well as being the scene of a double death, it is the focus of Judy/Madeleine's feigned 'memories' of her life as Carlotta. It is also in another important sense a repetition, as it mirrors the location of Nathaniel's attempt on Clara's life in 'The Sandman'.[105] Nathaniel's maddened scorn when he cries out 'spin round, wooden doll! Spin round, wooden doll!' matches the mood of Scottie, disgusted by Judy's deceit. The fake Madeleine 'remembers' the death of Carlotta by falling, a story from the past; outside the fiction of the film, *Vertigo* is also 'remembering' and reanimating Hoffman.

The film confronts us with the problems faced when trying to distinguish between the real and the unreal in the context of a category as uncertain as 'woman'. We can distinguish in *Vertigo* between two 'real' women – Judy and Midge – and one 'unreal' woman, Madeleine. Midge, plain and clever, completely fails to capture

Scottie's imagination. When she provokingly paints her own face onto a copy of Carlotta's portrait, the woman 'Madeleine' so resembles, he is disgusted by the joke. The disjuncture between Midge's face and the fantasy, fairytale body is a shock for both Scottie and the viewer, a shock, a sense of travesty, in some ways comparable to that faced by the narrator of T. M.'s poem in his encounter with the transvestite. It is almost as though Midge is somehow a 'not woman' (because she is plain and forceful) as opposed to the 'real' woman Madeleine, graceful and elegant, who is paradoxically a complete fiction. Judy is more attractive than Midge but this is not enough for Scottie who insists on turning her (back) into the cool and otherworldly Madeleine. The qualities that make Judy seem 'real', her earthy physicality and her working-class accent, must be ironed out. Pygmalion turned stone into a simulacrum of life. But because Scottie is working in flesh and blood, transforming her with dyes and paints, he seems to be following the opposite trajectory, from life to death. In order to approximate his illusory ideal, his own sense of a 'real' woman, she must become both more inert and more artificial. Although he doesn't plan her eventual death, the dynamic of the film suggests a need to complete the process, to turn her from an automaton into a corpse. Like Cocteau, Hitchcock reverses the sequence of events in the *Metamorphoses*, where a dead woman, Eurydice, is reinvented as a statue and finally becomes a living woman. Even though he is aiming for a kind of rebirth, the return of 'Madeleine', it is significant that the moment when the replication is finally completed is so deathly. A strange green light fills the hotel room and a prolonged shot of Scottie slowly turning to the opening door is accompanied by uncanny and dissonant music. Dressed in grey, 'Madeleine' at first seems shadowed in a ghostly fog, more Eurydice at this point than Galatea. Judy's dual role also flags the film's status as a complex *homage*; it is itself a reanimation, a revenant.

The film's trademark vortex denotes vertigo but might also suggest the sense of *mise en abyme* created by its complex plot. *Vertigo*'s vertiginous repetitions are markers of uncanny allusion. 'Madeleine' is supposedly haunted by a woman from the past, Carlotta, who fell to her death in the nineteenth century. As Judy she is in turn haunted by her crime as 'Madeleine', by the death of the real Madeleine thrown from the tower, and Scottie is of course also haunted by the apparent death of 'Madeleine' which itself echoes the similar death of his colleague. Judy's eventual death replays both her earlier feigned death and the death of the policeman which is the catalyst of the whole film. A further death by falling which is a persistent absent presence in the film is Scottie's own, which never happens but which he imagines again and again. (These persistent echoes, both for the viewer and the characters, may create that effect of being helplessly trapped in a dream which Freud associates with repetition.)[106] This dynamic of repetition is matched by the film's dialogue, especially as it reaches its climax when Scottie confronts Judy at the scene of the crime. 'You were the counterfeit', he says twice in succession, as he does another phrase: 'You were a very apt pupil.' This repetition is specifically reflexive as she has twice been a counterfeit Madeleine, once for Gavin Elster, once for Scottie himself. Similarly she was an apt pupil for both men. Scottie complains that she performed better on Elster's behalf than his own and the viewer may of course import a further third Pygmalion into the picture, Hitchcock himself. These layers are further complicated by the film's intertextual resonances. The sense of the characters' incessant and apparently inescapable urge to repeat is made more compelling if we are aware of its debts to the Eurydice story and to 'The Sandman'. In particular the repeated phrases used by Scottie echo Nathaniel's repetition of the phrase 'spin round, wooden doll', especially given the film's own emphasis on spinning in its trademark vortex visuals. We might also see an added significance in the repeated phrase 'you were a very apt pupil'. These doubled pupils, particularly given the prominent use of a single eye in the film's opening credits, suggest a pair of eyes, uncomfortably separated from their context like those of Hoffman's Olympia.

Motifs from both the 'stone Venus' and the 'Sandman/Vertigo' strands of this chapter collide in *Fables & Reflections*, Volume 6 of Neil Gaiman's *The Sandman*, a series of graphic novels which trace the story of the Sandman (usually referred to as Morpheus, or Dream) who inhabits a complex mythological world in which Greek gods rub shoulders with characters from English folklore and American popular culture. Each volume contributes to a developing story arc while also containing a number of apparently unrelated stories. *Fables & Reflections* opens with Todd Faber (his name might be translated as 'Death Smith'), a playwright and director, watching an unnamed film late at night: 'It had Jimmy Stewart and some blonde woman, Kim Novak maybe, or Tippi Hedren, and a plot I just couldn't follow. Someone was dead or maybe she wasn't. I don't know.'[107] Although this vague account might fit *Rear Window* or perhaps *Dial M for Murder*, the film's identity seems confirmed as *Vertigo* once Todd falls asleep. He dreams he is climbing up a rock face where he meets Morpheus, god of dreams, the Sandman of the series' title, and confronts his fear of heights. Although in one sense the dream appears to be inspired by watching *Vertigo*, Todd himself traces it back to an earlier dream he had as a small child of falling off the roof of a house. The roofscape and vortex-like swirl in the illustrations, however, invoke Hitchcock once again.

The implied association between Hitchcock and Hoffman is then extended when Gaiman returns to the ultimate source material of both. Within Gaiman's idiomythology, Morpheus has become the father of Orpheus, and the original story of Orpheus, the catalyst for Morpheus's own tragedy in *The Sandman*, is retold in the central section of *Fables & Reflections*. The artwork at the opening of the episode is a striking reprise of many motifs we have already encountered over the course of the story's afterlife. Eurydice is a dark and shadowy figure and the viewer's eye is drawn to the homoeroticised depiction of Orpheus, naked and with his back to us.[108] This Orpheus, like Cocteau's Orphée, seems to be half turning into a statue as his arms are cropped neatly below the shoulders, suggesting a broken sculpture rather than a mutilated body, particularly as his stance is otherwise upright and confident. Three stylised découpé eyes stick to his back, further examples of the many uncomfortable mutilations this narrative has attracted, although the viewer's own gaze may also be implicated.

I would like to end with a curious footnote to this analysis of the queer afterlife of Pygmalion and Orpheus. Oddly we can find a fusion of similar themes in a very different literary and cultural tradition, the Book of Genesis.[109] Orpheus loses his wife Eurydice to death a second time when he looks back at her before they have left the Underworld. Lot's wife also gets punished for looking back (at the destroyed cities of Sodom and Gomorrah). She is of course turned into a pillar of salt. If we think of this transformed woman as a kind of statue, Lot's wife can be linked with Galatea as well as with Eurydice. Because her own trajectory is in the opposite direction Lot's wife is still more like the Propoetides, women who turn into stone after becoming prostitutes, and whose scandalous behaviour helps confirm Pygmalion's aversion for women. The Genesis narrative, like the story of Orpheus, has homosexual associations – Sodom and Gomorrah were destroyed because of their inhabitants' homosexual acts. Moreover both tales have incestuous sequels. Lot slept with his daughters (they tricked him into this act by making him drunk) and Pygmalion's grandson slept, also unwittingly, with his daughter Myrrha. So we have ill-omened backward glances, women/statue transformations, homosexuality and incest in both these (ostensibly remote) narratives. Is this evidence for a deep-rooted association between such motifs or simply a coincidence? Even if the latter is the case it may be that the presence in the Bible itself of the same group of themes linked together by Ovid in Book 10 of the *Metamorphoses* reinforced the tendency for later artists, most of whom would have been well acquainted with the Old Testament, to recombine the same themes in their own works.

Notes

1 J. Milton, *Areopagitica* (Cambridge: Deighton, Bell & Co, 1973), p. 3.
2 G. Poulet, 'Criticism and the Experience of Interiority', in R. Macksey and E. Donato (eds), *The Languages of Criticism and the Sciences of Man: The Structuralist Controversy* (Baltimore and London: Johns Hopkins Press, 1970), pp. 56–88, p. 59.
3 *Ibid.*, pp. 62–3.
4 *Ibid.*, p. 63.
5 M. Shaneen, 'Adapting the occult: horror and the avant-garde in the cinema of Ken Jacobs', in R. J. Hands and J. McRoy (eds), *Monstrous Adaptations: Generic and Thematic Mutations in Horror Film* (Manchester: Manchester University Press, 2007), pp. 111–26, p. 111.
6 Ovid, *Metamorphoses*, 7.198–200.
7 Shakespeare, *The Riverside Shakespeare*, 5.1.48–9.
8 R. Lyne, 'Ovid, Golding and The Tempest', in A. B. Taylor (ed.), *Shakespeare's Ovid: The Metamorphoses in the Plays and Poems* (Cambridge: Cambridge University Press, 2000), pp. 150–64, p. 159.
9 This name only came into use in the eighteenth century – Ovid's statue has no name – but I use it throughout for reasons of convenience.
10 In this chapter I draw on the discourse of psychoanalysis and the writings of Freud because they provide a suggestive image or emblem of some of the complex intertextual processes at work in a literary tradition, rather than because I think Freud's theories are necessarily 'true'. Compare Stephen Hinds's pragmatic embrace of the convenient fiction of intentional allusion.
11 Freud suggests that, because small children may believe their dolls could come to life, the motif of the living doll or statue carries an

additional uncanny charge because it takes us back to forgotten or repressed fancies. S. Freud, 'The Uncanny', in *The Standard Edition of the Complete Works of Sigmund Freud*, trans. J. Strachey (London: Hogarth Press, 1955), 24 vols, vol. 17, pp. 219–52, pp. 247–8.

12　*Ibid.*, pp. 237–8.
13　H. Cooper, *The English Romance in Time: Transforming Motifs from Geoffrey of Monmouth to the Death of Shakespeare* (Oxford: Oxford University Press, 2004), p. 3.
14　N. Abraham and M. Torok, 'A Poetics of Psychoanalysis: The 'Lost Object' – Me', trans. N. Rand, *SubStance*, 43 (1984), 3–18, p. 17.
15　Ovid, *Metamorphoses*, 10.291–4.
16　T. Hughes, *Tales from Ovid* (London: Faber & Faber, 1997), p. 146.
17　A further dimension is added if we consider the possible perceived parallels between Eurydice and Plath. These are discussed by G. A Jacobsen, '"A Holiday in a Rest Home": Ted Hughes as *vates* in Tales from Ovid', in R. Rees (ed.), *Ted Hughes and the Classics*, pp. 156–76, pp. 173–4 and by G. Liveley, 'Birthday Letters from Pontus: Ted Hughes and the white noise of classical elegy', in R. Rees (ed.) *Ted Hughes and the Classics*, pp. 216–32, pp. 220–1.
18　Ovid, *Metamorphoses*, 10.220–46.
19　Hughes, *Tales from Ovid*, p. 145.
20　Ovid, *Metamorphoses*, 10.83–5.
21　Cf S. A. Brown, *Ovid: Myth and Metamorphosis* (London: Bristol Classical Press, 2005), pp. 35–6.
22　This aspect of the poem's dynamic seems to have been overlooked. *Sir Orfeo* is not, for example, mentioned in G. Burger and S. F. Kruger, *Queering the Middle Ages* (Minneapolis: University of Minnesota Press, 2001) or in T. Pugh, *Queering Medieval Genres* (New York and Basingstoke: Palgrave Macmillan, 2004).
23　*Sir Orfeo*, ed. A. J. Bliss (Oxford: Oxford University Press, 1954), pp. 37–8, pp. 44–5.
24　*Ibid.*, p. 46.
25　*Ibid.*, p. 18.
26　*Ibid.*, p. 46.
27　*Ibid.*, p. 16.
28　*Ibid.*, p. 46.
29　*Ibid.*
30　Mark Dooley offers a useful analysis of the play's gender confusion in 'Inversion, Metamorphosis, and Sexual Difference: Female Same-Sex Desire in Ovid and Lyly', in G. V. Stanivukovic (ed.), *Ovid and the Renaissance Body* (Toronto: University of Toronto Press, 2001), pp. 59–76.
31　J. Lyly, *Gallathea and Midas*, ed. A. Begor Lancashire (London:

Edward Arnold, 1970), 5.3.145–7. Freud explicitly excluded the miracle of Pygmalion's statue from the category of the uncanny (Freud, 'The Uncanny', p. 246), yet the more we note the way in which her story represents a repetition, the more we may feel inclined to dispute his judgement.

32 For a discussion of the significance and origin of the statue's name see E. Joshua, *Pygmalion and Galatea: The History of a Narrative in English Literature* (Aldershot: Ashgate, 2001), pp. 34–5.
33 P. Berry, *Of Chastity and Power: Elizabethan Literature and the Unmarried Queen* (London: Routledge, 1995), p. 125.
34 L. H. Newcomb touches briefly on the potential masculinity of the statue in '"If That Which is Lost be not Found": Monumental Bodies Spectacular Bodies in *The Winter's Tale*' in Stanivukovic (ed.), *Ovid and the Renaissance Body*, pp. 239–59, p. 244.
35 For a discussion of Marston's treatment of the Pygmalion myth see L. Enterline, *The Rhetoric of the Body from Ovid to Shakespeare* (Cambridge: Cambridge University Press, 2000), pp. 125–51.
36 *The Poems of John Marston*, ed. A. Davenport (Liverpool: Liverpool University Press, 1961), p. 52.
37 J. Rainolds, *Th'overthrow of Stage-plays* (London, 1599), p. 34.
38 T. Middleton, *Collected Works*, eds G. Taylor and J. Lavagnino (Oxford: Clarendon Press, 2007), p. 1,982.
39 *Ibid.*, p. 1,983.
40 P. Sidney, *The Countess of Pembroke's Arcadia* (Oxford: Oxford University Press, 1985), p. 25.
41 Ovid, *Metamorphoses*, 3.418–19.
42 *Ibid.*, 3.422.
43 Sidney, *Arcadia*, p. 106.
44 W. Shakespeare, *The Riverside Shakespeare*, ed. H. Baker *et al.* (Boston and New York: Houghton Mifflin Company, 1987), p. 1,847. The possible echo of Pygmalion's feat is noted by, *inter alia*, Richard Halpern in *Shakespeare's Perfume: Sodomy and Sublimity in the Sonnets, Wilde, Freud and Lacan* (Philadelphia: University of Pennsylvania Press, 2002), p. 25.
45 J. I. M. Stewart, *Character and Motive in Shakespeare: Some Recent Appraisals Examined* (London: Longmans, 1949). See also J. Ellis, 'Rooted Affection: The Genesis of Jealousy in *The Winter's Tale*', *College English*, 25.7 (1964), 545–7; N. Johnson, 'Ganymedes and Kings: Staging Male Homosexual Desire in *The Winter's Tale*', *Shakespeare Studies* 26 (1998), 187–217.
46 Compare M. Taylor, *Shakespeare' Darker Purpose: A Question of Incest* (New York: AMS Press, 1982), p. 36.
47 1.2.66–71.

48 1.2.116–17.
49 3.2.82.
50 5.1.127-30.
51 'Drama, more than any other literary form, seems to be associated in all cultures with the retelling again and again of stories that bear a particular religious, social, or political significance for their public. There clearly seems to be something in the nature of dramatic presentation that makes it a particularly attractive repository for the storage and mechanism for the continued recirculation of cultural memory.' M. Carsson, *The Haunted Stage: The Theatre as Memory Machine*, (Ann Arbor: University of Michigan Press, 2001), p. 8.
52 Another important related intertext is Euripides' *Alcestis*, in which a wife cheats death to be reunited with her husband.
53 5.1.13–16.
54 5.1.16–20.
55 5.1.56–60.
56 3.3. 19–20, 25–7, 36–7.
57 Cf Freud, 'The Uncanny', pp. 230–3.
58 A typical, and effective, example of the uncannily autonomous hand can be found in W. F. Harvey's 1928 short story 'The Beast with Five Fingers'.
59 *The Poems of John Keats*, ed. M. Allott (London: Longman, 1970), p. 701.
60 For a suggestive account of the poem's uncanny qualities see B. Hopkins, 'Keats and the Uncanny: "This Living Hand"', *The Kenyon Review* 11.4 (1989), 28–40.
61 William of Malmesbury, *Gesta Regum Anglorum*, ed. and trans. R. A. B. Mynors (Oxford: Clarendon Press, 1998), 2 vols, vol. 1, pp. 381–5. A very useful survey of the wider tradition can be found in T. Ziolkowski, *Disenchanted Images: A Literary Iconography*, (Princeton: Princeton University Press, 1977). See also J. Andriano's *Our Ladies of Darkness: Feminine Daemonology in Male Gothic Fiction* (Pennsylvania: Pennsylvania State University Press, 1993); P. F. Baum, 'The Young Man Betrothed to a Statue', *PMLA*, 34.4 (1919), 523–7.
62 P. Mérimée, *Colomba, La Vénus d'Ille, Les Ames du Purgatoire* (Paris : Editions Garnier Frères, 1962), p. 187. A. Burgess and P. Mérimée, *The Eve of Saint Venus and The Venus of Ille*, trans. A. Brown (London: Hesperus Press, 2006), p. 93.
63 *Ibid.*, p. 211, *Ibid.*, p. 111.
64 *Ibid.*, p. 183, *Ibid.*, p. 90.
65 *Ibid.*, *Ibid.*
66 *Ibid.*, p. 191, *Ibid.*, p. 96.
67 *Ibid.*, p. 185, *Ibid.*, p. 91.

68 Ibid., p. 205, Ibid., p. 107.
69 Ibid., Ibid., p. 106.
70 Amy J. Ransom notes this link but offers a different interpretation: 'The psychic imago they represent are Alphonse's own parental images, the mother and father between whom he must choose to identify.' (*The Feminine as Fantastic in the Conte Fantastique: Visions of the Other* (New York: Peter Lang, 1995), p. 161).
71 A ball game of some kind is present in many earlier versions of the story but without Mérimée's emphasis.
72 A briefer early version of parts of this analysis is included in Brown, *Ovid: Myth and Metamorphosis*, pp. 131–6.
73 Henry James, *Daisy Miller and other stories* (London: Penguin, 1983), p. 21.
74 Michèle Mendelssohn discusses James's use of the Pygmalion myth within a homoerotic context in 'Homosociality and the Aesthetic in Henry James's *Roderick Hudson*', *Nineteenth-Century Literature*, 57.4 (2003), 512–41, p. 514. See also L. S. Person Jr, 'James's Homo-Aesthetics: Deploying Desire in the Tales of Writers and Artists', *The Henry James Review*, 14.2 (1993), 188–203.
75 James, *Daisy Miller*, p. 20.
76 Ibid., pp. 28–9.
77 In 'The Hermes in Henry James's "The Last of the Valerii"' Michael Clark suggests that the Hermes is associated with pagan sexuality in marriage. (*The Henry James Review*, 10.3 (1989), 210–13.)
78 James, *Daisy Miller*, p. 30.
79 Ibid., p. 31.
80 Ibid.
81 Ibid., p. 33.
82 Ibid., p. 26.
83 Ibid.
84 Ibid., p. 23.
85 Ibid., p. 42.
86 Ibid., p. 24.
87 Stoppard, Tom, *The Invention of Love*, (London: Faber & Faber, 1997), p. 89. I am grateful to Peter O'Neill for drawing this play to my attention.
88 A. Burgess and P. Mérimée, *The Eve of Saint Venus and The Venus of Ille*, trans. A. Brown (London: Hesperus Press, 2006), p .6.
89 Ibid., p. 9.
90 Ibid., p. 19.
91 Ibid., p. 22.
92 Ibid., p. 60.
93 Ibid., pp. 83–4.

94 *Orphée*, dir. J. Cocteau (1949).
95 For a discussion of the points of contact between them, see J. Jervis, 'Uncanny Presences', in J. Collins and J. Jervis (eds), *Uncanny Modernity: Cultural Theories, Modern Anxieties*, (Basingstoke: Palgrave Macmillan, 2008), pp. 10–50.
96 This story has been extensively discussed by critics. Useful readings which place it within the context of Freud's own analysis include H. Cixous, 'Fiction and its Phantoms: A Reading of Freud's Das Unheimliche', *New Literary History*, 7.3–4 (1976), 525–48; Royle, *The Uncanny*, pp. 39–50; J. M. Todd, 'The Veiled Woman in Freud's 'Das Unheimleiche'", *Signs*, 2.3 (1988), 519–28.
97 Although Delibes' comic ballet *Coppélia* omits most of the more troubling elements of Hoffmann's tale on which it is loosely based, it is perhaps significant within a queer context that Dr Coppélius aims to transfuse the spirit of a man, Franz, into his doll rather than the spirit of the heroine Swanilda.
98 E. T. A. Hoffmann, *The Best Tales of Hoffmann*, trans. J. T. Bealby (New York: Dover, 1967), p. 200.
99 *Ibid.*, pp. 213–14.
100 Ken Mogg, 'Some Notes on *Rear Window*', http://labyrinth.net.au/~muffin/rear_window_c.html, accessed 18 March 2011.
101 On the film's Ovidian influences, see P. James, 'She's All That: Ovid's ivory statue and the legacy of Pygmalion on film', *Classical Bulletin* 79.1 (2003), 63–91.
102 T. Price, *Hitchcock and Homosexuality* (New Jersey and London: Scarecrow Press, 1992), pp. 94–5.
103 *Ibid.*, pp. 92–3.
104 R. Samuels, *Hitchcock's Bi-Textuality: Lacan, Feminisms and Queer Theory* (New York: State University of New York Press, 1998), p. 86.
105 Compare E. Berman, 'Hitchcock's *Vertigo*: The collapse of a rescue phantasy', *The International Journal of Psychoanalysis*, 78 (1997), 975–96.
106 See p. 117.
107 N. Gaiman, *Fables & Reflections* (New York: Vertigo, 1994), p. 2.
108 *Ibid.*, p. 150.
109 A number of commentators have identified the link between Lot's wife and Orpheus, although the fact both stories have incestuous sequels seems not to have been noted. See for example J. O. Lowrie, *Sightings: Mirrors in Texts, Texts in Mirrors* (Amsterdam: Rodopi, 2007), p. 165; J. Williams, *Jean Cocteau* (Manchester: Manchester University Press, 2006), p. 170.

6

The ghost in *Hamlet*

In *Spectres of Marx*, Jacques Derrida quotes the famous opening of the *Communist Manifesto*: 'A spectre is haunting Europe, the spectre of Communism.' Derrida explores the intergenerational slippage at work between the production of Marx's text and its reception, demonstrating how communism, described by Marx as a ghost from some unknown future, has been transformed into a spectre from the past which may return to haunt us:

> At bottom, the specter is the future, it is always to come, it presents itself only as that which could come or come back; in the future, said the powers of old Europe in the last century, it must not incarnate itself, either publicly or in secret. In the future, we hear everywhere today, it must not re-incarnate itself; it must not be allowed to come back since it is past.[1]

A quite different spectre haunts Derrida's own text, that of *Hamlet*. Although ostensibly a political response to the fall of the Berlin Wall, and a critique of capitalism, *Spectres of Marx* seems endlessly preoccupied by *Hamlet*, by the nature of its ghost and by the play's slippery, even uncanny, representation of time and causality.

It is possible to find affinities between Shakespeare's most famous ghost, the shade of Hamlet's father, and Derrida's spectre of communism. The ghost in *Hamlet*, like the spectre of communism, shifts and mutates over the course of the play's afterlife, sometimes manifesting itself as a voice or warning from the future, sometimes as a trace of the play's most remote ancestors.[2] It can be interpreted as an emblem of Shakespeare's sources, the play's textual ancestors, as well as of Hamlet's father.[3] In later responses to Shakespeare, the pattern is repeated. But now it is Shakespeare's *Hamlet* (and his Hamlet) which has become the spectre from the past, haunting more modern incarnations of the story. Each generation of the Hamlet tradition is haunted by its past as sons are transformed into fathers and ghosts. Sometimes this teleology is uncannily reversed; certain moments on the Hamlet spectrum – by which I mean the entire set of texts comprised by the play itself, its sources, and later adaptations and responses – can appear to be haunted by ghostly voices from their future as well as from their past, rather as some of the ruins described in Chapter 4 seem to be premonitions of the future.[4]

In addition to creating that special *frisson* associated with any of the uncanny allusion markers this book identifies, the effect of intergenerational confusion created by the various ghosts who populate *Hamlet*'s many intertexts, in particular the emphasis on the uncertain and shifting nature of the boundary which separates fathers from sons, invites the reader to return with renewed interest to a much discussed aspect of the play, Hamlet's preoccupation with his mother's sexuality; a preoccupation which some readers interpret as incestuous.[5] Freudian interpretations of *Hamlet*, foregrounding sexual jealousy as a motive for Hamlet's hostility towards Claudius, are not especially fashionable. Yet if we read *Hamlet* in the light of some of its principal intertexts, the threat of mother/son incest emerges still more strongly, less from any one individual text than from the gaps and hidden connections between them. Strange secrets lurk in the spaces between these texts, spaces whose spectral shape can only be perceived if we examine the play within its transhistorical literary context rather than as the product of one historical moment. These interstitial spaces can be seen as further 'ghost' texts on the Hamlet spectrum, created through collusion between the texts' authors and their readers, as well as through collisions between different generations of *Hamlet*'s *Nach* – and *Vor* – *leben*. These spaces sometimes serve to forge a bond between Hamlet and his father. Sometimes, on the other hand, they suggest a tacit identification between Hamlet and Claudius. Although these scenarios seem mutually contradictory, both have the effect of intensifying any perceived sexual charge between Hamlet and his mother.

These confusions also have the potential to mirror and comment on the workings of the textual 'family tree'. *Hamlet*, just like Hamlet, has forebears. The play, unlike the prince, also has progeny. With textual family trees, as with human ones, it is more difficult to locate the beginning than the end of the line. Where does *Hamlet* (in the widest sense) begin? An obvious starting point would seem to be

Saxo Grammaticus's version of the story, which is recounted in his early thirteenth-century *Gesta Danorum*.[6] Saxo's resourceful Amleth is more Last Action Hero than melancholy philosopher and his story doesn't end in tragedy. Yet Saxo's narrative certainly includes most of the key elements of Shakespeare's play: the father murdered by the brother, the mother's swift remarriage, the son's feigned madness and his eventual revenge are all present, and the text is recognisably *Hamlet*'s 'ancestor'. One of the most notable absences in Saxo is the ghost. The murder is open knowledge and there is no need for Amleth's father to return from the dead to spur his son to vengeance. It seems likely that the ghost was introduced for the first time, not in *Hamlet* itself, but in the *Ur-Hamlet*, a successful play which was probably first produced in the 1580s, no copies of which have survived. It is not certain whether *Hamlet*'s clear debts to Saxo were incurred directly or were mediated via this missing play.[7]

Hamlet is one of those texts which is so well known it is difficult to read or view with fresh eyes. Rereading it in the light of Saxo's early version of the story is one way of defamiliarising the play and prompting new questions. For example, when we look at the play in isolation we don't wonder why Hamlet and his father have the same name. In the past sons were frequently named after their fathers. But in Saxo this is not the case – Amleth's father's name is Horwendil. So we can assume that someone, whether Shakespeare or an earlier intermediary, made a conscious decision to rename Hamlet's father (reversing usual practice) after his son. This doubling of Hamlets in Shakespeare's *Hamlet* might be related to the play's conspicuous fondness for hendiadys, a doubling trope which inheres literally of course in the texture of the language but which also permeates its structure through its many doubles, parallels and repetitions.[8] It might also function as a kind of allusion trigger, intensifying the possibility that the ghost, in later responses to the play, might in some way represent the prince rather than his father.

As we've already seen, the introduction of a ghost into the Hamlet story seems to date back no earlier than the *Ur-Hamlet*. But although Amleth's father does not return from the dead there is a kind of 'ghost' in Saxo. This is Amleth himself:

> Covered with filth, he entered the banquet-room where his own obsequies were being held, and struck all men utterly aghast, rumour having falsely noised abroad his death. At last terror melted into mirth, and

the guests jeered and taunted one another, that he whose last rites they were celebrating as though he were dead, should appear in the flesh.[9]

Within the Saxo narrative there is no special invitation to identify this 'ghost' Amleth with his genuinely dead father. However if we read (and now who doesn't?) Saxo through a *Hamlet* lens we might well be reminded of the similar appearance of old Hamlet as a 'real' ghost.

If Hamlet *père* is a sign of a different kind of ancestor, the Saxo source, signalling its haunting presence in Shakespeare's play, and if his name is now the same as his son's because he is an avatar of Amleth – then Saxo's own revenant, though living, Amleth may be identified as the marker pointing to still earlier texts which may have had a part to play in the shaping of *Hamlet*. Although there are no ghosts in Saxo, this text has 'parents' too, and their ghostly traces can be detected in the text. As I suggested in the introduction, a text such as *Hamlet* makes the reader work harder to find any possible source material for the play. When such potential sources are themselves equally pre-eminent, the reader, or later writer, is more likely to hunt for, or even create, suggestive links between them. Although the two possible intertexts which I discuss here, Aeschylus's *Agamemnon* and Homer's *The Odyssey*, cannot be established with certainty as direct sources for either Saxo or Shakespeare, for today's reader, plotting significant paths through the landmarks of literature, the temptation to consider them as possible sources for *Hamlet* proves irresistible. The alluding poet, Stephen Hinds reminds us, is frequently at least a partial fiction, 'ultimately and necessarily a figure whom we ourselves read out from the text'.[10] Just as Amleth, though no ghost, looks like a spectre, so these texts certainly look like sources, and this fact in itself is significant when looking at the creative afterlife of the play. We can gloss the virtual cord which attaches two texts to one another in terms either of 'reception' or 'influence', depending on whether we want to put the weight on the earlier or later writer. However, some of these cords may have been created by neither writer but seem instead to have been forged, or at least strengthened, retrospectively by later writers and readers. More recent translators, as we shall see, have reinforced the links between *Hamlet* and its classical predecessors.

If we read the earlier Saxo version of Hamlet's story in the light of these possible 'sources', Homer and Aeschylus, the points of contact, I would suggest, work to confuse the roles of father and son and thus invite us to detect an incestuous subtext in Saxo's narrative.

We would of course be unlikely to consider such a subtext if *Hamlet* itself did not seem to hint at incest. And in Shakespeare's play too the potential for an incestuous reading is increased if we read it in the light of its classical sources, or precursors. The significance of characters' names in the play, for example, is, as we shall see, one important example of how ghosts from *Hamlet*'s past can help reveal some of its secrets.

Beginning with Homer (and post-Homeric additions to the story), we can easily identify parallels between the characters and situations of Odysseus and Amleth. They both combine guile and intelligence with a readiness to act decisively and destructively when necessary. More specifically both feign madness for tactical reasons. Odysseus assumed an antic disposition to avoid having to participate in the Trojan War. He ploughed his soil with salt instead of seeds, but the ruse was revealed when Palamedes thrust Odysseus's infant son Telemachus in front of the plough. (Interestingly in some versions of the story Odysseus uses a forged letter to frame Palamedes and thus secure his execution, a ruthless revenge similar to that taken by Hamlet on Rosencrantz and Guildenstern, who also use underhand methods to try to uncover a hero's secrets.)[11] Amleth uses a similar stratagem, feigning idiocy to make people think he won't revenge the death of his father. Another parallel can be identified if we also look at post-Homeric accounts of Odysseus.[12] Both men are cast in a detective role when on a visit to a foreign court. Odysseus works out which of the women of Lycomedes's court is really Achilles in disguise and Amleth is able to reveal various secrets about the English court to its king on the basis of clues that he has identified. Although many characters in literature might be described as 'detectives' at some point, the incidents involving Amleth and Odysseus have similar qualities as set pieces; both involve the unveiling of potentially shameful secrets by a stranger in a formal and public setting. Both have a slight quality of bathos too. Achilles falls very easily for the trick Odysseus sets, taking no trouble to hide the fact he is attracted to armour rather than domestic objects. Similarly, it is not clear why Amleth's super-subtle intelligence is needed to notice something a little unusual about the behaviour which betrays the king's mother to be a bondmaid by birth: muffling her head with a mantle, gathering up her skirt as she walks, and picking her teeth with a splinter.[13]

These similarities between the two men encourage the reader to follow the characters' example and turn detective, decoding other points of contact between the Homeric tradition and Saxo's narrative. One intriguing parallel links an episode from the *Odyssey* with the earliest surviving trace of Amleth. In the prose *Edda* there is a mysterious reference to Amloði's mill. Nine maids are said to have ground Amloði's meal in a sea-churn. The same incongruous link between flour and the sea is made in the *Odyssey* by Tiresias, who, in Book 11, tells Odysseus that he must take an oar, travel inland until he finds a people who don't recognise what it is and mistake it for a winnowing fan, and there make a sacrifice to Poseidon.

But the most significant links between the two narratives can be found in their scenes of revenge. When he leaves Denmark for England, Amleth 'gave secret orders to his mother to hang the hall with a knotted tapestry, and to perform pretended obsequies for him a year thence'.[14] It is later explicitly stated that his mother wove the tapestry herself. The return of Odysseus is also strongly associated with weaving, because his wife Penelope promises to marry again once her weaving is completed, and undoes her work every night to ensure this never happens. In Book 17 of *The Odyssey*, Odysseus, like Amleth, returns like a ragged beggar so he won't be recognised:

> At no long interval, Odysseus came
> through his own doorway as a mendicant,
> humped like a bundle of rags over his stick.[15]

Hence the returning Amleth is 'ghostly' not just because he was believed to be dead but because the manner of his return signals an allusion to (or affinity with) Homer's epic hero. A link with Homer might explain why there is something oddly skewed about the depiction of Amleth's eventual revenge. The real object of Amleth's hatred should be the Claudius character, Feng, but more space is devoted to a mass murder of everyone else in the banqueting hall. The killing of Feng himself is delayed, and only briefly narrated. One result of Amleth's apparent revenge overkill is, once again, to suggest an affinity with the narrative of Odysseus. He too takes revenge on a large group of men, the suitors, not a single enemy. And both Odysseus and Amleth then cause fires to be lit, although in *The Odyssey* the fire is intended merely to purge, whereas Amleth completely destroys the building. This link between the two characters effects a father/son confusion, intertextually. The woman Amleth is returning to, and who has been complicit in a deception against the massacred men, is his mother. But Penelope, in many ways a similar figure, is Odysseus's wife. Placing the two texts together has the effect of placing a decoding grid on top of a ciphered message. An incestuous secret hidden between the parent text (Homer) and the child text (Saxo) is revealed.

The intergenerational confusion in Saxo becomes still more complex if we look at its relationship with *The Odyssey* from a rather different perspective. Odysseus, resourceful, eloquent and strategically deceitful, has much in common with Hamlet but he is not troubled by parental problems. However at the beginning of *The Odyssey* the situation of his son Telemachus is similar to that faced by Hamlet. Telemachus is concerned not by the death but by the absence of his father and by the consequent danger that his mother may prove unchaste. The riotous suitors resemble the tipsy Danes and both are equally distasteful to a fastidious young prince. Like Hamlet, Telemachus is visited by a supernatural guest. Athena exhorts him to show more gumption:

> You need not bear this insolence of theirs,
> You are a child no longer. Have you heard
> What glory young Orestes won
> When he cut down that two-faced man, Aigisthos,
> For killing his illustrious father?
> Dear friend, you are tall and well set up, I see;
> Be brave – you, too – and men in times to come
> Will speak of you respectfully.[16]

Thus Amleth combines elements of Homeric father and son, of the jealous husband and the protective child. Once again a *Hamlet* intertext is working to blur the demarcation line between the generations.

Athena's invocation of Orestes's example is significant. Many have noted affinities between Hamlet and Aeschylus' troubled hero.[17] Haunted by his murdered father and horrified by his mother's liaison with his treacherous uncle, he returns unexpectedly from exile in disguise to take revenge, supported by his loyal friend Pylades, and is later driven almost to madness by the Furies. Although his father's ghost does not appear on stage, he is invoked powerfully and at length at the beginning of *The Libation Bearers*. Even though his mother is much more decidedly at fault than Hamlet's, the two women's relationships with their sons are similarly intense. But if we add Amleth as well as Hamlet into the intertextual equation, a more complex picture emerges. Orestes, the son who is torn between the wish to avenge his father's murder and his duty to his mother, is clearly the character in the trilogy who most resembles Hamlet. Yet Amleth's revenge invokes, not Orestes' revenge, but the crime which spurred him on: the original murder of his father Agamemnon by Aegisthus and Clytemnestra. Amleth kills the feasting Danes with the same hanging his mother had made, echoing the use of a woven cloth, or net, in the murder of Agamemnon:

> I threw his robe around him,
> A net on a haul of fish, and he couldn't see,
> Or fight, or escape, and I stabbed him. Twice![18]

> Then, cutting away its supports, he brought down the hanging his mother had knitted, which covered the inner as well as the outer walls of the hall. This he flung upon the snorers, and then applying the crooked stakes, he knotted and bound them up in such insoluble intricacy that not one of the men beneath, however hard he might struggle, could contrive to rise.[19]

Thus Amleth parallels simultaneously both Orestes and his mortal enemy Aegisthus; the narrative's climax echoes both the murder of Agamemnon and his son's revenge for that same murder. Amleth is his mother's son but (intertextually) he may also be identified both with her lover (via Aeschylus) and her husband (via Homer). A double sexual contact is thus hinted at between mother and son.

It is by no means certain that Saxo had first hand knowledge of either the *Odyssey* or the *Oresteia*. However William F. Hansen offers a useful survey of analogues for the Hamlet story and suggests that many of its features may be traced back to remote Indo-European roots.[20] Thus Saxo's narrative may be a collateral, if not a direct, descendent of its Greek predecessors. More to the point perhaps, a great many readers of *Hamlet* have certainly been fully familiar with Homer and Aeschylus and may import or reimport them into the Hamlet tradition.[21] Thus a conscious or unconscious awareness of the effect of intergenerational confusion engendered by Saxo's Greek 'sources' may be a factor behind the odd intimations of mother/son incest in François de Belleforest's French version of the Amleth story, first published in 1570 as part of his *Histoires Tragiques*. During the 'closet scene', Belleforest describes how the Queen:

> having long time fixed her eyes upon Hamlet, as being ravished into some great and deepe contemplation, and as it were wholy amazed, at

the last imbracing him in her armes (with the like love that a vertuous mother may or can use to kisse and entertaine her owne childe), shee spake unto him in this manner.[22]

His insistence on the innocence of the mother's embrace seems superfluous, and thus raises doubts in the reader's mind as to whether the narrator is protesting too much. And more subtly, the process whereby two characters from a source or analogue, such as Odysseus and Telemachus, appear to merge into one in Saxo (with the effect of intensifying hints at incest) is repeated in Shakespeare's own subsequent use of Saxo. Amleth neglects his first wife to court Hermetrude, the queen of Scotland, whom he also marries. The name given by Shakespeare to Hamlet's mother thus represents an uneasy hybrid of Amleth's mother Geruth and his second wife.[23] Yet Shakespeare's choice of the name 'Gertrude' will only have an incestuous resonance for those possessing the other half of the puzzle; those familiar with Saxo.

Elsewhere I have argued that the relationship between Shakespeare and the classics is in part created by Shakespeare's successors.[24] They have the power to forge or strengthen links between Shakespeare and classical texts, even classical texts which he almost certainly never read. This process in a sense mirrors the 'generational confusion' I've identified in the *Hamlet* spectrum, where the roles of fathers and sons are blurred. Just as Hamlet the father is named after Hamlet the son in Shakespeare's play, so in two translations of Aeschylus, one Victorian, one written in the early twentieth century, *Agamemnon* becomes, if not a proven source, certainly part of *Hamlet*'s afterlife.

The watchman, in his speech at the beginning of *The Oresteia*, looks forward to Agamemnon's return with hope, yet seems almost to foretell the disasters which await the king when his words tail off in uncertainty and he appears to hint at secrets which remain undisclosed, implying an ironic awareness of the fact that he is a character in a play being watched by an audience who knows what is going to happen. The following translation of these lines, written by John Connington and published in 1848, is a close and unremarkable version – except for one detail which jumps out from the page:

> O may I then in this my hand support
> The dear hand of the mansion's lord, when come
> But soft – the rest is silence – a huge ox
> Has passed upon my lips; but the house itself,

Could it find tongue, would tell the tale I mean
Excellent well: – for me, to those who know
I'd speak – to those who don't – why – I've forgotten.[25]

The allusion to *Hamlet* is obtrusive, and invites the reader to probe the connection further. Here is the original context within which the prince's last words appear:

But I do prophesy th'election lights
On Fortinbras, he has my dying voice,
So tell him, with th'occurrents, more and less,
Which have solicited – the rest is silence.[26]

The watchman's portentous final words might recall Hamlet's own hints that he knows more than he can reveal:

Had I but time – as this fell sergeant, Death,
Is strict in his arrest – O, I could tell you –
But let it be. Horatio, I am dead,
Thou livest. Report me and my cause aright
To the unsatisfied.[27]

The quotation from *Hamlet* may also reinflect the significance of Aeschylus's watchman's assertion that 'the house itself, could it find tongue, would tell the tale I mean'. The house is (or may be) the theatre which could indeed tell tales, that of Hamlet as well as that of Agamemnon. A reference which may, or may not, be a metatheatrical reference to the theatre itself, could even cue a memory of these lines:

Remember thee!
Ay, thou poor ghost, whiles memory holds a seat
In this distracted globe. Remember thee!
Yea, from the table of my memory
I'll wipe away all trivial, fond records,
All saws of books, all forms, all pressures past.[28]

If this 'globe' *is* the theatre (it is also the world and Hamlet's head) then it is one which, like the 'house' in *Agamemnon*, seems to know things. Hamlet may want to erase his memories, including those of old books, but *Hamlet* seems to acquire, not merely influence on new texts, but new, or newly strengthened, sources as well, once writers such as Connington read and rewrite classical texts in the light of Shakespeare.

The quotation from *Hamlet* is surely an unambiguously intentional allusion on the part of Connington. Yet my own reflections on that quotation, the journey it took me on through *Hamlet*, were probably not, or not all, anticipated by the translator. To quote John Hollander, 'we must always wonder what our own contribution was – how much we are always being writers as well as readers of what we are seeing'.[29] Yet my own response, although subjective, is a symptom of the great power of *Hamlet* within any allusive network. It is so well known that any allusion to it in a new work, or in a translation of an older work, has a huge capacity to attract other relevant details from the play into the allusive equation. Even the tiniest detail, the most insignificant phrase, can start to register as an 'allusion' – thus when I read the words 'excellent well' in Connington, I remember Hamlet's: 'Excellent well, you are a fishmonger.'[30] The play, as well as Old Hamlet, compels us to remember it.

Herbert Weir Smyth's 1922 translation of *Agamemnon* also alludes to *Hamlet*. Anticipating the murder of Agamemnon, the Chorus says: 'Why ever thus persistently doth this terror hover at the portals of my prophetic soul?'[31] The phrase 'prophetic soul' is memorably used by Hamlet when he learns that his father, like Agamemnon, has been treacherously slain: 'O my prophetic soul',[32] he exclaims to the ghost, apparently because he had already suspected the truth. Smyth's echo is reinforced by the description of terror hovering at the soul's portals, personifying the emotion as a malignant presence. In Act 3 of *Hamlet* the prince sees his father's ghost when he is closeted with Gertrude and calls: 'Look where he goes, even now out at the portal.'[33] As well as flagging an affinity between the Greek and the English revenge plays, Smyth creates a moment of uncanny charge because the echo occurs at a moment of prophecy, and (through the phrase 'thus persistently') suggests a repeated cycle. Within the immediate context of *The Oresteia*, the Chorus, when it asks, 'Why doth my song, unbidden and unfed, chant strains of augury',[34] is foretelling the imminent death of Agamemnon. But for the reader of Smyth's translation, the Chorus's foresight reaches a full two thousand years into the future and their lines enact as well as describe the act of prophecy, foretelling the tragic repetition of the pattern established by Aeschylus in another tale of a wronged father and a vengeful son, turning *Hamlet* into a ghost of the future haunting its textual 'father'.

This characterisation of *Hamlet* as a kind of palimpsest within which we can glimpse ghosts of its source texts may be reinforced by a further examination of its names. Once again, the play's overfamiliarity encourages us to take these for granted. But it may be significant that Greek, Roman and Danish names are combined apparently at random, and particularly significant that one of those Greek names, Laertes, is also the name of Odysseus's father.[35] The character of Laertes is defined with reference to his roles as a brother and a son, and the final duel is poignant because both young men are motivated by the same drive to avenge their father. But if we remember the many affinities between Hamlet and Odysseus then the duel adds fuel to a Freudian reading of the play, and the two combatants can be seen as ghostly shades of the Homeric father and son. Once again, the play's intertexts force the play's incestuous subtext, its hints at a rivalrous, even murderous, relationship between the two Hamlets, into the open.

The use of names to signal the presence of *Hamlet*'s complex source material is also prominent in a very recent response to *Hamlet*, John Updike's *Gertrude and Claudius*.[36] This prequel takes us from the time of Gertrude's first marriage to the moment when Shakespeare's own play begins, and maps the story's chronology onto the chronology of *Hamlet*'s sources. Thus in the first section Updike uses the same names as Saxo for the characters, and in the second the slightly different names adopted by Belleforest in his 1570 retelling. Only in the final section do the characters assume their familiar Shakespearean handles. The precise significance of Updike's tripartite structure is elusive, but one effect is to blur the divide between a character's personal history and the more drawn-out history of a complex text. Updike does offer some slightly half-hearted rationalisations for the internal name changes, suggesting, for example, that Feng changed his name to Claudius to suit the dignity of his new role as monarch. But these don't quite convince, and it becomes easier to see the people in his novel less as fictional characters, more as metacharacters who inhabit, not a single textual world, but the whole Hamlet spectrum. Gertrude seems almost to acknowledge this when, in the final section, she senses the presence of her dead husband 'calling her name, out of an agony – *Gerutha*, as she had been in the deeps of time'.[37] Here, as so often in the Hamlet tradition, the return of one sort of dead, a ghost, is associated with the return of another kind of dead, a distant source.

At one point, speaking to the king, his brother, Claudius describes the inhibiting weight of fathers and older brothers in terms which invite a textual, perhaps a Bloomian or Borgesian, reading: 'The son's world differs from the father's if only by the dominating presence of the father in it.'[38] This statement makes itself felt in the move from Part 1 (Saxo) to Part 2 (Belleforest). We are no longer in the earliest (or earliest extant) version of *Hamlet*, but in a later version, and this difference is made apparent within the text. The gulf between Saxo and Belleforest is highlighted by the fact that an epistemic shift seems to have taken place in just a few lived years. Gerutha, with comically improbable fluency, tries to explain this newfangled Renaissance business to her confused husband: 'Instead of arguing from first principles, you deduce your principles from a host of observed particulars. I'm sorry; I'm not making a great deal of sense.'[39] The characters seem haunted by the fact their story has already been written; they are not simply older but belated. Horwendile (old Hamlet) suffers from 'uncanny spells of fatigue'[40] and he seems almost a living skeleton: 'His skull showed its mineral hardness, its marmoreal gloss.'[41] If old Hamlet is already dead, Claudius and Gertrude are already adulterous, at least in Claudius's dreams: 'In my dreams, you were wanton, and I wore a crown.'[42] This sense of belatedness, of living on borrowed (or repeated) time, is combined with a stronger atmosphere of metatheatricality as though, because the story has been told already, this current manifestation is no more than a performance. Horwendile complains of Hamlet: 'What does he think life is – a theatrical performance to be minced through by boys in women's clothes?'[43]

As a figure who moves along the Hamlet spectrum, shifting out of Saxo into Shakespeare via Belleforest, it is perhaps not surprising that the character of Gerutha or Gertrude is receptive to messages from the future as well as voices from the past. In Part 1 of the novel, Updike describes the dissatisfied queen becoming aware of the days slipping past her:

> spring days tasting of salty wave-froth and of hearth-smoke blown down from the chimney pots, misty days of sifted sunshine and gentle fitful rain that glistened and purred on the windowsill like a silvery cat, days of luxurious tall clouds that brought thunder east from Jutland, days when the shoreline of Skäne lay vivid as a purple hem upon the Sund's rippling breadth, days of high ribbed skies like an angel's carcass.[44]

The images of the elemental cat at the window and of the landscape laid out like a surreal corpse may cause footfalls to echo in the reader's memory. Gerutha seems to have accessed a ghost from *Hamlet*'s afterlife, Eliot's J. Alfred Prufrock, who famously asserts, 'No, I am not Prince Hamlet nor was meant to be':[45]

> Let us go then, you and I,
> When the evening is spread out against the sky
> Like a patient etherised upon a table . . .
>
> The yellow fog that rubs its back upon the window-panes,
> The yellow smoke that rubs its muzzle on the window-panes,
> Licked its tongue into the corners of the evening . . .
> Curled once about the house, and fell asleep.[46]

Gerutha shares Prufrock's sense of life passing meaninglessly by. We are told that 'the days passed, and Gerutha felt them stealing away with her life',[47] echoing Prufrock's reflections on the chilling banality of mortality: 'I have measured out my life in coffee spoons.'[48] She even shares Prufrock's vision of Death as a polite subordinate – 'And I have seen the eternal Footman hold my coat, and snicker'[49] – when she reflects on 'sick days when she floated in a fever and received a parade of soft-spoken visitors one of whom might be faceless Death'.[50] It is as though, in the metafictional world of Updike's 'perpetually revised old castle of Elsinore',[51] 'time future [is] contained in time past'.[52]

Voices from the future become still more insistent in Part 3, when Shakespeare's own names are finally used. Perhaps reflecting the fact that Shakespeare's *Hamlet* has absorbed all future Hamlets (as well as all past ones) into its own orbit, Part 3 draws on phrases and ideas which seem to postdate Shakespeare. There is anachronistic talk of 'market values' and 'final solutions',[53] and Claudius coolly articulates a post-Freudian explanation for Hamlet's erratic behaviour: 'He blames himself, I believe, for his father's death,' Claudius smoothly explained. 'He feels he willed it, in desiring you.'[54]

One of the more suggestive effects created by Updike's palimpsest of names is an especially pronounced slippage between father and son. Within the timeframe of Updike's story, Old Hamlet only acquires that name posthumously. Whereas the reader or watcher of Shakespeare's play is unlikely to be worried by the shared name, the reader of Updike shares the (hypothetical) problem of Shakespeare's original audience – both have become accustomed to Hamlet's father being called Horwendil. Thus Gertrude (almost as though she were aware that the time is suddenly out of joint again) feels the need to acknowledge this rather awkward change when she explains to Claudius: 'And I couldn't stop myself from thinking that now there was no chance of Hamlet's, my husband Hamlet's, finding out about us.'[55] As well as renewing – by first defamiliarising – the resonance of the shared name, Updike surprises the reader who is expecting a ghostly revenant. At the very beginning of Part 3 Claudius complains to Gertrude that Hamlet's visit has been too brief: 'His best friend was ignored, and the populace could take no impression of an apparition so fleeting. Hamlet plays the ghost, a presence spun of rumor, to spite me.'[56] Hamlet's textual belatedness is signalled by his becoming, not simply a living ghost, like Amleth, but a ghost fashioned out of words.

Director Kenneth Branagh, like Updike, also seems to have brooded on the fact that father and son share a name. His 1996 film version of the play opens with the words 'William Shakespeare's' on the screen, immediately followed by a shot of the dead king's grave, with the name Hamlet carved on the headstone. Although 'Hamlet' here clearly signifies the father it also serves as the film's opening title shot, and hence represents the son. The full significance of Hamlet's dead father, here played by Brian Blessed, emerges more clearly if we bring a further, comparatively remote, *Hamlet* intertext into the equation: Mozart's *Don Giovanni* (1787). Certain patterns or moments in *Don Giovanni* might be said to recollect *Hamlet*, with its murdered, haunting father figure echoing old Hamlet and, though more weakly, Polonius.[57] But the opera's 'hero' is not related to the Commendatore, and Don Giovanni is the latter's murderer not his revenger. Don Giovanni demonstrates his hubris by inviting the statue of the Commendatore to dinner, and meets his downfall when the animated statue accepts. Although the spectacle of an uncanny aged revenant appearing before a young man, warning him 'my time is short'[58] could faintly recall Hamlet's encounter with his father's ghost, the parallel might seem comparatively inert, chance and unproductive. Whether or not this is the case, the relationship between *Hamlet* and *Don Giovanni* is retrospectively intensified by Branagh's film.[59] The first appearance of the ghost is ambiguous. If one did not know the play one would think that the revenant was in fact a metallic statue of the king (visible in the film's opening sequence) come to life. A mechanical crunch on the soundtrack strengthens the impression, and the choice of eighteenth-century Blenheim Castle to represent Elsinore might act as a further little nudge, encouraging viewers to be more receptive to echoes of Mozart. The effect of this apparent allusion is to sow seeds of doubt about the relationship between father and son. We cannot possibly say that here is a Hamlet who murdered his father. But if we see the ghost as a reincarnation of the Commendatore then we may wonder whether Branagh's Hamlet didn't subconsciously welcome his father's death. Even though we see the ghost dissolve, establishing its status as a shade rather than a statue, the Mozartian echo may still resonate. Thus, immediately after Claudius' sinister promise to Laertes that Ophelia's 'grave shall have a living monument',[60] we are shown another external shot of Blenheim, already associated in the viewer's mind with the appearance of that other apparent 'living monument', the statuesque ghost.

The *Don Giovanni* echoes are just one facet of the permeability of Branagh's film. This Elsinore is lined with mirrored doors, one of which seems to be a portal into our own world (for we see Ophelia's face crushed against a surface which is simultaneously a mirror and the screen we are watching). If the play thus seems almost to escape its textual (or filmic) confines, so does its inset, quoted drama of Troy which we see enacted before our eyes by players (including Judi Dench and John Gielgud) who are just as real as Branagh. In much the same way as Updike's novel excavated the play's sources, laying bare its textual layers for all to see, this recent film alludes to the play's performance history, with ageing actors who once played *Hamlet*'s leads now relegated to playing memories and quotations, ghosts from the distant past.

There is almost a kind of humour in the way these iconic figures from the stage are relegated to playing silent non-characters, a humour similar to that deployed in an earlier celebrated response to *Hamlet,* Tom Stoppard's 1966 play *Rosencrantz and Guildenstern are Dead*. Here the main characters have been summoned to (re)play their roles by a mysterious and rather ghostly figure. Ros and Guil describe how they were woken up that morning by 'a messenger . . . pale sky before dawn'.[61] Guil then elaborates: 'An awakening, a man standing on his saddle to bang on the shutters, our names shouted in a certain dawn, a message, a summons.'[62] They have been summoned, or quoted, into existence. Some time later Guil returns to the same memory: 'A man standing in his saddle in the half-lit half-alive dawn banged on the shutters and called two names. He was just a hat and a cloak levitating in the grey plume of his own breath, but when he called we came.'[63] The plume denotes his ghostly breath but perhaps also a feather, and thus his identity as a writer who has (re)called them into existence from limbo which is neither dark nor light, day nor night.

The play both famously relegates Hamlet to the (comparative) margins and acknowledges *Hamlet*'s iconicity, and its own status as a repetition. Later when they give Ros and Guil a preview of *The Murder of Gonzago* the players act out scenes which are closely and explicitly modelled on *Hamlet*, showing not simply the events leading up to *The Mousetrap*, but also its aftermath, the 'closet scene' and even the deaths of Rosencrantz and Guildenstern themselves. Earlier I quoted Updike's Claudius claiming that 'the son's world differs from the father's if only by the dominating presence of the father in it'.[64] With textual genealogies this isn't usually precisely true, for most updates of canonical works are set in a universe in which the original source does not exist. But *Hamlet* cannot be kept out of Stoppard's play in this way. Baffled by the fact that his coin always comes up heads, Ros starts to reflect on the nature of probability:

> Guil (musing): The law of probability, it has been oddly asserted, is something to do with the proposition that if six monkeys (he has surprised himself.) . . . if six monkeys were . . .[65]

His momentary confusion conquered, he goes on to finish the thought:

> The law of averages, if I have got this right, means that if six monkeys were thrown up in the air for long enough they would land on their tails about as often as they would land on their – [66]

However it is the *wrong* conclusion, for this is of course an allusion to Arthur Eddington's infinite monkey theorem which states that a monkey typing at random would, given an infinite amount of time, eventually produce an accurate text of *Hamlet*. Whereas the audience is likely to know of this whimsical and striking illustration of probability theory, Ros should have no knowledge of this particular little instance of cultural trivia. The mild *frisson* of the uncanny – he seems, a bit like Aeschylus's watchman, to half know something he shouldn't have access to – is enhanced if we compare this reference to monkeys with one in the original play. We understand a monkey reference which a character himself does not understand. In *Hamlet* itself, by contrast, another monkey reference has proved ephemeral, and is understood by Hamlet but not by the (modern) audience.

> No, in despite of sense and secrecy,
> Unpeg the basket on the house's top.
> Let the birds fly, and, like the famous ape,
> To try conclusions in the basket creep,
> And break your own neck down.⁶⁷

The effect of this chiastic pairing of monkey references is perhaps to enhance our sense of Hamlet's strange aura of knowledge and awareness. We may know more than Ros and Guil, but Hamlet, in his turn, still knows something that eludes the modern, 'real' reader.

Stoppard's play depends heavily on its audience's knowledge of *Hamlet*, and sensitivity to its iconic cultural status. *Hamlet*'s iconicity is similarly foregrounded in Michael Almereyda's 2000 film of the play. One of the most significant effects of the film's pervasive and much discussed use of technology is to draw attention to its status as an act of representation, a repetition.⁶⁸ Although the emphasis on technological reproduction has generally been discussed as a sign of postmodern alienation, repetition also has both an uncanny and an allusive charge in the film.⁶⁹ The fact that hundreds of Hamlets intervene between 1600 and 2000 is repeatedly articulated within its self-reflexive layers.⁷⁰ Once again textual and personal pasts collide. Both Hamlet and his father are repeatedly seen on film within the film, bringing their past and present together. When the 'ghost' appears, his initial fuzzy form – a fuzziness whose resonances are more suggestive of a technological glitch than of the supernatural – is swiftly brought into sharp focus to make him seem just as real as Hamlet, an effect which is compounded by their conspicuous physical interactions. Both Hamlets, we are reminded, are simultaneously real – in that they are actors – and illusions – because they are digitised.

The film dramatises the many Hamlet layers which intervene between 1600 and 2000 in various ways. At one point the prince is disturbed by Polonius as he watches a recording of himself on a video camera. In the play, but not in the film, Polonius at this point asks Hamlet what he is reading and is told it is a book about foolish old men. If we map play onto film we can say that Hamlet is, as it were, reading *Hamlet* – and the actor Ethan Hawke in Almereyda's film is indeed watching himself read part of the authentic *Hamlet* script. 'Sources' and 'ghosts' are brought tellingly close in the film as both are frequently presented as recordings to be accessed on a screen. A similar effect of belatedness is created when 'To be, or not to be' is shown on a video tape which is being watched by the 'later' Hamlet; later both within the fiction of the film and within the Hamlet tradition. The iconic quality of this most famous speech is emphasised by the continual replays of the opening words – those six words that everyone knows here stand in place of the whole speech – as though even within the fictional world of the film it is pointless to pretend that the speech is new or fresh.[71]

A little later Almereyda creates a similarly paradoxical and self-reflexive effect by implying that Hamlet's plan for *The Mousetrap* was derived from *Hamlet*. At the moment when he muses 'I have heard / That guilty creatures sitting at a play',[72] we see on an inset screen behind him footage of John Gielgud playing Hamlet, clutching a skull. Hamlet's line can thus be seen as a little allusion trigger, becoming self-referential through repetition. As we watch or read *Hamlet* now, that play which even to first-time readers seems 'full of quotations', Hamlet's 'I have heard / That guilty creatures sitting at a play' becomes inevitably reflexive. Perhaps it did to *Hamlet*'s first audiences too, if the *Mousetrap* scene was an echo from the *Ur-Hamlet*. For in drawing attention to its own status as a repetition, the film is in fact building on characteristics already present in Shakespeare's play itself. *Hamlet* produces such astonishing textual energy that it seems to be the origin (in effect if not in reality) of its sources as much as of its derivations. But although we have to make an active effort to remember that *Hamlet* has ancestors, Hamlet himself, like Ethan Hawke, seems strangely aware of his textual forebears. Both Hamlet and his Ethan Hawke avatar live in a world where *Hamlet* already exists.

It is tempting to speculate further about possible allusions to the *Ur-Hamlet*, that missing link on the *Hamlet* spectrum. Might the *Ur-Hamlet* explain why Hamlet's verses to Ophelia, so (comparatively) clichéd and banal, seem so unworthy of their author?

> Doubt thou the stars are fire,
> Doubt that the sun doth move,
> Doubt truth to be a liar,
> But never doubt I love.[73]

In other words, could this trace of Hamlet's mysterious past as the 'expectation and rose of the fair state',[74] a trace which we glimpse in this earlier correspondence with Ophelia when it is 'quoted' on the stage, also be a trace of his textual past as a forgettable revenge hero in a second-rate play?[75] I've already suggested that we forget to ask questions about *Hamlet* because everything in the play seems like a given, not to mention a quotation. But perhaps the introduction of Yorick (or rather his skull) in Act 5 can be seen as another variant on the uncanny allusion marker.[76] The physical, like the spectral, remains of a character might figure the bones of Hamlet's sources showing through the play's flesh. Although such speculation is perhaps creative (or fanciful) rather than critical, it is intriguing to hypothecate an *Ur-Hamlet* which included a jester called Yorick, whose jokes would be remembered by the audience as well as by the prince himself. The whole episode would make more sense if he had been a living character in the *Ur-Hamlet*. In seeing the skull Hamlet would confront simultaneously both his personal and his textual past.

Even without speculating on *Hamlet*'s relationship with its probable immediate source, we can identify a self-consciously textual quality in Shakespeare's prince, a trait which paradoxically makes him appear more 'real'. Hamlet at times seems haunted by a sense of his own fictionality. In this he resembles other belated avatars of a long-established literary tradition such as Medea. Wilamowitz-Moellendorff observes that Seneca's Medea seems to have read Euripides's *Medea*, and we might equally say that Shakespeare's play-going prince seems to have watched the *Ur-Hamlet*.[77] Hamlet at times seems on the verge of puncturing the membrane between the stage world and reality, most obtrusively when he links personal with literary memory by apparently alluding to the Globe Theatre (although the world and his head are the more immediately obvious referents):

> Remember thee!
> Ay, thou poor ghost, whiles memory holds a seat
> In this distracted globe.[78]

His outburst when Gertrude suggests he has mourned his father too long reveals a similarly literary self-consciousness:

> 'Tis not alone my inky cloak, [good] mother,
> Nor customary suits of solemn black,
> Nor windy suspiration of forc'd breath,

> No, nor the fruitful river in the eye,
> Nor the dejected havior of the visage,
> Together with all the forms, moods, [shapes] of grief,
> That can [denote] me truly. These indeed seem,
> For they are actions that a man might play,
> But I have that within which passes show,
> These, but the trappings and the suits of woe.[79]

Hamlet seems to be differentiating himself from earlier, less convincing Hamlets, almost convincing us, in defiance of logic, that he is neither a textual 'inky' artefact nor an actor playing a part.

His frustrations, his feelings of being overlooked, of being 'th'observed of all observers',[80] almost implicate the audience as well as Elsinore's courtiers and, like the protagonist of *The Truman Show*,[81] we sense him grasping towards consciousness of his own constructedness. Ophelia tells him that he is 'as good as a chorus'[82] and he does indeed seem to share the choric quality of liminality, of being in transit between stage and audience, a quality most hauntingly apparent in his dying words:

> You that look pale, and tremble at this chance,
> That are but mutes or audience to this act,
> Had I but time – as this fell sergeant Death
> Is strict in his arrest – oh I could tell you –
> But let it be.[83]

Here Hamlet – rather like Othello in his speech beginning 'Soft you; a word or two before you go'[84] – appears to address the 'real' as well as the inset audience. The uncanny boundary between this world and the next thus figures the more familiar boundary between stage and audience. Whereas most dramatic characters know less than their audiences, Hamlet actually gives the impression of knowing more, of being privy to secrets which must remain tantalisingly hidden not just from Horatio but from us as well. His apparent transformation at the end of the play, his passive acceptance of his fate, might be attributed to a knowledge that Act 5 has been reached as much as to any special change of heart. In his melodramatic assertion, 'This is I, Hamlet the Dane'[85], we hear an echo of Medea's similar articulation of a role fulfilled: 'Medea nunc sum.' If the Senecan Medea is catching up with her Euripidean ancestor, so is Hamlet at last filling Amleth's shoes, living up both to his father and to his source, laying two ghosts in the process.

Notes

1. J. Derrida, *Specters of Marx*, trans. Peggy Kamuf (New York and London: Routledge, 1994), p. 39. Much has been written about Derrida's essay. See for example R. Halpern, 'An Impure History of Ghosts: Derrida, Marx, Shakespeare', in J. E. Howards and S. C. Shershow (eds), *Marxist Shakespeares* (Routledge: London and New York, 2001), pp. 31–52; C. Prendergast, 'Derrida's Hamlet', *SubStance*, 34.1 (2005), 44–7.
2. For an excellent discussion of Hamlet's haunting iconicity see Carlson, *The Haunted Stage*, pp. 78–81. Emma Smith offers a particularly suggestive account of the play's haunted intertextuality in 'Ghost Writing: Hamlet and the Ur-Hamlet', in A. Murphy (ed.) *The Renaissance Text: Theory, Editing, Textuality* (Manchester: Manchester University Press, 2000), pp. 177–96.
3. See for example Garber: 'Whatever else it is, the *Hamlet* Ghost is an animation of the earlier theatrical genre known as revenge tragedy, come to summon protagonist and play to a genre already beginning to fade' (M. Garber, *Shakespeare's Ghost Writers* (New York and London: Methuen, 1987), p. 172) and Scofield: 'the Ghost in *Hamlet* as an image [in Valéry] for the phantoms of tradition seems significant'. (M. Scofield, *The Ghosts of Hamlet: The Play and Modern Writers* (Cambridge: Cambridge University Press, 1980), p. 33.
4. 'Hamlet remains proleptically in tune with the latest present'. (M. de Grazia, *Hamlet without Hamlet* (Cambridge: Cambridge University Press, 2007), p. 22.
5. The classic study of the topic is E. Jones, *Hamlet and Oedipus* (London: Gollancz, 1949).
6. A useful recent discussion of the sources of *Hamlet* can be found in M. W. Hunt, *Looking for Hamlet* (New York and Basingstoke: Palgrave Macmillan, 2007), pp. 13–30.
7. François de Belleforest's 1570 *Histoires Tragiques*, which included a version of the story, is another probable source.
8. For a full account of the trope's importance in the play see G. T. Wright, 'Hendiadys and Hamlet', *Proceedings of the Modern Language Association*, 96:2 (1981), 168–93.
9. G. Bullough (ed.), *Narrative and Dramatic Sources of Shakespeare* (London: Routledge and Kegan Paul, 1973), vol. 7, p. 69.
10. Hinds, *Allusion and Intertext*, p. 144.
11. See, for example, Hyginus' *Fabulae*, ed. P. K. Marshall (Stuttgart: Teubner, 1993), pp. 95–6.
12. See for example Philostratus, *Imagines*, trans. A. Fairbanks (London: William Heinemann, 1960), pp. 287–91.
13. Bullough, *Narrative and Dramatic Sources*, vol. 7, pp. 68–9.

14 *Ibid.*, p. 66.
15 Homer, *The Odyssey*, trans. Robert Fitzgerald (London: Heinmann, 1962), p. 289.
16 *Ibid.*, p. 10.
17 See for example G. Murray, *Hamlet and Orestes: A Study in Traditional Types* (London: H. Milford, 1914).
18 Aeschylus, *The Oresteia*, trans. David R. Slavitt (Philadelphia: University of Pennsylvania Press, 1998) ll.1156–8.
19 Bullough, *Narrative and Dramatic Sources*, vol. 7, p. 70.
20 William F. Hansen, *Saxo Grammaticus and the Life of Hamlet* (Lincoln and London: University of Nebraska Press, 1983), pp. 36–7.
21 I have given a fuller account elsewhere of the way Shakespeare's classical sources become intensified in importance over the course of the plays' reception. S. A. Brown, 'There is no End but Addition: The Later Reception of Shakespeare's Classicism' in C. Martindale and A. B. Taylor (eds) *Shakespeare and the Classics* (Cambridge: Cambridge University Press, 2004), pp. 277–93.
22 Bullough, *Narrative and Dramatic Sources*, p. 98.
23 The echo of Hermetrude in Gertrude's name is discussed by Alexander Welsh in *Hamlet in his Modern Guises* (Princeton: Princeton University Press, 2001), p. 23.
24 See note 21.
25 Aeschylus, *Agamemnon*, trans. J. Connington (Oxford: Clarendon Press, 1907), p. 2.
26 W. Shakespeare, *The Riverside Shakespeare*, 5.2.355–8.
27 5.2.336–40.
28 1.5.95–100.
29 Hollander, *The Figure of Echo*, p. 99.
30 2.2.174.
31 Aeschylus, *Works*, trans. H. W. Smyth 2 vols, vol. 2 (London: William Heinemann, 1963), p. 83.
32 1.5.41.
33 3.4.127.
34 Aeschylus, *Works*, vol. 2, p. 83.
35 Laertes' name is discussed by William Jones in 'Shakespeare's Sources for the Name "Laertes"', *The Shakespeare Newsletter* 10 (1960), 9.
36 For discussions of this novel see S. Greenblatt, 'With Dirge in Marriage', *The New Republic*, 222.8 (2000), 32–9; L. E. Savu, 'In Desire's Grip: Gender, Politics, and Intertextual Games in Updike's *Gertrude and Claudius*', *Papers on Language and Literature*, 39.1 (2003), 2–48.
37 John Updike, *Gertrude and Claudius* (London: Hamish Hamilton, 2000), p. 194.
38 *Ibid.*, p. 140.

39 *Ibid.*, p. 80.
40 *Ibid.*, p. 81.
41 *Ibid.*
42 *Ibid.*, p. 88.
43 *Ibid.*, p. 81.
44 *Ibid.*, pp. 45–6.
45 T. S. Eliot, *Collected Poems 1909-62* (London: Faber & Faber, 1963), p. 7.
46 *Ibid.*, p. 3.
47 Updike, *Gertrude and Claudius*, pp. 46–7.
48 Eliot, *Collected Poems*, p. 4.
49 *Ibid.*, p. 6.
50 Updike, *Gertrude and Claudius*, p. 46.
51 *Ibid.*
52 'Burnt Norton' (Eliot, *Collected Poems*, p. 177).
53 Updike, *Gertrude and Claudius*, *Ibid.* p. 164, p. 176.
54 *Ibid.*, p. 199.
55 *Ibid.*, p. 165.
56 *Ibid.*, p. 164.
57 Mozart clearly gave some thought to the depiction of the ghost in Hamlet. In 1780 he wrote in a letter to his father: 'if the speech of the ghost in *Hamlet* were not so long, it would be far more effective' (E. Bloom (ed.) *Mozart's Letters: Selected from the letters of Mozart and his family* (London: Penguin, 1968), 2 vols, vol. 2, p. 150).
58 W. A. Mozart and L. da Ponte, *Don Giovanni* (Philips, 1990), p. 280.
59 Scott Rosenberg offers a useful discussion of the potential parallels between Branagh's film and Mozart's opera in his review for Salon, 'Something's Misbegotten in the State of Denmark', http://www.salon.com/jan97/hamlet970120.html, accessed 2 March 2011. See also L. Hopkins, *Screening the Gothic* (Texas: University of Texas Press, 2005), p. 11. The potential similarity between *Don Giovanni* and *Hamlet* is also strengthened, as Marjorie Garber notes, in Peter Shaffer's *Amadeus* where the figure of the Commendatore becomes fused with Mozart's father (Garber, *Shakespeare's Ghost Writers*, pp. 140–3).
60 5.1.297.
61 Tom Stoppard, *Rosencrantz and Guildenstern are Dead* (London: Faber & Faber, 1967), p. 9.
62 *Ibid.*, p. 10.
63 *Ibid.*, p. 30.
64 Updike, *Gertrude and Claudius*, p. 140.
65 Stoppard, *Rosencrantz and Guildenstern are Dead*, pp. 2–3.
66 *Ibid.*, p. 3.
67 3.4.192–6.
68 One of the most suggestive readings of the film is W. B. Worthen's 'Fond

Records: Remembering Theatre in the Digital Age' in Peter Holland (ed.) *Shakespeare, Memory and Performance* (Cambridge: Cambridge University Press, 2006), pp. 55–72.
69 See for example A. Abbate, 'To be or inter-be': Almereyda's end-of-millennium *Hamlet*', *Literature/Film Quarterly* 32.2 (2004), 82–9; C. Jess, 'The Promethean Apparatus: Michael Almereyda's Hamlet as Cinematic Allegory', *Literature/Film* 32:2 (2004), 90–6. Jess is more conscious of the film's allusions to past versions, but her discussion is confined to the tradition of cinema.
70 Judith Buchanan discusses the multiple Hamlets of Almereyda in *Shakespeare on Film* (London: Longman, 2005), p. 239. See Terence Hawkes's essay 'Telmah' for an analysis of the recursive qualities of the original play. (*That Shakespeherian Rag: Essays on a Critical Process* (Methuen: London and New York, 1986), pp. 92–119.)
71 For a discussion of Stéphane Mallarmé's suggestive description of Hamlet as himself already a ghost see Garber, *Shakespeare's Ghost Writers*, p. 151.
72 2.2.588–9.
73 2.2.16–19.
74 3.1.152.
75 For an attempted scene by scene reconstruction of the *Ur-Hamlet* see H. D. Gray, 'Reconstruction of a Lost Play', *Philological Quarterly,* 7.3 (1928), 254–74.
76 For a suggestive discussion of Yorick's skull on film see Pascale Aebischer, *Shakespeare's Violated Bodies: Stage and Screen Performance* (Cambridge: Cambridge University Press, 2004), pp. 93–101.
77 U. von Wilamowitz-Moellendorff, *Griechische Tragödien* (Berlin, 1919), vol. 3, p.162.
78 1.5.95–7.
79 1.2.77–86.
80 3.1.154.
81 *The Truman Show*, dir. Peter Weir (1998).
82 3.2.245.
83 5.2.334–8.
84 5.2.338.
85 5.1.257–8.

7

A familiar compound ghost: *katabasis* and *The Tempest*

In this final chapter I discuss two separate uncanny strands within Western literature, both sites of haunting repetition. The first has its roots in classical literature, in the journeys to the underworld, or *katabases*, performed by daring heroes. This trope is then repeated and transformed by post-classical poets, including T. S. Eliot in *The Four Quartets*, whose own variation on the theme of *katabasis* provides the starting point for this chapter, as well as my book's title. The second is the ghostly afterlife of *The Tempest*, which seems not simply derived from, but haunted by, Shakespeare's play, its own earlier sources and other intertexts. Although initially distinct, these two traditions will, like Eliot's narrator and the compound ghost, meet one another at the end of the chapter, and speak with one voice. Central to both strands is a process that the Italian classicist Gian Biagio Conte calls 'refraction'. This is when source and derived text coexist on the page creating a moment of startlingly obtrusive allusivity: 'Thus the new poetic word becomes for a moment a sign of something outside itself, the word of a poet who has not been assimilated. Then two different voices are heard within the poem as if they were engaged in dialogue.'[1] And indeed, as we shall see, one way in which this effect of 'refraction' can be achieved is by representing two or more co-present texts as separate characters within the fictional world of the later text.

Eliot's encounter with the 'familiar compound ghost' in 'Little Gidding' displays many of the hallmarks of the uncanny. Like the ghostly figure who summons Rosencrantz and Guildenstern to take their places for Stoppard's play he inhabits a liminal space. He is encountered at the end of a night which is interminable, between three districts, thus dwelling in the interstices of time and space, simultaneously loitering and hurrying.

> I caught the sudden look of some dead master
> Whom I had known, forgotten, half recalled
> Both one and many; in the brown baked features
> The eyes of a familiar compound ghost
> Both intimate and unidentifiable.
> So I assumed a double part, and cried
> And heard another's voice cry: 'What! are you here?'
> Although we were not.²

He is both known and not known, canny and uncanny. Like the mysterious doubles discussed in the first two chapters, the ghost seems to have a special bond with the narrator. The epithet 'compound' suggests that he is made up of several different elements, and one of these elements would seem to be the narrator himself, whose voice is oddly echoed, or doubled, as he speaks. After he has 'assumed a double part' it is significant that the narrator hears *another's* voice cry 'What! are *you* here?' as though he and the ghost were speaking in unison.

Recognition is a powerful allusion marker and here the narrator's familiarity with the ghost is matched by our own possible sense that we have read something like this before. The most obvious source, and one that was explicitly signaled in an earlier draft of the poem, is the meeting between Dante and the shade of his sinful mentor Brunetto Latini in Canto 15 of the *Inferno*.³

> Eyed in this way by this company
> I was recognised by one of them, who seized me
> By the edge of my cloak, and cried: 'How marvellous!'
>
> And, when he had stretched out his arm to me,
> I fixed my eyes upon his scorched appearance
> So that his burnt face should not prevent
>
> The recognition of him by my intellect;
> And, bending my face towards his,
> I answered him: 'Are you here, ser Brunetto?'⁴

So when Eliot's narrator addresses the ghost and hears another voice speak instead of (or in unison with) his own, the voice could be identified with that of Dante. But if Dante is to be heard in the poem it is not only as an additional voice addressing the compound ghost but as itself part of that compound. For Dante – in the *Inferno*, only a visitor to the underworld – has with the passing of time become himself a ghost. Eliot's own narrator borrows Dante's words but the shade whom he recognises is no longer Dante's teacher but (at least in part) Dante himself. The half recognition in the *Inferno* of a transformed former friend is refigured as the reader's recognition of a half-concealed source. The compound ghost has traditionally been seen as an amalgamation of several poets, including Yeats and Mallarmé.[5] But 'compound' has connotations of 'increase' as well as 'combination' and it is this transhistorical, refractive and cumulative aspect of the ghost on which I want to focus, on the possibility that this spectral palimpsest has absorbed a succession of formerly distinct and living interlocutors, and will in time absorb others.

The origins of the compound ghost can be traced back much further than the *Inferno*; Dante's poem is a comparatively recent example of the ancient epic motif of *katabasis*.[6] Such journeys have a clear potential to act as uncanny allusion markers. A hero visits the dead and recognises former comrades, unearthing buried memories, and the new text (and its readers) perform similar acts of memory and excavation, for each recurrence of *katabasis* invites comparisons with its predecessors. Many of the most charged connections between *katabases*, the most active invitations to make comparisons with earlier occurrences of the trope, are associated with encounters with troubled former comrades, such as the meeting between Dante and Latini. The *locus classicus* for the whole tradition is Homer's account of Odysseus's descent to the underworld. The first ghost Odysseus meets is the shade of Elpenor, his foolish former companion who had fallen to an accidental death from a rooftop after binge-drinking at Circe's house:

> Now when I saw him there I wept for pity
> and called out to him:
> How is this, Elpênor,
> how could you journey to the western gloom
> swifter afoot than I in a black lugger?[7]

Elpenor is anxious to receive a proper burial:

> do not abandon me unwept, unburied,
> to tempt the gods' wrath, while you sail for home;
> but fire my corpse, and all the gear I had,
> and build a cairn for me above the breakers.[8]

When Virgil sent his own hero down into the underworld he seems to have had his predecessor's example in mind as there are several parallels between the experiences of Odysseus and Aeneas.⁹ Both hear prophecies of the future. Both have similarly frustrating meetings with shades who refuse to acknowledge them; Odysseus with Ajax (whom he beat in a contest for Achilles's armour) and Aeneas, more famously, with Dido. Both heroes adduce the will of the gods as an excuse for the actions which caused the indignant shades' displeasure. But the most interesting point of contact between the Greek and Roman *katabases* comes when Aeneas learns that he will meet an unburied comrade. Aeneas had been forewarned of this encounter by the Sybil, though not of the man's identity, while still in the upper world, and he mulls over the prophecy with his friend Achates:

> Multa inter sese vario sermone serebant,
> quem socium exanimem vates, quod corpus humandum
> diceret.¹⁰
>
> (Much varied discourse were they weaving, each with each – of what dead comrade spoke the soothsayer, of what body for burial?)

The mingled voices could also be seen as the voices of these two tangled texts as Homer and Virgil converge. *Vates* can mean 'poet' as well as 'soothsayer', and if Aeneas has the Sybil's words in mind, the reader may have Homer's. Virgil seems to be inviting his readers to remember Homer's Elpenor, that other dead comrade who awaited burial, in order to ensure that any ghost Aeneas encounters will be, in some sense, a compound one.

In fact two such shades are encountered. The first is Palinurus, the helmsman who fell to his death from the stern of his boat while sleeping. The parallels between the fate of Palinurus and the death of Elpenor confirm the idea that text and source are being woven together. The second ghost is one of Priam's sons, Deiphobus, who had briefly been married to Helen following the death of Paris, and whose body Aeneas had sought for in vain. Aeneas now learns that he was savagely murdered by Menelaus, with the help of Helen herself. His unburied status echoes that of Elpenor, and is also a suggestive emblem for a poetic predecessor who cannot quite be laid to rest.

> Atque hic Priamiden laniatum corpore toto
> Deiphobum videt et lacerum crudeliter ora,
> ora manusque ambas, populataque tempora raptis
> auribus, et truncas inhonesto volnere nares.

Vix adeo agnovit pavitantem et dira tegentem
supplicia, et notis compellat vocibus ultro.[11]

(And here he sees Deiphobus, son of Priam, his whole frame mangled and his face cruelly torn – his face and either hand – his ears wrenched from despoiled temples, and his nostrils lopped by a shameful wound. Scarce, indeed, did he know the quivering form that tried to hide its awful punishment; then, with familiar accents, unhailed, he accosts him.)

Familiarity and strangeness are jumbled together here as they are in 'Little Gidding'. Aeneas does recognise Deiphobus, yet only with difficulty as his face is horribly mutilated. He addresses him in familiar accents, which are familiar to Deiphobus (because Aeneas was his kinsman) but also familiar to the reader who remembers *The Odyssey*. Deiphobus's disfigurement delays the moment of recognition, in the same way that even a well-known source is harder to spot the more it is transformed. (It also invites a more uneasy reading of the relationship between the two poets.) The possibility that the double significance of the word *notis*, 'familiar', may register as a deliberate rather than a chance effect is strengthened if we examine closely what the unfortunate Deiphobus has to say. He gives an embittered account of his murder, particularly focusing on Helen's treachery:

egregia interea coniunx arma omnia tectis
emovet, et fidum capiti subduxerat ensem;
intra tecta vocat Menelaum et limina pandit,
scilicet id magnum sperans fore munus amanti,
et famam exstingui veterum sic posse malorum.
quid moror?[12]

(Meanwhile, this peerless wife takes every weapon from the house – even from under my head she had withdrawn my trusty sword; into the house she calls Menelaus and flings wide the door, hoping, I doubt not, that her lover would find this a great boon, and so the fame of old misdeeds might be blotted out. Why prolong the story?)

His account seems calculated to echo the parallel episode in *The Odyssey*'s *katabasis* where Agamemnon tells of his own murder at the hands of his wife. Two additional factors make this parallel particularly pungent: the identity of Menelaus's comrade, Odysseus himself (Deiphobus's antagonist but the hero of the earlier *katabasis* of course) and Deiphobus's own final impassioned wish: 'di, talia

Grais / instaurate, pio si poenas ore reposco' ('O gods, with like penalties repay the Greeks, if with pious lips I pray for vengeance!').[13] Deiphobus's wish is both prophetic (given the fate of Agamemnon) and allusive.

All three earlier *katabases*, those of Homer, Virgil and Dante, can be said to lie behind the encounter in 'Little Gidding', making the ghost truly compound, 'both one and many'; his fractured, composite form connotes not just one source but a complex and shifting intertextual continuum, the sum of several previous moments of charged recognition. Indeed, existing as it does in the interstices of space and time, it becomes an emblem less for any specific poet or text than for intertextuality itself. The ghost hovers between the literature of past and future like those shades who, as Aeneas's dead father Anchises explains, hover between one incarnation and the next as they await rebirth:

> animae, quibus altera fato
> corpora debentur, Lethaei ad fluminis undam
> securos latices et longa oblivia potant.[14]
>
> (Spirits there are, to whom second bodies are owed by fate, and at the waters of Lethe's stream they drink the soothing draught and long forgetfulness.)

The double voice we hear in 'Little Gidding' may take us back to Dante but may also take us forward to the future when some new poet will, in his turn, accost Eliot, astonished to discover him in an unexpected place. Eliot's compound ghost is thus potentially an allusion trigger as well as an allusion marker and sure enough, at the end of this chapter, we will find Eliot himself in hell.

As I noted earlier, the most recent incarnations of the compound ghost are also part of another allusive spectrum where the ghosts of successive texts rise up to haunt latecomers. We have seen how a whole sequence of individual *katabases* have become entangled together in a cumulative weave in which the wider intertextual relations are somehow referenced or even instantiated as an additional layer or character in each new occurrence of the tradition. A similar 'compound' effect can be identified in the afterlife of *The Tempest*,[15] an afterlife in which T. S. Eliot will once again have an important part to play and which will eventually cross paths with the onward journey of the 'compound ghost' from 'Little Gidding'. The *Tempest* tradition is full of its own 'compound ghosts', occasions when a character or moment becomes unexpectedly doubled or multiplied, translating the play's own intertextual workings – and each derived text's status as a repetition or reanimation – into some, tangible, concrete fictive form through allusive refraction, that process described by Conte. Thus adaptations of *The Tempest* (and other slighter allusions to the play) themselves go on to become part of what the play means to us, forming a kind of compound ghost text composed of many layered memories. Some of the memories contained in these responses to *The Tempest* predate the play itself. Partially submerged classical sources which have to be excavated with some care from Shakespeare's original play are displayed on the page for all to see in several later works which adapt or allude to *The Tempest*. Like the responses to *Hamlet* I examined in the previous chapter, these texts demonstrate how the relationship between Shakespeare and his classical predecessors is one which continues to evolve and strengthen, even now.

And there is another link with *Hamlet*. The play's capacity to generate a series of haunted responses is in part explained by the fact that the play already seems, in a sense, to be haunted by itself, just as Hamlet, even before Almereyda, seemed to have read his own play. Echoes and memories, internal stutters of repetition, inhere in *The Tempest*'s verbal texture. This echo chamber effect is created partly through use of simple repetitions – in the very first scene we find 'Bestir, bestir', 'Lay her a-hold, a-hold' and 'we split, we split'[16] – and through rather more complex and subtle patterns, offering a kind of sampler of repetitive rhetorical devices such as anadiplosis, the repetition of the final words of a line at the beginning of the next: 'I have done nothing, but in care of thee / Of thee my dear one'[17] and chiasmus: 'All lost! To prayers, to prayers! All lost!'[18] At the level of narrative we see a different kind of repetition, in the double attempt made by Antonio and Sebastian to assassinate Alonso and Gonzalo. It is as though two versions of the play were being heard nearly, but not quite, simultaneously. In his analysis of the play's internal echoes Russ McDonald suggests that 'the tendency of words and phrases to repeat themselves may be linked to the play's profound concern with reproduction, in various senses from the biological to the political.'[19] These are all legitimate points, but I would argue that, at least for the play's imitators, *textual* reproduction is the key correlative of these verbal echoes, and it is an effect which is compounded by the introduction of still more obtrusive repetitions.

Dryden and Davenant's *The Enchanted Island* (1670) is an

important early vector for the *Tempest* tradition. This version (like Nahum Tate's 1681 rewrite of *King Lear*) held the stage for many years and is thought to have mediated several later creative responses to *The Tempest*, including *Robinson Crusoe*.[20] One striking feature of the play is the way so many characters from *The Tempest* have been given a mate or double. These new pairings, like the various encounters between the living and the dead in *katabases*, might be seen as visible signs of the co-presence of source and adaptation, signaling the play's status as an adaptation, a repetition: Ferdinand acquires a rival, Ariel a mate, and both Miranda and Caliban are given sisters. Even the play's collaborative authorship is a kind of doubling. But more clearly uncanny and allusive are the parallels drawn between the play's source material and ghosts haunting the text. The link is acknowledged most explicitly in the epilogue:

> The ghosts of poets walk within this place,
> And haunt us Actors whereso'er we pass,
> In visions bloodier than King Richard's was.[21]

As we shall see, the textual ancestors of *The Enchanted Island*, like the ghostly ancestors of Richard, are imagined hovering over the performance, even appearing as participants in the play.

Dryden and Davenant's awareness of ghostly literary precursors – most obviously *The Tempest* itself – is not limited to the epilogue, but bleeds into the fiction of the play itself. In *The Tempest* characters are aware of mysterious invisible presences, spirits such as Ariel we assume, who inhabit the island. In its Restoration incarnation the island seems haunted rather than simply enchanted, rather as Pygmalion seemed haunted by an unovidian ghost in Hughes's *Tales from Ovid*. Dryden and Davenant's Antonio anticipates his creators' own reference to haunting in their epilogue when he says:

> This Isle's inchanted ground, for I have heard
> Swift voices flying by my Ear, and groans
> Of lamenting Ghosts.[22]

Links can be drawn between the textual ghosts of the epilogue and the more literal ghosts of the play. Alonzo (sic) notes a creepy detail quite absent from Shakespeare's island: 'I pull'd a Tree, and Blood pursued my hands.'[23] This recalls an episode from the *Aeneid* – Polydorus's metamorphosis into a bleeding tree – later imitated by both Dante and Spenser:[24]

> accessi, viridemque ab humo convellere silvam
> conatus, ramis tegerem ut frondentibus aras,
> horrendum et dictum video mirabile monstrum.
> nam quae prima solo ruptis radicibus arbos
> vellitur, huic altro liquuntur sanguine guttae
> et terram tabo maculant.[25]

> (I drew near; and essaying to tear up the green growth from the soil, that I might deck the altar with leafy boughs, I see an awful portent, wondrous to tell. For from the first tree, which is torn from the ground with broken roots, drops of black blood trickle and stain the earth with gore.)

Although the central story of *The Tempest*, unusually for Shakespeare, has no clearly identifiable source, the *Aeneid* has long been acknowledged as a key influence on the play.[26] Thus the uncanny bleeding plant which Dryden and Davenant import into *The Tempest* is like a visible sign of the play's source material, one of those 'ghosts of poets' which haunt the stage. In adding a further Virgilian element to an already Virgilian play, the *Aeneid*'s bond with *The Tempest* has been not merely acknowledged but strengthened, and a new point of contact between the two works has been created. Although the fact the bough bleeds implies a link with Polydorus, we should perhaps also remember another important bough from the *Aeneid*; the golden bough which Aeneas must tear off the tree in order to enter the underworld.[27] In *The Enchanted Island*, tearing the bough effects a metaphorical *katabasis*, a return to a source from the remote past.

But Shakespeare himself is the most important ghostly presence in *The Enchanted Island*.[28] The first marvel, the bleeding tree, spawns another ghostly detail. Antonio exclaims that:

> The shadows of the Trees are poisonous too:
> A *secret venom* slides from every branch.[29] (my italics)

The innovation of the bleeding and venomous tree gains a fresh significance if we look back to the prologue. Here the authors associate their adaptation of the earlier play with the positive processes of pruning and regrowth:

> As when a Tree's cut down *the secret root*
> Lives underground, and thence new Branches shoot
> So, from old Shakespeare's honour'd dust, this day
> Springs up and buds a new reviving play. (my italics)

But lurking beneath this rather buoyant account of their relationship with Shakespeare, and joined to it by the word 'secret', reflexively acting as a 'secret root' between the trees in prologue and play, is that bleeding bough. The far more uneasy resonances of mutilation and poison which attend the adaptors' references to trees in the play itself suggest a more anxious, even guilty, sense of their relationship with Shakespeare. If Shakespeare is a tree, he is a resentful, if not malevolent, presence in *The Enchanted Island*, damaged rather than nurtured, and none too pleased at being hacked about. For the accounts of ghosts in *The Enchanted Island* enact as well as describe haunting, exemplifying a parallel drawn by Marjorie Garber: 'A quotation is a ghost: a revenant taken out of context, making an unexpected, often disconcerting experience – the return of the expressed.'[30] Influence troped as necromancy haunts *The Enchanted Island*.

The image used to express the relationship between adapting Shakespeare and pruning a tree, quoted above, is not entirely coherent. The (positive) metaphor of the reshooting root is contaminated by other possibilities. One is that of Shakespeare as revenant, springing up from the grave. The other is that of Shakespeare as a decaying corpse like that Eliot describes in *The Waste Land*:

> That corpse you planted last year in your garden,
> Has it begun to sprout? Will it bloom this year?[31]

This uneasy interplay between the explicit reference to Shakespeare in the prologue and the implicit invocation of him in the play may invite us to look again at the epilogue.

> The Ghosts of Poets walk within this place,
> And haunt us Actors whereso'er we pass,
> In visions bloodier than King Richard's was.[32]

The uncanny violence of this picture suggests some discomfort with their own imitative project on the writers' part. In particular the fact that they think of the ghosts that appeared to Richard III betrays a guilty conscience and figures them as haunted usurpers rather than godlike reanimators. For the ghosts in Shakespeare's *Richard III* appear simultaneously to both Richard and Richmond (later Henry VII, and presented in the play as England's rightful king). It is therefore perhaps telling that the epilogue only mentions Richard, the deformed villain of the piece. It is with the vanquished usurper Richard rather than with the virtuous and conquering Richmond that these two playwrights would seem to identify. Audiences have often felt that one of *The Tempest*'s characters has a counterpart in real life; Prospero the magician has traditionally been associated with his creator.[33] But in *The Enchanted Island* there are several more such links. Two usurpers, aware that they have wronged Prospero, are haunted by the island's ghosts. And two literary 'usurpers', Dryden and Davenant, are haunted by the shade of Shakespeare. Dryden and Davenant, rather like Spenser in his response to Horace 3.30, discussed in Chapter 4, are simultaneously reanimating and ousting the original *Tempest*, and casting themselves as Antonio and Sebastian in the process.

Other writers swell the ranks of *The Enchanted Island*'s visibly compound authorship. As well as Virgil, Dryden and Davenant, we can identify Fletcher and Jonson on stage. In the Prologue Dryden and Davenant describe these playwrights' debts to the play.

> Shakespear, who (taught by none) did first impart
> To Fletcher wit, to labouring Johnson Art . . .
> The storm which vanish'd on the neighbouring shore,
> Was taught by Shakespear's Tempest first to roar.
> That innocence and beauty which did smile
> In Fletcher, grew on this Enchanted Isle.

The allusion in the preface to Fletcher's qualities 'growing' on the 'enchanted isle' encourages us to conceptualise the play as a geographical space rather than simply as a text. Earlier Shakespeare himself becomes a physical location for it is claimed that:

> Fletcher reach'd that which on his [Shakespeare's] heights did grow,
> Whilst Johnson crept and gather'd all below.

This division may encourage us to visualise Fletcher as a kind of Ariel, and 'labouring Johnson' as Caliban. The parallels are telling, for Jonson responded to *The Tempest* in a rather surly and grudging way, attacking all Shakespeare's late plays as 'tales, tempests and such like drolleries'[34] in the Induction to *Bartholomew Fair*, whereas Fletcher collaborated with Shakespeare on several plays.

Thus Dryden and Davenant created a stage haunted by other poets: earlier imitators of Shakespeare, Shakespeare himself, even one of his influences, Virgil. In other responses to *The Tempest*, fictional characters from the play's intertexts, rather than those texts' real creators, clutter the page. A comparatively early and striking example of this pattern can be found in Keats's *Endymion* (1818), although the debt to *The Tempest* is localised in just one episode in Book 3. Endymion encounters an old man, dressed in a blue cloak which is 'o'erwrought with symbols by the deepest groans / Of ambitious magic'.[35] He bears a 'pearly wand' and a book lies in his lap.[36] This magician with his staff and book might most obviously recall Prospero, but turns out to be the Ovidian Glaucus.[37] As with *Hamlet*, the process of adapting or reinventing the play has the effect of dredging up its more submerged sources. In Ovid, Glaucus is the subject of a mysterious 'sea change' when he eats a herb which transforms him into a merman. Although there is no strong affinity between Prospero and Ovid's original Glaucus, the phase of the *Metamorphoses* in which the latter appears lent much to *The Tempest*'s atmosphere.[38] Having further fused the Ovidian Glaucus and Prospero together, Keats draws attention to their kinship within a literary line of descent when he makes his Glaucus describe how once, Prospero-like, he beheld a vessel in trouble:

> On a day
> Sitting upon a rock above the spray,
> I saw grow up from the horizon's brink
> A gallant vessel . . .
> . . . therefore all the billows green
> Tossed up the silver spume against the clouds.
> The tempest came. I saw that vessel's shrouds
> In perilous bustle, while upon the deck
> Stood trembling creatures. I beheld the wreck;
> The final gulfing; the poor struggling souls.[39]

From the wreck emerged one survivor, another old man, who clutches the same scroll and wand now in Glaucus's care, but is lost in the sea before he can be rescued. Glaucus's account of the moment he read the scroll is suggestive in its repetition, and in the way it seems to hint at a link between scroll and poem:

> I read *these words*, and *read again*, and tried
> My eyes against the heavens, and *read again*.[40] (my italics)

In fact 'these words' turn out to refer to an inset quotation from the scroll rather than to *Endymion* itself – yet as the subject of these lines seems to be Glaucus himself, and the scroll a strange prophecy, the effect of circularity is compounded:

> In the wide sea there lives a forlorn wretch,
> *Doomed with enfeebled carcase to outstretch.*[41]

But the 'forlorn wretch' cannot perhaps simply be identified as Glaucus; he is rather a kind of eternal sea mage figure, something like the compound ghost, in whom Prospero and Glaucus are merged, together with nameless others.[42] It is significant that Glaucus's encounter with his doomed double is a moment of pressure and anxiety. He, like Keats himself, seems to be 'wrestling with the dead':[43]

> I knelt with pain – reached out my hand – had grasped
> These treasures – touched the knuckles – they unclasped –
> I caught a finger. But the downward weight
> O'erpowered me – it sank.[44]

The note of desperation in Keats's description of the attempted rescue half suggests that the speaker was himself in peril of drowning and was 'o'erpowered' before sinking. The confusion between subject and object resembles that between ghost and narrator in 'Little Gidding' as well as between many of the paired and antagonistic doubles discussed in the opening chapters. And in a sense the drowning man was only another version of Glaucus himself. The scroll imposes a burden on him:

> He must pursue this task of joy and grief
> Most piously: all lovers tempest-tossed,
> And in the savage overwhelming lost,
> He shall deposit side by side.[45]

Thus numberless lovers are now in his care, held in suspended animation:

> Turn to some level plain where haughty Mars
> Has legioned all his battle . . .
> . . . Imagine further, line by line,
> These warrior thousands on the field supine –
> So in that crystal place, in silent rows,
> Poor lovers lay at rest from joys and woes.[46]

These lovers can be woken only by the tearing of the scroll, the Prospero-like shattering of the wand, the breaking of the continuous loop in which Glaucus is trapped. The presence of a literary line of lovers, culminating in Endymion himself, mirrors the poem's accumulation of textual traces, providing the play's sources and influences with a concrete correlative within the fiction of the poem, a striking example of allusive refraction.

A contemporary writer, the inventive and prolific Russell Hoban who is perhaps best known as the author of the post-apocalyptic novel *Riddley Walker* (1980), also uses the idea of a hall of mirrors to figure textual repetition in his 1992 libretto *Some Episodes in the History of Miranda and Caliban*. Hoban's text opens, briefly, with its *dramatis personae*:

> Miranda and all other female characters: mezzo soprano
> Caliban and all other male characters: baritone.[47]

Although we might assume 'all other characters' could be glossed 'all other characters from *The Tempest*', Hoban actually goes rather further than this. Caliban and Miranda are not simply archetypes, they are *über*-archetypes containing within themselves the seeds of all possible characters. Caliban subsumes Prospero and Ferdinand certainly, but he also figures (among others) Icarus and Adam. The inclusion of references to the Icarus myth in Hoban's libretto, another narrative of imprisonment on a mazy island, is an example of the way in which a classical text, whose logical relationship to *The Tempest* should be that of source, in fact emerges more significantly as part of the play's creative afterlife.

The importance of unearthing *The Tempest*'s buried sources informs a key conceit in Hoban's libretto. He presents Shakespeare's play as a moment on a spectrum, one of several competing possibilities, rather than a complete, inevitable and self-contained creation. Here the play's central characters are shown to have a life which pre-existed *The Tempest*; in a prologue Hoban explains:

> The way I see it Shakespeare didn't invent Caliban; Caliban invented Shakespeare (and Sigmund Freud and one or two others). Caliban is one of the hungry ideas, he's always looking for someone to word him into being so he can have another go and maybe win Miranda this time or next time.[48]

This view of the play is upheld when Miranda and Caliban are shown in a surreal limbo which both pre- and post-dates *The Tempest*, and where they apparently existed before they acquired any textual reality. The libretto opens with Caliban and Miranda 'crossing a vast and meaningless desolation'[49] looking for the sea. Water, already an agent of metamorphosis in *The Tempest*, is here the medium in which literary archetypes are reborn: 'The submerged father is changed into something rich and strange so that the daughter can re-encounter him as Caliban-Icarus'.[50] They are like the souls of future generations waiting to be reborn in Book VI of the *Aeneid*. Indeed Hoban's depiction of the way texts, characters and motifs are endlessly recycled through different incarnations is itself recycled from the vision of Rome's future the Sibyl grants Aeneas in the underworld. She shows Aeneas how the spirits of the dead lose their memories in the river Lethe before being reborn, rather as Miranda explains to Caliban how one day they will emerge from literary limbo:

> animae, quibus altera fato
> corpora debentur, Lethaei ad fluminis undam
> securos lattices et longa oblivia potant.[51]

> (Spirits they are, to whom second bodies are owed by Fate, and at the water of Lethe's stream they drink the soothing draught and long forgetfulness.)

> Out of now will come the future, our unknowing will be lost and never found again and we shall forget.[52]

So, once again, a writer responding to *The Tempest* seems driven to trace the play back to its classical sources, and to present an adaptation which is not a single text, but a complex compound of *The Tempest*'s sources and derived texts. Hoban may not of course have had the *Aeneid* in mind when he wrote his libretto – but perhaps Virgil's limbo is just another one of those 'hungry ideas', waiting to be (re)worded into being, to which Hoban refers in the prologue.

Later in the libretto, appropriately considering the vision she has evoked of her own limitless potential for reinterpretation and reinvention along a textual continuum, Miranda 'becomes a mirror maze':

> There's no time for reflection; imagine my distress,
> Trapped in multiplicity and infinite regress.[53]

We are encouraged to visualise multiple Mirandas in a *mise en abyme* which figures the now long-established tradition of *Tempest* imitations and, in particular, echoes the way *The Tempest* seemed to be playing on a continuous loop in *Endymion*. Hoban reminds us that his libretto follows in the footsteps not just of *The Tempest* itself but of its many imitators, and indeed of its many 'sources', whether real or retroactive. Gian Biagio Conte's idea of allusive 'refraction', yet again, finds physical, literal expression within the fictional world of Hoban's fantasy. His mirror maze, the strange continuum described by Keats, and Dryden and Davenant's *pièce à clef*, are all, like the encounter with the compound ghost in 'Little Gidding', sites where multiple texts meet and merge.

Hoban's use of the phrase 'rich and strange' in his vision of the characters' endless cycle of reincarnations into other stories suggests how easily Ariel's famous 'Full Fathom Five' can become a sign of a text's, as well as a body's, rebirth:[54]

> Full fadom five thy father lies,
> Of his bones are coral made:
> Those are pearls that were his eyes:
> Nothing of him that doth fade,
> But doth suffer a sea-change
> Into something rich and strange.
> Sea-nymphs hourly ring his knell
> *Burthen* [*within*] Ding-dong.
> Hark, now I hear them: ding dong bell.[55]

The corpse which Ariel invokes is uncannily elusive. It is perhaps surprising that Ariel's song is so memorable and resonant given that Ferdinand's father Alonso has neither died nor been metamorphosed. Its power can be located in its fugitive, dream-like quality, in part created by its confusing play with tenses, the way it contrives almost to suspend time.

Other factors further complicate what could be, on the surface, a clear cut description of the transition from one substance to another. The line 'Of his bones are coral made' prepares us, in the next line, to expect the original substance – in this case 'eyes' – to be first named. But the order is inverted. 'Pearls' occupies the same position in the line as 'bones' had previously, and 'eyes' is withheld until the end of the line. The potential for some confusion in the reader's mind is compounded by the very first word of this same line, 'Those'. 'Those' suggests distance, probably of place but possibly of time, as in the phrase 'those days'. In other words we expect 'those' to qualify the pre-metamorphic rather than the post-metamorphic substance. Had Shakespeare written 'these' we would have been able to orient ourselves in the line, internalise which substance has replaced which, a little more securely. The temporal limbo in which Ariel's song seems suspended, the confusion over the precise nature of the metamorphosis described, reflects larger confusions in the play as a whole. Ferdinand thinks Alonso is dead but will soon be amazed to find him alive, apparently reanimated, a movement from death to life just hinted at in the counterintuitive word order of Ariel's song, ostensibly about a movement from life to death.

This quality of the song, its mysterious metamorphic power, intensifies its aptness for reinvention as an uncanny allusion marker, anticipating its own metamorphosis in future *Tempest* texts. When we read 'Full Fathom Five' we might speculate whether a literary corpus as well as a literal corpse is being metamorphosed. The answer is yes, but not yet. Because it is not itself a quotation or adaptation of some still earlier work, within *The Tempest* itself the built-in reflexivity of Ariel's song is still potential, a trap waiting to be sprung by future texts. Ariel's song of metamorphosis is still only an allusion trigger, but will become a fully functioning allusion marker in later responses to the play when it is transformed into a comment on the transformation of *The Tempest* itself. For as a memorable moment in one of Shakespeare's best-known plays, any later recontextualisation or reinvention of 'Full Fathom Five', by metamorphosing one of literature's most famous accounts of metamorphosis, has the power to render it unmistakably and precisely reflexive.

Eliot is conspicuously susceptible to the reflexive potential of 'Full Fathom Five'.[56] 'Those are pearls that were his eyes' is quoted twice in *The Waste Land*, and the song may be read as an emblem of Eliot's collagist poetic procedures. Ariel describes the metamorphosis of a corpse into a strangely beautiful if confusing artifact and Eliot uses scraps and fragments from other poets' works to create his own works of art:

(Those are pearls that were his eyes. Look!)[57]

I remember
Those are pearls that were his eyes.[58]

Memory is one of the most effective and common allusion markers. Usually it acts as an invitation to the reader to import an earlier text into a later adaptation. (We saw in an earlier chapter how the strange atavistic 'memories' of a character in Ballard's *The Drowned World* could cue for the reader textual memories of Conrad.) But in *The Waste Land* it operates intra- as well as intertextually and encourages the reader to remember not simply an earlier text, *The Tempest*, but the derived text, itself in other words, as well. Eliot's cue to memory is forceful (and memorable), functioning, rather like Hamlet's father's ghost's 'Remember me', as an imperative rather than just a statement. His tacit injunction to remember *The Waste Land* if we remember *The Tempest* proved successful. In later literature, as we shall see, *The Waste Land* and *The Tempest* are associated together, each acting as a Pavlovian stimulus for the other. Each has become part of the other.

The double reference to eyes turning into pearls is an obtrusive repetition which reflects the poem's reliance on acts of repetition or quotation. Another significant instance of duplication comes when Eliot adjusts a line of Ferdinand's:

> On a winter evening round behind the gashouse
> Musing upon the king my brother's wreck
> And on the king my father's death before him.[59]

This proliferation of mourned relatives reflects the way the play itself has proliferated, having been alluded to and adapted so many times, three times already in *The Waste Land* alone. But has Eliot really altered *The Tempest* so much by giving Ferdinand a mysterious dead brother? In thus doubling the moment when Ferdinand is described weeping for his dead father, revisioning the prince as a Glaucus-like character doomed to repeat himself, the poem draws attention to an odd little fault line in *The Tempest* itself, a subtle anticipation of the many doublings and compounds we have already identified in the play's reception. For a similarly superfluous corpse makes a brief appearance in *The Tempest*, although its presence can probably be ascribed to careless editing. Ferdinand tells Prospero and Miranda of the shipwreck, which he thinks has killed everyone but himself. He says: 'Yes, faith, and all his lords, the Duke of Milan / and his brave son being twain.'[60] The reference to the Duke of Milan's son is unexplained – Antonio has no son in the play – it is probably just a slip of the pen, but this strange moment might suggest other versions of the play lying behind the one we have, rather like those visions of infinite regress conjured up by Keats and Hoban. The play's self-proliferation anticipates Eliot's own adjustments – and is more visible because of them. Ferdinand also explains that he has been 'sitting on a bank, / Weeping again the King my father's wrack'.[61] For those who now may read *The Tempest* only after they have read *The Waste Land*, there is an uncanny aptness in Ferdinand's use of the word 'again' in the original play. It is an example of the way in which reading a tradition within literature 'backwards' may shift our focus. This tiny detail, 'again', only lights up with any significance when seen through the lens of Eliot. For readers who know Eliot, the word functions as a kind of prophetic allusion marker.

Ferdinand's reference to weeping 'again' and his unexplained allusion to Antonio's absent son, as well as other repetitive gestures – Ferdinand's assertion that Prospero has given him a second life for example – are all individually plausible yet become cumulatively disquieting, implying that the characters are caught in a loop, continually re-enacting the same tale, but with variations, anticipating the play's complex afterlife. The only one that cannot be explained away is the reference to Antonio's son. In most other plays such a glitch would seem just that – of no greater significance than a wristwatch in the film *Gladiator*. But in *The Tempest*, particularly given the nature of the play's afterlife, the atmosphere invests such a mistake with more resonance, as though the island's fabric of reality were actually being disrupted.

By repeating and intensifying the odd repetitions and continuity errors in Shakespeare's play, Eliot encouraged later writers and readers to experience or create an imaginative fusion of *The Waste Land* with *The Tempest*. In Barry Unsworth's *Sacred Hunger* (1992), a novel about the impact of the slave trade in the eighteenth century and a failed attempt to establish a multiracial paradise, the free association of ideas in a character's mind neatly reflects similar associations in the mind of both author and reader. But within a historical novel, the thought processes which are natural and explicable for the modern reader represent an uncanny prolepsis, a prophetic moment parallel to one in another modern novel discussed in the previous chapter, Updike's *Gertrude and Claudius*. Unsworth, like Updike, fuses a Shakespeare play with an Eliotic allusion to that play. Towards the beginning of *Sacred Hunger* we learn how the coming of spring has a powerful impact upon the novel's hero, Erasmus, who is acting in a production of *The Tempest*. The season is heralded by:

> The deepening colours of the hawthorn blossom on the slopes above the lake, the appearance of soft spikes of flower on the chestnut trees in the grounds. Amidst this slow flushing of the season experiences took on an importance for Erasmus that somehow belonged rather to their associations than to themselves and made odd fusions in his mind. Already there, the virulent speck that would curdle his memories,

already working among the impressions of the time, a man sniffing at timber, another the sport of rats in an alley, a haunting song of deep seas and dead fathers that came to him while he waited for his cue.[62]

This is rather an uncanny anticipation of memory – his shipbuilder father will shortly die – than a memory itself. Just as Erasmus's personal memories are anticipated, so are larger literary memories, although logically both should be equally inaccessible to the eighteenth-century hero. Unsworth simultaneously omits and alludes to a silent third text, *The Waste Land*, between his own novel and *The Tempest*.[63] It is significant that Unsworth refers to 'deep seas and dead fathers' in the plural as though acknowledging the complex refractive layers of the *Tempest* tradition. The rats too resemble Eliot's. A few lines before 'I remember / Those are pearls that were his eyes' come the lines:

I think we are in rats' alley
Where the dead men lost their bones.[64]

And in 'The Fire Sermon' there is another reference to rats within a *Tempest* context:

A rat crept softly through the vegetation
Dragging its slimy belly on the banks
While I was fishing in the dull canal
On a winter evening round behind the gashouse
Musing upon the king my brother's wrack.[65]

The 'odd fusions' Erasmus forges are thus also forged (by both Unsworth and his readers) between *The Tempest* and *The Waste Land*. Unsworth's account of spring's capacity to generate 'odd fusions' is itself derived from Eliot, whose description of how spring prompts memories may cue reflexively for the reader memories of Geoffrey Chaucer's very different account of April as the time of soft showers rather than the 'cruellest month':

April is the cruellest month, breeding
Lilacs out of the dead land, mixing
Memory and desire, stirring
Dull roots with spring rain.[66]

Unsworth's readers may similarly find that their own literary memories are alerted by the novelist's account of one character's reflections on individual memory. Here however it is Eliot rather than Chaucer who is brought to mind. Eliot finds himself taking the place of his own predecessor, just as Dante did in his own 'Little Gidding', becoming himself a canonical author to be reanimated in the works of his successors and remembered by their readers. Although the memory-curdling speck is described as virulent, within the context of 'Full Fathom Five', the speck might recall the grit which forces an oyster to form a pearl. In literary terms the pearl is the later poet's response to the intrusion of a foreign body from the past into his own poem, the product of the writer's urge to metamorphose old texts into something new and strange.

In a little-known, curious, yet striking work, *Black Anima* (1973) by the African-American poet Norman Loftis, Eliot's *Waste Land* again undergoes a sea change.[67] *Black Anima* is essentially a revisioning of Eliot's poem, yet as *The Tempest* is part of the fabric of *The Waste Land*, it is also in part a response to Shakespeare's play. Loftis relocates *The Waste Land* to New York, and, although it is as full of literary and historical references as Eliot's poem, nearly all Loftis's allusions are to African-American culture.[68] One of Eliot's many *Tempest* moments:

> 'This music crept by me upon the waters'
> And along the Strand, up Queen Victoria Street.[69]

is thus transformed by Loftis:

> This music shuffled
> past me in 633
> at the Alamac
> while Miss Brown
> seductively
> exposed her thighs
> her eyes meeting my eyes.[70]

Ariel's music makes another appearance in *Black Anima*, mediated through Section 4 of *The Waste Land*, 'Death by Water', which describes the drowned body of Phlebas the Phoenician:

> A naked figure flowed
> along the Harlem River
> turning, turning in sunlight . . .
> it fell under sea
> but at Wall Street was free
> fish nipping in the Bay
> picked its fingers clean.[71]

Loftis's repetitive 'Turning, turning' perhaps picks up on the end of the section of *The Waste Land* which immediately precedes 'Death by Water', 'The Fire Sermon', which concludes:

> Burning burning burning burning
> O Lord thou pluckest me out
> O Lord thou pluckest
>
> Burning.[72]

Loftis's 'turning' thus suggests the corpse's movement but also change – just as the word itself is the product of a metamorphosis from burning to turning, and Eliot's Phoenician (himself a metamorphosed Alonso) has been changed to an African-American. The body in the Harlem river is changing, picked clean just like Phlebas, but so is Eliot's poem and indeed *The Tempest*. Loftis's poem harnesses the reflexive power of 'Full Fathom Five' in order to articulate a riposte to the hegemony of Western culture. The corpse becomes the corpus, which must be transformed and not simply revived. In one of *Black Anima*'s prose sections Loftis returns to the image of a bone picked clean of flesh to describe his journey back into a cultural past in which echoes of Eliot and other Western texts such as the story of Pygmalion are combined with images of African and African-American history, parading in front of the narrator like the shades of Aeneas's ancestors.

> images from your past rushed on you, and you sucked them clean as a bone. The dead king searching the shore of the Nile for the perfect ebony figure. The hanged man drenched with gasoline and set aflame down in Mississippi. And the grass that year grew green as fire, the cotton heaped high as the Alps and an old man covered with wheat rose out of the river wet with water and ambergris. All this filed past you sorting itself out in your feeling, already frayed from the journey.[73]

The image of exposing the past, as a skeleton is exposed when the flesh decays, reflects Loftis's self-conscious literary practice in *Black Anima*. We are sent right back to *The Waste Land*'s roots, uncovering traces of earlier sources, including the *Aeneid*. The narrator of *Black Anima* is led down to the catacombs by 'Sibby' who shows him the shades of dead writers. 'Sibby', Loftis informs us, denotes Dame Sibyl Leek, a supposed witch, as well as Virgil's Sibyl. This double explanation operates reflexively – Sibby, simply through her role and her name, fulfils the prophesies of Virgil's Sibyl who had offered

Aeneas a vision of the dead being reborn, and of stories being endlessly recycled.

This Sibyl offers Loftis the chance to join the long line of figures who experience a moment of uncanny and allusive recognition in the underworld. One of the ghosts Loftis's narrator meets in the underworld, in a group of nude bathers walking in circles on smouldering sands, seems to be a disguised T. S. Eliot, disguised yet recognisable. It is significant that although Loftis is quite as fond of footnotes as T. S. Eliot he makes no reference to Eliot or *The Waste Land* in his extensive annotations. As with the suspected appearance of Chuck Palahniuk in *Glamorama*, discussed in Chapter 3, the appearance of Eliot would be less playful and pleasurable if Loftis hadn't built some 'plausible deniability' into his allusion by adjusting the poet's name:

> And I recognize the poet
> admiring himself in his bikini
> and I said, 'Mr Elicut, what a sad
> day for poetry, what are you doing
> in this dismal city?'
>
> And Mr. Elicut said, 'When I lived
> above I wrote only of sin and body's
> contamination, now I'm forced to feel life's fascination.'[74]

The verb 'recognize' functions here as an allusion marker, for just as the narrator recognises 'Elicut' (the altered third syllable 'cut' reflexively signals the deformation of Eliot's name, the way his poem is cut down to size in *Black Anima*) we recognise the informing presence of Eliot in *Black Anima* as a whole. The incongruous bikini may be a comic sideswipe at Eliot's adoption of a Tiresian voice in *The Waste Land*, even a hint at emasculation. Eliot is perhaps now 'Elicut' because, like Deiphobus, he has been subjected to mutilation. This moment of recognition is anticipated when Loftis first descends to the catacombs and notes 'dead footfalls echoing through the halls',[75] a line which reflexively echoes, and may spark memories of, a line from 'Burnt Norton': 'Footfalls echo in the memory'.[76]

The narrator's expressions of sympathy and dismay at finding 'Elicut' in hell may be read as an ironic reflection of his own displacement of the poet from *The Waste Land* into *Black Anima*. His recognition of Elicut/Eliot is a complicated moment. He recognises the (slightly metamorphosed) poet as we recognise the similarly distorted presence of *The Waste Land* in Black Anima. At the same time we are also invited to recognise Dante because we are reminded of the parallel moment where he recognised Latini. A further ghost may of course be detected lying behind Mr Elicut, the Dantean 'familiar compound ghost' of 'Little Gidding':

> I caught the sudden look of some dead master
> Whom I had known, forgotten, half recalled
> Both one and many; in the brown baked features
> The eyes of a familiar compound ghost
> Both intimate and unidentifiable.
> So I assumed a double part, and cried
> And heard another's voice cry: 'What! Are *you* here?'[77]

Loftis's 'Mr. Elicut' thus fulfils Eliot's own tacit acknowledgement that he would one day himself become the 'familiar compound ghost', or part of him at least. 'Another's voice' is, at least in part, now that of Loftis.

A later text, although not one apparently influenced by Loftis, also offers the reader a *katabasis* to an underworld where the souls of dead poets reside, and where Homer, Virgil, Dante, Shakespeare and Eliot all make their presence felt. This is Derek Walcott's *Omeros* (1990) which, like *Black Anima*, dramatises the racial distance between the living poet and his many influences. Homer is, as is evident from the title, the most obvious influence, and it is he who eventually takes the narrator down to the underworld in a repetition, perhaps a kind of overtopping, of Dante's descent with Virgil. Characters from the *Iliad*, in particular Hector, Achilles and Helen, are reborn in the modern Caribbean. Yet again *The Tempest* is added to the mix; Walcott's most obvious engagement with the play is perhaps this extravagant *imitatio* of 'Full Fathom Five':

> In the corals' bone kingdom his skin calcifies.
> In that wavering garden huge fans on hinges
> Swayed, while fingers of seaweed pocketed the eyes
>
> Of coins with the profiles of Iberian kings;
> Here the sea-floor was mud, not corrugating sand
> That showed you its ribs . . .
>
> The shreds of the ocean's floor passed him from corpses
> That had perished in the crossing, their hair like weeds,
> Their bones were long coral fingers, bubbles of eyes
>
> Watched him, a brain-coral gurgled their words.[78]

In a kind of chiastic response to Shakespeare's transformation of flesh and bone into other substances, Walcott reverses the procedure and invests the corpse's surroundings with attributes associated with the human body. The seaweed has fingers, the eyes turn out to be coins, the sand has ribs and the coral is uncannily given a voice.

Philoctetes, as well as the more conventional Homeric heroes, Achilles and Hector, finds an avatar in *Omeros*. Walcott's Philoctete has been associated with Caliban by some critics.[79] Going back to Sophocles' depiction of Philoctetes as a lonely, ostracised, and repulsive figure, leading a primitive life on a small island, it is certainly possible to detect parallels with Caliban. But Caliban is not the only character from *The Tempest* we can link with Philoctetes. The lonely exile, abandoned by his own people, who eventually returns home and becomes reassimilated, has just as much in common with Prospero. And perhaps this is why Walcott's 'colonial', Plunkett, as well as the St Lucian Philoctete, is troubled by a wound, like the sore which affects the original Philoctetes. 'This wound I have stitched into Plunkett's character,'[80] observes Walcott, in a line which seems to invite a comparison with Eliot's 'these fragments I have shored against my ruin'.[81] This apparent acknowledgement that colonialism causes damage to both sides is reflected in another moment of hybridity. Whereas Loftis makes ebony displace ivory, Walcott offers us a vision of fusion between black and white.

> between two Helens:
>
> yours is here and alive; their classic features
> were turned into silhouettes from the lightning bolt
> of a glance. These Helens are different creatures,
> one marble, one ebony.[82]

But a still more interesting moment of complex fusion occurs towards the beginning of *Omeros*. Returning to his family home, where his father had once run a printing business, the narrator has a strange encounter:

> And there was a figure
> Framed in the quiet window for whom this was home,
>
> Tracing its dust, rubbing thumb and middle finger,
> Then coming to me, not past, but through the machines,
> Clear as a film and as perfectly projected

As a wall cut by the jalousies' slanted lines.
He had done a self-portrait, it was accurate.
In his transparent hand was a book I had read.[83]

The figure is a ghost of some of the many other ghosts described in this chapter, a further addition to Eliot's compound. The fact that he is carrying 'a book I had read' seems like a reflexive nod towards his own textuality, and towards his creator's immersion in the works of his precursors. However it soon becomes clear that this is a ghost of a real rather than a literary ancestor, and the volume is a simple notebook rather than a well-known classic.

'In this pale blue notebook where you found my verses' –
My father smiled – 'I appeared to make your life's choice,
And the calling that you practice both reverses

And honours mine from the moment it blent with yours.
Now that you are twice my age, which is the boy's,
Which the father's?'

'Sir' – I swallowed – 'they are both one voice.'[84]

This suggestion that the son and his paradoxically younger father are speaking in unison again seems to echo Eliot's compound ghost, and this hint is strengthened when Walcott describes his former home, in the next stanza, as uncannily 'familiar and unfamiliar', a description which might be applied to the alluding poem as well as to the house. The father's terse autobiographical sketch is reminiscent of several encounters in the *Inferno*, particularly given the use of terza rima, and there are also odd parallels between the life of the narrator's real father and one of his literary 'fathers', Shakespeare:

'I was raised in this obscure Caribbean port,
Where my bastard father christened me for his shire:
Warwick. The Bard's country. But never felt part

Of the foreign machinery known as Literature.
I preferred verse to fame, but I wrote with the heart
Of an amateur. It's that Will you inherit.

I died on his birthday, one April

I believe the parallel has brought you some peace.
Death imitating Art, eh?'[85]

(It has sometimes been said that Shakespeare too died on his own birthday, a coincidence which contributes to this ghost's literary, 'compound' quality.) Later in the poem the narrator describes a visit to Ireland in which he makes many allusions to the works of Joyce, whom he refers to as 'our age's Omeros'.[86] Joyce's own most famous epic, like *Omeros*, immediately signals its debts to Homer through its name, and Walcott's poem can be seen as a response to Joyce's *Ulysses*, to its own engagement with the *Odyssey*, as well as a response to Homer himself.[87] Thus perhaps the 'ghost' the narrator encounters invokes Joyce as well as Warwick Walcott, Dante, Shakespeare, Eliot and the rest. And if we are encouraged to think of *Ulysses* we may also be reminded of that novel's own fixation on the relationship between fathers and sons: Shakespeare and his father, Hamlet and the ghost, Stephen and the father figure of Bloom, Ulysses and Telemachus.

So Joyce, Homer, Shakespeare, and other textual fathers are present here, just as they are in 'Little Gidding'. But this seems a more unanxious encounter. Whereas Eliot's narrator seems haunted, almost possessed, by the ghost who speaks with his voice, Walcott's narrator courteously articulates his sense of union with his father in a move which has the paradoxical effect of asserting the distinctiveness of his own voice. He is polite and respectful, yet older than his father, and a better poet too. We may infer that Walcott feels a similar independence from, if not superiority to, his poetic ancestors as well, and this is again perhaps signaled by his readiness to acknowledge them, just as he acknowledges the humanity and interest of the white characters in his poem. Loftis refuses to name Eliot or *The Waste Land* in *Black Anima*, but Walcott names *Omeros* after Homer and lets the earlier poet, literally, take him by the hand in the poem's climactic *katabasis*, when Homer will prevent him from falling into the underworld to join the poets in hell who are:

> Condemned in their pit to weep at their own pages.
> And that was where I had come from. Pride in my craft.
> Elevating myself. I slid, and kept falling
>
> Towards the shit they stewed in; all the poets laughed,
> Jeering with dripping fingers, then Omeros gripped
> My hand in enclosing marble and his strength moved
>
> Me away from that crowd.[88]

But there is just a little uncertainty here after all; a hint at struggle recalling the tensely ambiguous moment when the hands of Glaucus and the unnamed old man meet in the water in *Endymion*. For it is not at first clear whether the marble grip of Omeros is going to support the narrator, or whether, like the other poets with their 'dripping fingers', he wants to drag him down to hell, as though reenacting the Commendatore's final punishment of Don Giovanni. Not until the beginning of the next stanza is this question resolved, as though Walcott himself has had to struggle to work with rather than against his predecessor. With Homer, as with Walcott's father, the narrator's respect is qualified by a clear assertion of his own personality and perspective. The name 'Omeros' seems like an attempt at authenticity, a refusal to anglicise the poet's name, but it is simultaneously updated and Caribbeanised for the reader once we realise how Walcott himself responds to that name:

> and O was the conch shell's invocation, *mer* was
> both mother and sea in our Antillean patois,
> *os*, a grey bone, and the white surf as it crashes.[89]

Homer is now always a compound, one way or another, always haunted by his future, by his reception. By contrast with Eliot, who appeared to be usurped by the voice of another, and implicitly invited later poets, such as Loftis, to put him in hell, Walcott effects a kind of reverse-colonisation, maintaining a securely separate identity, freeing himself from the mass of unworthy poets in hell, and making sure that any influence from his predecessors is uncannily reciprocated.

Notes

1 G. B. Conte, C. Segal, *The Rhetoric of Imitation: Genre and Poetic Memory in Virgil and other Latin Poets* (Ithaca: Cornell University Press, 1996), p. 66.
2 T. S. Eliot, *Collected Poems*, p. 204.
3 A useful account of the presence of traces of Dante and other poets in the 'compound ghost' is offered by H. Blamires, *Word Unheard: A Guide through Eliot's Four Quartets* (London: Methuen, 1969), p. 147, p. 154.
4 Dante, *The Divine Comedy*, trans. C. H. Sisson (London: Carcanet, 1980), p. 107.
5 H. Kenner, *The Invisible Poet: T. S. Eliot* (London: W. H. Allen, 1960), p. 274.
6 Philip Hardie offers some particularly interesting reflections on *katabasis* within the context of classical and postclassical epic traditions. (P. Hardie, *The Epic Successors of Virgil: A Study in the Dynamics of a*

Tradition (Cambridge: Cambridge University Press, 1993), pp. 57–87. See also E. J. Bellamy, 'From Virgil to Tasso: The Epic Topos as an Uncanny Return', in V. Finucci and R. Schwartz (eds), *Desire in the Renaissance: Psychoanalysis and Literature* (Princeton: Princeton University Press, 1994).

7 Homer, *Odyssey*, pp. 166–7.
8 *Ibid.*, p. 167.
9 The *Aeneid*'s debts to Homer have been much discussed. See for example R. D. Williams, 'The *Aeneid* and its Literary Background', in E. J. Kenney and W. V. Clausen (eds), *The Cambridge History of Classical Literature* (Cambridge: Cambridge University Press, 1982), 2 vols, vol. 1, pp. 339–44, p. 340.
10 Virgil, *Aeneid*, 6.160–2.
11 *Ibid.*, 6.494–9.
12 *Ibid.*, 6.523–8.
13 *Ibid.*, *Aeneid*, 6.529–30.
14 *Ibid.*, 6.713–15.
15 Although my own focus is on just one small aspect of this rich tradition, entire books have of course been written on the subject of *The Tempest*'s afterlife and I only seek to illuminate one aspect of the topic. See for example P. Hulme and W. H. Sherman (eds), *'The Tempest' and its Travels* (London: Reaktion, 2000); C. J. Zabus, *Tempests after Shakespeare* (New York and Basingstoke: Palgrave Macmillan, 2002).
16 1.1.4, 49, 67.
17 1.2.16–17.
18 1.1.51.
19 R. McDonald, 'Reading *The Tempest*', *Shakespeare Survey*, 43 (1991), 15–28, p. 26.
20 J. W. Loofbourow, 'Robinson Crusoe's Island and the Restoration *Tempest*', *Enlightenment Essays*, 2 (1971), 201–7.
21 J. Dryden and W. Davenant, *The Tempest or The Enchanted Island* (London, 1670), p. 83.
22 *Ibid.*, p. 15.
23 *Ibid.*
24 *Faerie Queene* Book I, canto 2; *Inferno* 13.
25 Virgil, *Aeneid*, 3.24–9.
26 Many commentators have discussed the presence of the *Aeneid* in *The Tempest*. For an extended account of the relationship see D. Hamilton, *Virgil and The Tempest: The Politics of Imitation* (Columbus: Ohio State University Press, 1990).
27 Virgil, *Aeneid*, 6.201–11.
28 Compare Marjorie Garber's suggestion that the ghost in Hamlet originally signified Shakespeare's past (the play's sources, the revenge

tradition, Shakespeare's own father) but now, after four centuries of performance and reception, signifies Shakespeare himself. (*Shakespeare's Ghost Writers*, pp. 172–6.)
29 Dryden and Davenant, *The Enchanted Island*, p. 17.
30 Garber, *Shakespeare's Ghost Writers*, p. 52.
31 Eliot, *Collected Poems*, p. 55.
32 Dryden and Davenant, *The Enchanted Island*, p. 83.
33 For a useful brief account of this tradition see D. E. Henderson, 'The Tempest in Performance' in R. Dutton and J. E. Howard (eds), *A Companion to Shakespeare's Works, Volume IV: The Poems, Problem Comedies, Late Plays* (Oxford: Blackwell, 2003), pp. 216–30, pp. 217–18.
34 B. Jonson, *The Oxford Jonson*, eds C. H. Herford Percy and E. Simpson (Oxford: Clarendon Press, 1938), 11 vols, vol. 6, p. 16.
35 Keats, *The Complete Poems*, 214.
36 *Ibid.*, p. 215.
37 Ovid, *Metamorphoses*, 13.906–68.
38 For a discussion of Ovid's influence on *The Tempest* see J. Bate, *Shakespeare and Ovid*, (Oxford: Clarendon Press, 1994), pp. 247–9. The importance of *The Tempest* for Keats is discussed by R. S. White in *Keats as a Reader of Shakespeare* (London: Athlone, 1987), pp. 88–103.
39 Keats, *Complete Poems*, pp. 231–2.
40 *Ibid.*, p. 233.
41 *Ibid.*
42 Karen Swann suggests that he encompasses 'Wordsworth's Leech-Gatherer, Coleridge's Ancient Mariner, Milton's Lycidas, and Spenser's Archimago.' ('*Endymion*'s Beautiful Dreamers', in S. J. Wolfson (ed.), *The Cambridge Companion to Keats* (Cambridge: Cambridge University Press, 2001), pp. 20–36, p. 26.
43 H. Bloom, *The Anxiety of Influence: A Theory of Poetry*, 2nd ed. (Oxford: Oxford University Press, 1997), p. 80.
44 Keats, *Complete Poems*, p. 232.
45 *Ibid.*, p. 233.
46 *Ibid.*, p. 234.
47 R. Hoban, *The Moment under the Moment* (London: Picador, 1993), p. 83.
48 *Ibid.*
49 *Ibid.*
50 *Ibid.*, p. 86.
51 Virgil, *Aeneid*, 6.713–15.
52 Hoban, *The Moment under the Moment*, p. 88.
53 *Ibid.*, p. 108.
54 For discussions of 'Full Fathom Five' see R. A. Brower, *The Fields of Light: An Experiment in Critical Reading* (Oxford: Oxford University

Press, 1951), p. 113; M. Garber, *Shakespeare After All* (New York: Pantheon, 2005), pp. 859–60.
55 1.2.397–405.
56 The use of *The Tempest* in *The Waste Land* is discussed in N. Corcoran, *Shakespeare and the Modern Poet* (Cambridge: Cambridge University Press, 2010), pp. 110–13.
57 Eliot, *Collected Poems*, p. 54.
58 *Ibid.*, p. 57.
59 *Ibid.*, p. 60.
60 1.2.438–9.
61 1.2.390–1.
62 B. Unsworth, *Sacred Hunger* (London: Doubleday, 1992), pp. 54–5.
63 For discussions of metaleptic allusion see Cook, *Against Coercion*, pp. 148–55; Hollander, *The Figure of Echo*, pp. 113–49.
64 Eliot, *Collected Poems*, p. 57.
65 *Ibid.*, p. 60.
66 *Ibid.*, p. 53.
67 Compare S. A. Brown, '"Hail, Muse! Et Cetera": Greek Myth in English and American Literature', in R. D. Woodard (ed.), *The Cambridge Companion to Greek Mythology* (Cambridge: Cambridge University Press, 2008), pp. 425–52, pp. 447–8.
68 Comparatively little has been written on *Black Anima*. For a useful account of the poem's sources see J. W. Ward, 'N. J. Loftis's *Black Anima*: A Problem in Aesthetics', *Journal of Black Studies*, 7.2 (1976), 195–210.
69 Eliot, *Collected Poems*, p. 62.
70 N. J. Loftis, *Black Anima* (New York: Liveright, 1973), p. 10.
71 *Ibid.*, p. 7.
72 Eliot, *Collected Poems*, p. 64.
73 Loftis, *Black Anima*, p. 86.
74 *Ibid.*, pp. 61–2.
75 *Ibid.*, p. 44.
76 Eliot, *Collected Poems*, p. 177.
77 *Ibid.*, p. 204.
78 D. Walcott, *Omeros* (London: Faber and Faber, 1992), pp. 45–6.
79 J. Ramazani, 'The Wound of Postcolonial History: Derek Walcott's *Omeros*', in H. Bloom (ed.), *Derek Walcott* (Broomall: Chelsea House, 2003), pp. 174–204.
80 *Ibid.*, p. 28.
81 Eliot, *Collected Poems*, p. 69. For an account of Walcott's relationship with Dante, Eliot and other precursors, see C. W. Pollard, *New World Modernisms: T. S. Eliot, Derek Walcott and Kamau Brathwaite* (Charlottesville: University of Virginia Press, 2004), pp. 149–73.
82 Walcott, *Omeros*, p. 313.

83 *Ibid.*, p. 68.
84 *Ibid.*
85 *Ibid.*, pp. 68–9.
86 *Ibid.*, p. 200.
87 On the relationship between Walcott and Joyce see C. W. Pollard, 'Travelling with Joyce: Derek Walcott's Discrepant Cosmopolitan Modernism', *Twentieth Century Literature*, 47.2 (2001), 197–216.
88 *Ibid.*, p. 298.
89 *Ibid.*, p. 14.

8

Afterword: 'You'd think she would remember all this from the first time'[1]

I opened this book with an example of an uncannily allusive moment which brought together two young heroines of children's literature, C. S. Lewis's Lucy and Philip Pullman's Lyra. I'd like to conclude with a discussion of a third heroine, Lewis Carroll's Alice – or perhaps I should say, Tim Burton's Alice. Burton's 2010 film, *Alice in Wonderland*, is a complexly allusive work, which cleverly stirs and shakes the memories both of Alice herself, within the fiction of the film, and of the audience, encouraging us (and her) to remember experiences from our childhood. And perhaps, as it turns out that Wonderland's real name is Underland, the film can also be seen as a kind of final *katabasis* too.

The film is predicated on the idea that Alice, now nineteen, visited 'Underland' as a child but has since almost forgotten the journey and remembers it only as something which perhaps happened in a dream. When pressured into marriage with an eligible but unappealing suitor she flees after a white rabbit and, for a second time, falls down a rabbit hole. If Burton only appealed to our memories of *Alice*, then there would be no great interest in the fact that we remember events from the famous children's book at the same time as his grown-up heroine begins to realise that she has visited Underland before. If we have read Carroll's books then we will naturally expect to be reminded of them, and will probably be on the lookout for both similarities and differences.

More interesting and potentially uncanny are the many other more unexpected flashbacks which we may experience as we watch the film, and which we cannot at first perhaps trace to their origins. These moments bring us closer to the experience of Burton's Alice, as she slowly begins to piece her memories together again, unprepared for the various discoveries she makes. At one point the Mad Hatter complains plaintively, 'I don't like it in here, it's terribly crowded', apparently reflecting on the confused thoughts and voices inside his head. The film is crowded with different voices too, traces of other texts, particularly children's books. The first such trace can be found in the film's opening sequence in the 'real' world. Although we are never told the surname of Carroll's Alice, here we learn that she is Alice Kingsley, and that her father's name was Charles. Charles Kingsley was (in a sense) a 'father' of the original *Alice* as his strange and magical *The Water-Babies* (1863) was published two years before Carroll's novel. Like *Alice*, it deals with a child's adventures in a magical world which is filled with talking animals and other wonders.

Echoes intensify once Alice has arrived in Wonderland, which has become a wasteland under the rule of the evil Red Queen.[2] Alice falls into her clutches and faces the threat of execution, but is then unexpectedly rescued by the fierce Bandersnatch, who carries her on his back to the White Queen's castle. I suggested in the introduction that when Lyra rides on the back of Iorek Byrnison, an armoured bear, we are invited to remember Lucy's ride on Aslan. Tim Burton's own variation on the theme might cue memories of both earlier scenes, and there are further parallels between Underland and Narnia. Alice, like Lucy, must rescue a magical land which has been taken over by a malevolent queen. Burton's Dormouse has a little sword which she is fond of flourishing, a detail which owes nothing to Carroll, but does recall Lewis's talking mouse, Reepicheep. Alice's poignant relationship with the Hatter, whom she has to rescue when he is captured by the wicked Red Queen, echoes Lucy's friendship with the lovable if not entirely reliable Mr Tumnus, taken prisoner by the White Witch in *The Lion, the Witch and the Wardrobe*. Burton reinvents Carroll's tea party as a perilous episode, in which Alice has to be hidden by the Hatter, Hare and Dormouse, lest she be captured by Stayne (the Knave of Hearts, sidekick to the Red Queen). If we have already been reminded of Narnia by other echoes, we might think back to the sad moment in *The Lion, the Witch and the Wardrobe* when a merry group of assorted woodland creatures, also enjoying an alfresco meal, are questioned and then turned to stone by the menacing white witch. *The Wizard of Oz* is yet another resonant intertext. Burton's languidly charming White Queen and vindictive Red Queen have little in common with Carroll's original characters, but they strongly resemble Glinda and the Wicked Witch of the West. These parallels emerge particularly clearly in the final scene, in which Alice, like Dorothy, is offered a talisman which will take her home by the White Queen, and is torn between her family and her new friends. And, as a curious sequel which begins with the heroine fearing she may be going mad, Burton's film also invites comparisons with the rather dark *Return to Oz* which opens with young Dorothy facing electrotherapy to cure her of her delusions.[3]

A particularly interesting allusion is cued by Burton's ingenious use of a Tenniel illustration which turns out to be both a prophecy and an allusion trigger. This depicts a small figure slaying the Jabberwocky. Although the figure ought to be the son, the 'beamish boy' of Carroll's nonsense poem, it looks suspiciously like Alice herself, although, as we can only see his (or her) back, this cannot be established with certainty. In the film this image becomes part of a magical scroll, the Oraculum, which illustrates, not a fictional text, but the future. Both Lewis's poem and its ambiguous illustration are revealed to be veiled prophecies of Alice's eventual defeat of the Jabberwocky, a victory which will restore the White Queen to power. Rather fearfully, Alice agrees to take up the vorpal sword, because she knows that she is fated to be the White Queen's champion. Burton cleverly manipulates Alice's fight in order to create a more richly allusive moment. We are of course reminded of Tenniel when we see her raise her sword to cut off the monster's head. But many viewers will be reminded of another famous victory, another fulfilment of prophecy, the moment in *The Lord of the Rings* when cross-dressing Éowyn slays the Nazgûl, caught off his guard because he has been assured that he will never meet his death 'by the hand of man'.[4]

At the end of the film the Hatter sadly tells the troubled Alice that she may return to Underland one day but she will no longer remember who he is. I felt certain, as I watched this scene, that I had encountered similar moments in children's fiction before – but could not quite remember where. I'm still (rather reflexively) unsure that I've pinned down exactly why that particular moment seemed so familiar, although one key precursor may be the poignant scene at the end of J. M. Barrie's play *Peter Pan* (1904) when we learn that Peter barely remembers that Wendy has visited Neverland before and has forgotten all about Tinkerbell and Captain Hook.

In his new Alice, Burton has created a kind of belated Ur-heroine, who re-enacts the heroic deeds performed by many other brave girls. But his film also draws on older archetypes, including the legends surrounding the figure of the Fisher King, another narrative about a wasteland waiting to be healed. Alice's festering Bandersnatch scratches can only be cured when they are licked by her own attacker, creating an apparent echo of Wagner's *Parsifal*, in which Amfortas can only be healed by the touch of the spear which wounded him. By invoking such a rich and varied array of earlier texts, Burton puts the allusion marker of memory to uncannily effective use, demonstrating that the bonds between allusion and the uncanny can resonate within film, popular culture and genre fiction as well as within more classical and canonical texts.

Notes

1 *Alice in Wonderland*, dir. Tim Burton (2010).
2 She is in fact a compound of the Red Queen from *Alice Through the Looking Glass* and the Queen of Hearts from *Alice in Wonderland*, and her character is closer to the latter.
3 Dir. W. Murch (1985).
4 J. R. R. Tolkien, *The Return of the King* (London: George Allen & Unwin, 1960), p. 92.

Bibliography

Abbate, A., 'To be or inter-be': Almereyda's End-of-Millennium *Hamlet*', *Literature/Film Quarterly* 32.2 (2004), 82–9.
Abi-Ezzi, N., *The Double in the Fiction of R. L. Stevenson, Wilkie Collins and Daphne du Maurier* (Oxford: Peter Lang, 2003).
Abraham, N., and M. Torok, 'A Poetics of Psychoanalysis: The 'Lost Object' – Me', trans. N. Rand, *SubStance*, 43 (1984), 3–18.
Aebischer, P., *Shakespeare's Violated Bodies: Stage and Screen Performance* (Cambridge: Cambridge University Press, 2004).
Aeschylus, *Agamemnon*, trans. J. Connington (Oxford: Clarendon Press, 1907).
Aeschylus, *Works*, trans. H. W. Smyth (London: William Heinemann, 1963), 2 vols, vol. 2.
Aeschylus, *The Oresteia*, trans. David R. Slavitt (Philadelphia: University of Pennsylvania Press, 1998).
Alexander, M., *Old English Literature* (London: Macmillan, 1983).
Amalric, J., 'Un Conte d'hiver? Note sur un sous-titre', *Cahiers Victoriens et Edouardiens*, 40 (1994), 121–5.
Andersen, H. C., *Longer Stories*, trans. Jean Hersholt (New York: Heritage Press, 1943).
Andriano, J., *Our Ladies of Darkness: Feminine Daemonology in Male Gothic Fiction* (Pennsylvania: Pennsylvania State University Press, 1993).
Anonymous, *Sir Orfeo*, ed. A. J. Bliss (Oxford: Oxford University Press, 1954).
Atwood, M., *Negotiating with the Dead: A Writer on Writing* (Cambridge: Cambridge University Press, 2002).
Atwood, M., *The Handmaid's Tale* (London: Everyman, 2006).
Auerbach, A., *Du Maurier, Haunted Heiress* (Philadelphia: University of Pennsylvania Press, 2000).
Ballard, J. G., *The Drowned World* (London: Harper Perennial, 2006).
Barkan, L., *Unearthing the Past: Archaeology and Aesthetics in the Making*

of Renaissance Culture (New Haven and London: Yale University Press, 1999).
Barkan, L, 'Ruins and Visions; Spenser, Pictures, Rome', in J. K. Morrison and M. Greenfield (eds), *Edmund Spenser: Essays on Culture and Allegory* (Aldershot: Ashgate, 2000).
Bate, J., *Shakespeare and Ovid* (Oxford: Clarendon Press, 1994).
Baum, P. F., 'The Young Man Betrothed to a Statue', *PMLA*, 34.4 (1919), 523–7.
Bellamy, E., 'From Virgil to Tasso: The Epic Topos as an Uncanny Return', in V. Finucci and R. Schwartz (eds), *Desire in the Renaissance: Psychoanalysis and Literature* (Princeton: Princeton University Press, 1994).
Benjamin, W., 'Excavation and Memory' in *Selected Writings*, ed. M. W. Jennings (Cambridge, Mass.: Harvard University Press, 1999), vol. 2.
Benjamin, W., *The Work of Art in the Age of Mechanical Reproduction*, trans. J. A. Underwood (London: Penguin, 2008).
Bennett, A. and N. Royle, *Introduction to Literature, Criticism and Theory*, 3rd edition (Harlow: Pearson Education, 2004).
Berman, E., 'Hitchcock's Vertigo: The Collapse of a Rescue Phantasy', *The International Journal of Psychoanalysis*, 78 (1997), 975–96.
Berry, P., *Of Chastity and Power: Elizabethan Literature and the Unmarried Queen* (London: Routledge, 1995).
Blamires, H., *Word Unheard: A Guide through Eliot's Four Quartets* (London: Methuen, 1969).
Blazer, A. E., '*Glamorama, Fight Club*, and the Terror of Narcissistic Abjection', in J. Prosser (ed.), *American Fiction of the 1990s: Reflections of History and Culture* (London and New York: Routledge, 2008), pp. 177–89.
Bloom, E., (ed.) *Mozart's Letters: Selected from the Letters of Mozart and his Family* (London: Penguin, 1968), 2 vols, vol. 2.
Bloom, H., *The Anxiety of Influence: A Theory of Poetry*, 2nd edition (Oxford: Oxford University Press, 1997).
Booker, M. K., *Alternate Americas: Science Fiction Film and American Culture* (Westport: Greenwood, 2006).
Braddon, M., *Lady Audley's Secret* (London: Penguin, 1998).
Bradshaw, M., 'Mary Shelley's Last Man (The End of the World as we know it)', in D. Littlewood and P. Stockwell (eds) *Impossibility Fiction* (Amsterdam: Rodopi, 1996), pp. 163–75.
Brower, R. A., *The Fields of Light: An Experiment in Critical Reading* (Oxford: Oxford University Press, 1951).
Brown, S. A., '"There is No End but Addition": The Later Reception of Shakespeare's Classicism', in C. Martindale and A. B. Taylor (eds), *Shakespeare and the Classics* (Cambridge: Cambridge University Press, 2004), pp. 277–93.

Brown, S. A., *Ovid: Myth and Metamorphosis* (London: Bristol Classical Press, 2005).
Brown, S. A., '"Plato's Stepchildren": SF and the Classics', in L. Hardwick and C. Stray (eds), *A Companion to Classical Receptions* (Oxford: Blackwell, 2008), pp. 415–27.
Brown, S. A., '"Hail, Muse! Et Cetera": Greek Myth in English and American Literature', in R. D. Woodard (ed.), *The Cambridge Companion to Greek Mythology* (Cambridge: Cambridge University Press, 2008), pp. 425–52.
Brown, S. A., 'Classics Reanimated: Ted Hughes and Reflexive Translation', in R. Rees (ed.), *Ted Hughes and the Classics* (Oxford: Oxford University Press, 2009), pp. 282–99.
Bruster, D., *Quoting Shakespeare: Form and Culture in Early Modern Drama* (Lincoln: University of Nebraska Press, 2000).
Buchanan, J., *Shakespeare on Film* (London: Longman, 2005).
Buckton, O. S., 'Reanimating Stevenson's Corpus', *Nineteenth-Century Literature*, 55.1 (2000), 22–58.
Buckton, O. S., *Cruising with Robert Louis Stevenson: Travel, Narrative and the Colonial Body* (Athens: Ohio University Press, 2007).
Bullough, G. (ed.), *Narrative and Dramatic Sources of Shakespeare* (London: Routledge and Kegan Paul, 1973), vol. 7.
Burger, G., and S. F. Kruger, *Queering the Middle Ages* (Minneapolis: University of Minnesota Press, 2001).
Burgess, A., and P. Mérimée, *The Eve of Saint Venus and The Venus of Ille*, trans. A. Brown (London: Hesperus Press, 2006).
Burian, P., 'Myth into *Muthos*: The Shaping of the Tragic Plot' in P. E. Easterling (ed.), *The Cambridge Companion to Greek Tragedy* (Cambridge: Cambridge University Press, 1997), pp. 178–208.
Buse, P., and A. Stott, 'Introduction: A Future for Haunting', in P. Buse and A. Stott (eds) *Ghosts: Deconstruction, Psychoanalysis, History* (Basingstoke: Macmillan, 1999), pp. 1–20.
Butt, J. (ed.), *The Poems of Alexander Pope* (London: Routledge, 1993), 6 vols, vol. 6.
Byron, G., *The Complete Poetical Works*, ed. J. J. McGann (Oxford: Clarendon Press, 1980), 7 vols, vol. 2.
Carsson, M., *The Haunted Stage: The Theatre as Memory Machine* (Ann Arbor: University of Michigan Press, 2001).
Cartelli, T., 'Taymor's *Titus* in Time and Space: Surrogation and Interpolation', *Renaissance Drama* 34 (2005), 163–84.
Christopher, J., *The White Mountains* (New York: Simon Pulse, 2003).
Cixous, H., 'Fiction and its Phantoms: A Reading of Freud's Das Unheimliche', *New* Literary History, 7.3–4 (1976), 525–48.
Clark, M., 'The Hermes in Henry James's "The Last of the Valerii"', *The Henry James Review*, 10.3 (1989), 210–13.

Clunas, A. B., in '"A Double Word": Writing and Justice in *The Master of Ballantrae*', *Studies in Scottish Literature*, 28 (1993), 55–74.
Cojocaru, D., 'Confessions of an American Psycho: James Hogg's and Bret Easton Ellis's Anti-Heroes' Journey from Vulnerability to Violence', *Contagion: Journal of Violence, Mimesis and Culture*, 15/16 (2008–9), 185–200.
Collins, W., *The Woman in White* (London: Everyman, 1969).
Collins, W., *Armadale* (London: Penguin, 1995).
Connolly, J. W., 'The Function of Allusion in Nabokov's *Despair*', *Slavic and East European Journal*, 26.3 (1982), 302–13.
Connolly, J. W., 'Nabokov's (re)visions of Dostoevsky', in J. W. Connolly (ed.), *Nabokov and his Fictions* (Cambridge: Cambridge University Press, 1999), pp. 141–57.
Connolly, J. W., 'The Major Russian Novels', in J. W. Connolly (ed.), *The Cambridge Companion to Nabokov* (Cambridge: Cambridge University Press, 2005), pp. 135–50.
Conrad, J., *Heart of Darkness* (Oxford: Oxford University Press, 2002).
Conrad, J., *Typhoon and other Tales* (Oxford: Oxford University Press, 2006).
Conte, G. B. and C. Segal, *The Rhetoric of Imitation: Genre and Poetic Memory in Virgil and other Latin Poets* (Ithaca: Cornell University Press, 1996).
Cook, E., *Against Coercion: Games Poets Play* (Stanford: Stanford University Press, 1998).
Cooper, H., *English Romance in Time: Transforming Motifs from Geoffrey of Monmouth to the Death of Shakespeare* (Oxford: Oxford University Press, 2004).
Corcoran, N., *Shakespeare and the Modern Poet* (Cambridge: Cambridge University Press, 2010).
Daemmrich, I. G., 'The Ruins Motif as Artistic Device in French Literature, Part 1', *The Journal of Aesthetics and Art Criticism*, 30.4 (1972), 449–57.
Dante, *The Divine Comedy*, trans. C. H. Sisson (London: Carcanet, 1980).
Dean, J., 'The Sick Hero Reborn: Two Versions of the Philoctetes Myth', *Comparative Literature Studies*, 17.3 (1980), 334–40.
De Grazia, M., *Hamlet without Hamlet* (Cambridge: Cambridge University Press, 2007).
Derrida, J., *Specters of Marx*, trans. Peggy Kamuf (New York and London: Routledge, 1994).
Dooley, D., 'Inversion, Metamorphosis, and Sexual Difference: Female Same-Sex Desire in Ovid and Lyly', in G. V. Stanivukovic (ed.), *Ovid and the Renaissance Body* (Toronto: University of Toronto Press, 2001), pp. 59–76.
Dryden, J., and W. Davenant, The Tempest or The Enchanted Island (London, 1670).

Du Maurier, D., *Rebecca* (London: Pan, 1975).
Du Maurier, D., *The Scapegoat* (Philadelphia: University of Pennsylvania Press, 2000).
Dyer, J., *Poems 1761* (Menston: Scolar Press, 1971).
Easton Ellis, B., *Glamorama* (London: Picador, 2000).
Edwards, C., *Writing Rome: Textual Approaches to the City* (Cambridge: Cambridge University Press, 1996).
Eliot, T. S., *Collected Poems 1909–62* (London: Faber & Faber, 2002).
Ellis, J., 'Rooted Affection: The Genesis of Jealousy in *The Winter's Tale*', *College English*, 25.7 (1964), 545–7.
Enterline, L., *The Rhetoric of the Body from Ovid to Shakespeare* (Cambridge: Cambridge University Press, 2000).
Forster, M., *Daphne du Maurier* (London: Arrow, 1994).
Freud, S., 'The Uncanny', in *The Standard Edition of the Complete Works of Sigmund Freud*, trans. J. Strachey (London: Hogarth Press, 1955), 24 vols, vol. 17.
Freud, S., *Civilisation and its Discontents*, trans. James Strachey (New York: W. W. Norton, 1961).
Gaiman, N., *Fables & Reflections* (New York: Vertigo, 1994).
Garber, M., *Shakespeare's Ghost Writers* (New York and London: Methuen, 1987).
Garber, M., *Shakespeare After All* (New York: Pantheon, 2005).
Gifford, D., 'Stevenson and Scottish Fiction: The Importance of *The Master of Ballantrae*', in H. Bloom (ed.), *Robert Louis Stevenson* (Philadelphia: Chelsea House, 2005), pp. 53–78.
Ginsberg, R., *The Aesthetics of Ruins* (Amsterdam and New York: Rodopi, 2004).
Goldstein, L., *Ruins and Empire: The Evolution of a Theme in Augustan and Romantic Literature* (Pittsburgh: University of Pittsburgh Press, 1977).
Gray, H. D., 'Reconstruction of a Lost Play', *Philological Quarterly*, 7.3 (1928), 254–74.
Greenblatt, S., 'With Dirge in Marriage', *The New Republic*, 222.8 (2000), 32–9.
Greene, T. M., *The Light in Troy* (New Haven: Yale University Press, 1982).
Greene, T. M., 'Resurrecting Rome: the Double Task of the Humanist Imagination', in P. Ramsay (ed.), *Rome in the Renaissance: The City and the Myth* (Binghampton, N.Y.: Center for Medieval and Early Renaissance Studies, 1982), pp. 41–54.
Grene D., and R. Lattimore, *Euripides V* (Chicago and London: University of Chicago Press, 1959).
Günther, *Ligurinus*, ed. E. Assmann (Hannover: Hahn, 1987).

Halpern, R., 'An Impure History of Ghosts: Derrida, Marx, Shakespeare', in J. E. Howards and S. C. Shershow (eds), *Marxist Shakespeares* (Routledge: London and New York, 2001), pp. 31–52.

Halpern, R., *Shakespeare's Perfume: Sodomy and Sublimity in the Sonnets, Wilde, Freud and Lacan* (Philadelphia: University of Pennsylvania Press, 2002).

Hamer, R., *Choice of Anglo-Saxon Verse* (London: Faber & Faber, 1970).

Hamilton, D., *Virgil and The Tempest: The Politics of Imitation* (Columbus: Ohio State University Press, 1990).

Hansen, W. F., *Saxo Grammaticus and the Life of Hamlet* (Lincoln and London: University of Nebraska Press, 1983).

Hardie, P., 'Augustan Poets and the Mutability of Rome', in A. Powell (ed.), *Roman Poetry and Propaganda in the Age of Augustus* (Bristol: Bristol Classical Press, 1992).

Hardie, P., *The Epic Successors of Virgil: A Study in the Dynamics of a Tradition* (Cambridge: Cambridge University Press, 1993).

Hart, L., *Fatal Women: Lesbian Sexuality and the Mark of Aggression* (Princeton: Princeton University Press, 1994).

Hatlen, B., 'His Dark Materials, a Challenge to Tolkien and Lewis', in Lenz and Scott (eds), *His Dark Materials Illuminated: Critical Essays on Philip Pullman's Trilogy* (Detroit: Wayne State University Press, 2005), pp. 75–94.

Hawkes, T., *That Shakespeherian Rag: Essays on a Critical Process* (Methuen: London and New York, 1986).

Henderson, D. E., 'The Tempest in Performance', in R. Dutton and J. E. Howard (eds), *A Companion to Shakespeare's Works, Volume IV: The Poems, Problem Comedies, Late Plays* Oxford: Blackwell, 2003), pp. 216–30.

Herdman, J., *The Double in Nineteenth-Century Fiction* (London: Macmillan, 1990).

Herford, C. H., and P. Simpson (eds), *Ben Jonson* (Oxford: Clarendon Press, 1986), 11 vols, vol. 4.

Hinds, S., *Allusion and Intertext: Dynamics of Appropriation in Roman Poetry* (Cambridge: Cambridge University Press, 1998).

Hoban, R., *The Moment under the Moment* (London: Picador, 1993).

Hoffmann, E. T. A., The Best Tales of Hoffmann, trans. J. T. Bealby (New York: Dover, 1967).

Hogg, J., *Selected Stories and Sketches* (Edinburgh: Scottish Academic Press, 1982).

Hogg, J., *The Private Memoirs and Confessions of a Justified Sinner* (Peterborough, Ontario: Broadview Books, 2001).

Hollander, J., *The Figure of Echo: A Mode of Allusion in Milton and After* (Berkeley: University of California Press, 1981).

Homer, *The Odyssey*, trans. Robert Fitzgerald (London: Heinmann, 1962).
Hopkins, B., 'Keats and the Uncanny: "This Living Hand"', *The Kenyon Review* 11.4 (1989), 28–40.
Hopkins, L., *Screening the Gothic* (Texas: University of Texas Press, 2005).
Horace, *Satires, Epistles and Ars Poetica*, trans. H. Rushton Fairclough (Cambridge, Mass.: Harvard University Press, 1978).
Horace, *Odes and Epodes*, trans. C. E. Bennett (Cambridge, Mass.: Harvard University Press, 1999).
Horner, A., and S. Zlosnik, *Daphne du Maurier: Writing, Identity and the Gothic Imagination* (Basingstoke: Macmillan, 1998).
Hughes, T., *Tales from Ovid* (London: Faber & Faber, 1997).
Hulme, P., and W. H. Sherman (eds), *'The Tempest' and its Travels* (London: Reaktion, 2000).
Hunt, M. W., *Looking for Hamlet* (New York and Basingstoke: Palgrave Macmillan, 2007).
Hyginus, *Fabulae*, ed. P. K. Marshall (Stuttgart: Teubner, 1993).
Jacobsen, G. A., '"A Holiday in a Rest Home": Ted Hughes as *vates* in Tales from Ovid', in R. Rees (ed.), *Ted Hughes and the Classics* (Oxford: Oxford University Press, 2009), pp. 156–76.
James, H., Daisy Miller and Other Stories (London: Penguin, 1983).
James, P., 'She's All That: Ovid's Ivory Statue and the Legacy of Pygmalion on Film', *Classical Bulletin* 79.1 (2003), 63–91.
Jameson, F., *The Political Unconscious: Narrative as a Socially Symbolic Act* (Ithaca, N.Y.: Cornell University Press, 1981).
Janowitz, A., *England's Ruins: Poetic Purpose and the National Landscape* (Oxford: Basil Blackwell, 1990).
Jauss, H. R., 'Literary History as a Challenge to Literary Theory', *New Literary History* 2.1 (1970), 7–37.
Jefferies, R., *After London* (Oxford: Oxford University Press, 1980).
Jervis, J., 'Uncanny Presences' in J. Collins and J. Jervis (eds), *Uncanny Modernity: Cultural Theories, Modern Anxieties* (Basingstoke: Palgrave Macmillan, 2008), pp. 10–50.
Jess, C., 'The Promethean Apparatus: Michael Almereyda's Hamlet as cinematic allegory', *Literature/Film* 32.2 (2004), 90–6.
Johnson, N., 'Ganymedes and Kings: Staging Male Homosexual Desire in The Winter's Tale', *Shakespeare Studies* 26 (1998), 187–217.
Jones, E., *Hamlet and Oedipus* (London: Gollancz, 1949).
Jones, W., 'Shakespeare's Sources for the Name "Laertes"', *The Shakespeare Newsletter* 10 (1960), 9.
Jonson, B., *The Oxford Jonson*, eds C. H. Herford Percy and E. Simpson (Oxford: Clarendon Press, 1938), 11 vols, vol. 6.
Joshua, E., *Pygmalion and Galatea: The History of a Narrative in English Literature* (Aldershot: Ashgate, 2001).

Keats, J., *The Poems of John Keats*, ed. M. Allott (London: Longman, 1970).
Kenner, H., *The Invisible Poet: T. S. Eliot* (London: W. H. Allen, 1960).
Kincaid, P., *What It Is We Do When We Read Science Fiction* (London: Beccon Publications, 2008).
Koestler, A., *The Act of Creation* (London: Hutchinson, 1976).
Lewis, C. S., *The Lion, the Witch and the Wardrobe* (London: Harper Collins Publishers, 2001).
Liveley, G., 'Birthday Letters from Pontus: Ted Hughes and the white noise of classical elegy', in R. Rees (ed.), *Ted Hughes and the Classics* (Oxford: Oxford University Press, 2009), pp. 216–32.
Llewellyn, P., *Rome in the Dark Ages* (London: Faber & Faber, 1971).
Loftis, N. J., *Black Anima* (New York: Liveright, 1973).
Loofbourow, J. W., 'Robinson Crusoe's Island and the Restoration *Tempest*', *Enlightenment Essays*, 2 (1971), 201–7.
Lowrie, J. O., *Sightings: Mirrors in Texts, Texts in Mirrors* (Amsterdam: Rodopi, 2007).
Lucan, *Pharsalia*, trans. J. D. Duff (Cambridge, Mass.: Harvard University Press, 1969).
Lucan, *Pharsalia*, eds S. A. Brown and C. Martindale, trans. Nicholas Rowe (London: Everyman, 1997).
Lydenberg, L., 'Freud's Uncanny Narratives, *PMLA*, 112.5 (1997), 1072–86.
Lyly, J., *Gallathea and Midas*, ed. A. Begor Lancashire (London: Edward Arnold, 1970).
Lyne, R., 'Ovid, Golding and *The Tempest*', in A. B. Taylor (ed.), *Shakespeare's Ovid: The Metamorphoses in the Plays and Poems* (Cambridge: Cambridge University Press, 2000), pp. 150–64.
Macaulay, R., *Pleasure of Ruins* (London: Thames & Hudson, 1966).
Marston, J., The Poems of John Marston, ed. A. Davenport (Liverpool: Liverpool University Press, 1961).
Marvell, A., *The Complete English Poems*, ed. E. Story Donno (London: Allen Lane, 1972).
Massie, E., 'Scottish Gothic: Robert Louis Stevenson, *The Master of Ballantrae*, and *The Private Memoirs and Confessions of a Justified Sinner*', in W. Jones (ed.), *Robert Louis Stevenson Reconsidered: New Critical Perspectives* (Jefferson: McFarland & Co Inc, 2002), pp. 163–74.
McCarthy, P. A., 'Allusions in Ballard's *The Drowned World*', *Science Fiction Studies*, 24.2 (1997), 302–10.
McDonald, R., 'Reading *The Tempest*', *Shakespeare Survey*, 43 (1991), 15–28.
McGann, J. J., 'Rome and its Romantic Significance', in A. Patterson (ed.), *Roman Images* (Baltimore: Johns Hopkins University Press, 1984), pp. 83–104.

McGlamery, G., 'The Three Tropographies of Ronald Wright's *A Scientific Romance*', *Canadian Literature*, 185 (2005), 92–109.

McSweeney, K., 'Literary Allusion and the Poetry of Seamus Heaney', *Style*, Spring (1999) http://findarticles.com/p/articles/mi_m2342/is_1_33/ai_58055908/pg_2/, accessed 15 June 2010.

Mendelsohn, M., 'Homosociality and the Aesthetic in Henry James's *Roderick Hudson*', *Nineteenth-Century Literature*, 57.4 (2003), 512–41.

Mérimée, P., *Colomba, La Vénus d'Ille, Les Ames du Purgatoire* (Paris: Editions Garnier Frères, 1962).

Michie, H., *Sororophobia: Differences among Women in Literature and Culture* (Oxford: Oxford University Press, 1992).

Middleton, T., *Collected Works*, eds G. Taylor and J. Lavagnino (Oxford: Clarendon Press, 2007).

Miller, K., *Doubles: Studies in Literary History* (Oxford: Oxford University Press, 1985).

Miller, K., *The Electric Shepherd: A Likeness of James Hogg* (London: Faber, 2003).

Milton, J., *Areopagitica* (Cambridge: Deighton, Bell & Co, 1973).

Mitchell, D., *Cloud Atlas* (London: Sceptre, 2004).

Mogg, K., 'Some Notes on *Rear Window*', http://labyrinth.net.au/~muffin/rear_window_c.html, accessed 18 March 2011.

Mozart, W. A., and L. da Ponte, *Don Giovanni* (Philips, 1990).

Murray, G., *Hamlet and Orestes: A study in traditional types* (London: H. Milford, 1914).

Nabokov, V., *Despair* (New York: G. P. Putnam Son's, 1966).

Nabokov, V., *Lolita* (London: Penguin, 1997).

Neill, M., 'Monuments and Ruins as Symbols in The Duchess of Malfi', in J. Redmond (ed.), *Drama and Symbolism* (Cambridge: Cambridge University Press, 1982), pp. 71–87.

Newcomb, L. H., '"If that which is lost be not found": Monumental Bodies Spectacular Bodies in *The Winter's Tale*', in Stanivukovic (ed.), *Ovid and the Renaissance Body* (Toronto: University of Toronto Press, 2001), pp. 239–59.

Nielsen, H. S., 'Telling Doubles and Literal-minded Reading in Bret Easton Ellis's *Glamorama*', in A. Durand and N. Mandel (eds), *Novels of the Contemporary Extreme* (London: Continuum, 2006), pp. 20–30.

Novak, D. A., 'Sexuality in the Age of Technological Reproducibility', in J. Brister (ed.), *Oscar Wilde and Modern Culture: The Making of a Legend* (Chicago: University of Chicago Press, 2009), pp. 63–95.

Paganoni, M. C., *The Magic Lantern: Representation of the Double in Dickens* (New York and London: Routledge, 2008).

Perri, C., 'On Alluding', *Poetics*, 7 (1978), 289–307.

Person Jr, L. S., 'James's Homo-Aesthetics: Deploying Desire in the Tales of Writers and Artists', *The Henry James Review*, 14.2 (1993), 188–203.

Phelan, J., *Narrative as Rhetoric: Technique, Audiences, Ethics, Ideology* (Columbus: Ohio State University Press, 1996), pp. 119–31.

Philostratus, *Imagines*, trans. A. Fairbanks (London: William Heinemann, 1960).

Pigman III, G. W., 'Du Bellay's Ambivalence Towards Rome in the *Antiquitez*', in *Rome in the Renaissance: The City and the Myth* (New York: Medieval and Renaissance Texts and Studies, 1982), pp. 321–32.

Pollard, C. W., 'Travelling with Joyce: Derek Walcott's Discrepant Cosmopolitan Modernism', *Twentieth Century Literature*, 47.2 (2001), 197–216.

Pollard, C. W., *New World Modernisms: T. S. Eliot, Derek Walcott and Kamau Brathwaite* (Charlottesville: University of Virginia Press, 2004).

Poulet, G., 'Criticism and the Experience of Interiority', in R. Macksey and E. Donato (eds), *The Languages of Criticism and the Sciences of Man: The Structuralist Controversy* (Baltimore and London: Johns Hopkins Press, 1970).

Prendergast, C., 'Derrida's Hamlet', *SubStance*, 34.1 (2005), 44–7.

Price, T., *Hitchcock and Homosexuality* (New Jersey and London: Scarecrow Press, 1992).

Priest, C., *The Prestige* (London: Touchstone, 1995).

Priest, C., *The Affirmation* (London: Touchstone, 1996).

Priest, C., *The Separation* (London: Gollancz, 2004).

Propertius, *Elegies*, trans. G. P. Goold (Cambridge, Mass.: Harvard University Press, 2000).

Pugh, T., *Queering Medieval Genres* (New York and Basingstoke: Palgrave Macmillan, 2004).

Pullman, P., *His Dark Materials: Northern Lights* (London: Scholastic Publications Ltd, 1995).

Punter, D., 'Spectral Criticism' in J. Wolfreys (ed.), *Introducing Criticism at the 21st Century* (Edinburgh: Edinburgh University Press, 2002), pp. 259–78.

Pykett, L., *The Sensation Novel: from The Woman in White to The Moonstone* (Plymouth: Northcote House, 1994).

Rainolds, J., *Th'overthrow of Stage-plays* (London, 1599).

Ramazani, J., 'The Wound of Postcolonial History: Derek Walcott's *Omeros*', in H. Bloom (ed.), *Derek Walcott* (Broomall: Chelsea House, 2003), pp. 174–204.

Rank, O., *The Double: A Psychoanalytic Study*, trans. H. Tucker Jr (London: Karnac, 1989).

Ransom, A. J., *The Feminine as Fantastic in the Conte Fantastique: Visions of the Other* (New York: Peter Lang, 1995).

Ricks, C., *Allusion to the Poets* (Oxford: Oxford University Press, 2004).

Rogers, R., *A Psychoanalytical Study of the Double in Literature* (Detroit: Wayne State University Press, 1970), pp. 42–4.
Rosenberg, S., 'Something's Misbegotten in the State of Denmark', www.salon.com/jan97/hamlet970120.html, accessed 2 March 2011.
Royle, N., *The Uncanny* (Manchester: Manchester University Press, 2003).
Ruddick, N., 'Reticence and Ostentation in Christopher Priest's Later Novels: *The Quiet Woman* and *The Prestige*', in A. M. Butler (ed.), *Christopher Priest: The Interaction* (London: The Science Fiction Foundation, 2005).
Sajé, N., *Red under the Skin* (Pittsburgh: University of Pittsburgh Press, 1994).
Samuels, R., *Hitchcock's Bi-Textuality: Lacan, Feminisms and Queer Theory* (New York: State University of New York Press, 1998).
Sandison, A., *Robert Louis Stevenson and the Appearance of Modernism: A Future Feeling* (London: Palgrave, 1996).
Satzinger, C., *The French Influences on Oscar Wilde's The Picture of Dorian Gray and Salome* (Lampeter: Edwin Mellen Press, 1994).
Savu, L. E., 'In Desire's Grip: Gender, Politics, and Intertextual Games in Updike's *Gertrude and Claudius*', *Papers on Language and Literature*, 39.1 (2003), 2–48.
Schwyzer, P., *Archaeologies of English Renaissance Literature* (Oxford: Oxford University Press, 2007).
Scofield, M., *The Ghosts of Hamlet: The play and modern writers* (Cambridge: Cambridge University Press, 1980).
Sedgwick, E. K., *Tendencies* (London: Routledge, 1994).
Self, W., *Dorian* (London: Viking, 2002).
Shakespeare, W., *The Riverside Shakespeare*, ed. H. Baker *et al* (Boston and New York: Houghton Mifflin Company, 1987).
Shaneen, M., 'Adapting the Occult: Horror and the Avant-Garde in the Cinema of Ken Jacobs', in R. J. Hands and J. McRoy (eds), *Monstrous Adaptations: Generic and Thematic Mutations in Horror Film* (Manchester: Manchester University Press, 2007), pp. 111–26.
Shelley, M., *Collected Tales and Stories* (Baltimore: Johns Hopkins University Press, 1976).
Shelley, M., *The Last Man* (Peterborough, Ontario: Broadview, 1996).
Showalter, E., *Sexual Anarchy: Gender and Culture at the 'Fin de Siècle'* (London: Bloomsbury, 1990).
Sidney, P., *The Countess of Pembroke's Arcadia* (Oxford: Oxford University Press, 1985).
Slethaug, G. E., *The Play of the Double in Postmodern American Fiction* (Carbondale: Southern Illinois University Press, 1993), pp. 33–57.
Smith, A., 'Death, Art, and Bodies: Queering the Queer Gothic in Will Self's *Dorian*', in W. Hughes and A. Smith (eds), *Queering the Gothic* (Manchester: Manchester University Press, 2009) pp. 177–92.

Smith, E., 'Ghost Writing: *Hamlet* and the Ur-Hamlet' in A. Murphy (ed.) *The Renaissance Text: Theory, Editing, Textuality* (Manchester: Manchester University Press, 2000), pp. 177–96.
Smith, H., *The Poetical Works* (London: Henry Colburn, 1846).
Spencer, D., 'Lucan's Follies: Memory and Ruin in a Civil-War Landscape', *Greece and Rome*, 52.1 (2005), 46–69.
Spenser, E., *Shorter Poems*, eds. W. A. Oram, *et al.* (New Haven and London: Yale University Press, 1989).
Stevenson, R. L., *The Master of Ballantrae* (London: Penguin, 1996).
Stewart, J. I. M., *Character and Motive in Shakespeare: Some Recent Appraisals Examined* (London: Longmans, 1949).
Stewart, V., 'The Other War: Christopher Priest's *The Separation*', in Butler (ed.), *Christopher Priest: The Interaction* (London: The Science Fiction Foundation, 2005), pp. 115–27.
Stirling, K., 'Dr Jekyll and Mr Jackass: *Fight Club* as a Refraction of Hogg's *Justified Sinner* and Stevenson's *Dr Jekyll and Mr Hyde*', in C. Gutleben and S. Onega (eds), *Refracting the Canon in Contemporary British Literature and Film* (Amsterdam: Rodopi, 2004), pp. 83–94.
Stoppard, T., *Rosencrantz and Guildenstern are Dead* (London: Faber & Faber, 1967).
Stoppard, T., *The Invention of Love (*London: Faber & Faber, 1997).
Swann, K., '*Endymion*'s Beautiful Dreamers', in S. J. Wolfson (ed.), *The Cambridge Companion to Keats* (Cambridge: Cambridge University Press, 2001), pp. 20–36.
Tambling, J., *Becoming Posthumous: Life and Death in Literary and Cultural Studies* (Edinburgh: Edinburgh University Press, 2002).
Tatar, M., and J. K. Allen (eds), *The Annotated Hans Christian Andersen* (New York and London: W. W. Norton, 2008).
Taylor, J. B., *In the Secret Theatre of Home: Wilkie Collins, Sensation Narrative, and Nineteenth Century Psychology* (London: Routledge, 1998).
Taylor, J. B., 'Armadale: The Sensitive Subject as Palimpsest', in L. Pykett (ed.), *Wilkie Collins* (Basingstoke: Macmillan, 1998), pp. 149–74.
Taylor, M., *Shakespeare's Darker Purpose: A Question of Incest* (New York: AMS Press, 1982).
Tennant, E., *The Bad Sister* (Edinburgh: Canongate, 2000).
Todd, J. M., 'The Veiled Woman in Freud's "Das Unheimleiche"', Signs, 2.3 (1988), 519–28.
Tolkien, J. R. R., *The Return of the King* (London: George Allen & Unwin, 1960).
Unsworth, B., Sacred Hunger (London: Doubleday, 1992).
Vaughan, A. T., and V. M. Vaughan, *Shakespeare's Caliban: A Cultural History* (Cambridge: Cambridge University Press, 1991).
Updike, J., *Gertrude and Claudius* (London: Hamish Hamilton, 2000).

Virgil, *Aeneid*, trans. H. Rushton Fairclough (Cambridge, Mass.: Harvard University Press, 2000).
Walcott, D., *Omeros* (London: Faber & Faber, 1992).
Wallace, J., *Digging the Dirt: The Archaeological Imagination* (London: Duckworth, 2004).
Ward, J. W., 'N. J. Loftis's *Black Anima*: A Problem in Aesthetics', *Journal of Black Studies*, 7.2 (1976), 195–210.
Ward, M., 'C. S. Lewis and Philip Pullman' in www.planetnarnia.com/assets/documents/74/Lewis_and_Pullman.pdf, accessed 15 June 2010.
Waters, S., *Fingersmith* (London: Virago, 2002).
Waters, S., 'Sensational Fiction: Sarah Waters on the echoes of 'sensation novels' in *Fingersmith*', *The Guardian*, 17 June 2006 www.guardian.co.uk/books/2006/jun/17/fiction.sarahwaters, accessed 27 June 2010.
Webster, J., *Three Plays*, ed. J. R. Brown (London: Penguin, 1972).
Welsh, A., in *Hamlet in his Modern Guises* (Princeton: Princeton University Press, 2001).
Welsh, L., *The Bullet Trick* (Edinburgh: Canongate, 2006).
White, R. S., *Keats as a Reader of Shakespeare* (London: Athlone, 1987).
Wilde, O., *The Major Works* (Oxford: Oxford University Press, 2000).
Wilde, O., *The Picture of Dorian Gray* (Oxford: Oxford University Press, 2008).
William of Malmesbury, *Gesta Regum Anglorum*, ed. and trans. R. A. B. Mynors (Oxford: Clarendon Press, 1998), 2 vols, vol. 1.
Wilamowitz-Moellendorff, U. von, *Griechische Tragödien* (Berlin, 1919).
Williams, J., *Jean Cocteau* (Manchester: Manchester University Press, 2006).
Williams, R. D., 'The *Aeneid* and its Literary Background', in E. J. Kenney and W. V. Clausen (eds), *The Cambridge History of Classical Literature* (Cambridge: Cambridge University Press, 1982), 2 vols, vol. 1, pp. 339–44.
Winchell, J., 'Wilde and Huysmans: Autonomy, Reference, and the Myth of Expiation', in R. Gagnier (ed.), *Critical Essays on Oscar Wilde* (New York: G. K. Hall, 1991), pp. 223–40.
Wolfreys, J., in *Writing London: The Trace of the Urban Text from Blake to Dickens* (Basingstoke: Macmillan, 1998).
Woodward, C., *In Ruins* (London: Chatto & Windus, 2001).
Worthen, W. B., 'Fond Records: Remembering Theatre in the Digital Age', in Peter Holland (ed.), *Shakespeare, Memory and Performance* (Cambridge: Cambridge University Press, 2006), pp. 55–72.
Wright, G. T., 'Hendiadys and Hamlet', *Proceedings of the Modern Language Association*, 96:2 (1981), 168–93.
Wright, R., *A Scientific Romance* (London: Transworld, 1997).
Zabus, C. J., *Tempests after Shakespeare* (New York and Basingstoke: Palgrave Macmillan, 2002).

Zetzel, J. E. G., '*Romane memento*: Justice and Judgement in *Aeneid* 6', *Transactions and Proceedings of the American Philological Association*, 119 (1989), 263–8.

Ziolkowski, T., *Disenchanted Images: A Literary Iconography* (Princeton: Princeton University Press, 1977).

Index

Abraham, N. 115
Aeschylus 5–6
   Oresteia 156, 159–63, 169
allusion triggers 5, 85, 171, 183, 194, 212
Almereyda, M.
   Hamlet 15, 170–1
Andersen, H. C.
   'Shadow, The' 19, 39, 51–2, 73
Apuleius
   Golden Ass, The 11
Atwood, M.
   Handmaid's Tale, The 72
Austen, J.
   Northanger Abbey 43

Ballard, J. G.
   Drowned World, The 14, 98–9, 194
Barkan, L. 91
Barrie, J. M.
   Peter Pan 212
Benjamin, W. 87, 94
Bennett, A. 53
Bible, The 89, 146–7
Blessed, B. 167
Blanchot, M. 13
Bloom, H. 12
Bracciolini, P. 88
Bradbury, R.
   Fahrenheit 451 71

Braddon, M. 13, 34
   Lady Audley's Secret 28–32, 33, 56, 66–8
Branagh, K.
   Hamlet 15, 167–8
Bruster, D. 16
Burgess, A. 15
   Eve of Saint Venus, The 137–9
Burton, T.
   Alice in Wonderland 210–13
Byron, G. G.
   Childe Harold's Pilgrimage

Carroll, L.
   Alice in Wonderland 210–13
Catullus 5
Chaucer, G.
   Canterbury Tales, The 197
Christopher, J.
   Tripods Trilogy 99–100, 101
Cinyras 114
cloning 14, 71–2
Cocteau, J.
   Orphic Trilogy, The 15, 113, 139–40, 144, 146
Collins, W. 13
   Armadale 32–3, 34, 68
   Legacy of Cain, The 66
   Mad Monkton 32
   No Name 66
   Woman in White, The 27–33, 66–8

Connington, J. 161–3
Conrad, J.
    Heart of Darkness 98–9, 194
    'Secret Sharer, The' 14, 40–6, 52, 54
Conte, G. B. 12, 178, 184, 193
Cooper, H. 12, 115
Cowley, A. 12

Dante, 12, 15, 201, 204
    Inferno 179–80, 183, 185, 198, 201, 203
Davenant, W. See Dryden, J.
de Belleforest, F.
    Histoires Tragiques 160–1, 164, 165
Defoe, D. 185
Dench, J. 168
Derrida, J.
    Spectres of Marx 153
Dick, P. K.
    Time out of Joint 86
Dickens, C. 31
    Bleak House 27
    Dombey and Son 27
    Tale of Two Cities, A 27
Dostoevsky, F.
    Double, The 51
doubles 13–14, 19–46, 51–73, 127
Dryden, J. and Davenant, W.
    Enchanted Island, The 184–8, 193
du Bellay, J.
    Antiquités de Rome 89–90, 92
Dumas, A.
    Le Vicomte de Bragelonne 32
du Maurier, D. 14
    Rebecca 54–8
    Scapegoat, The 54–8
Dyer, J.
    Ruins of Rome 92–4

Easton Ellis, B. 14, 58
    American Psycho 62
    Glamorama 62–4, 68, 73, 200, 203–4
Edda 158
Eddington, A. 169
Edwards, C. 104
Eliot, T. S.
    Four Quartets, The 15, 178–80, 182, 183, 190, 193, 198, 200, 201, 204
    'Love Song of J. Alfred Prufrock, The' 166
    Waste Land, The 8, 82, 97–8, 101, 187, 194, 201, 202, 204
Empson, W. 87
Euripides
    Electra 5–6
    Medea 172, 173

Fanshawe, R. 3
Fleischer, R.
    Soylent Green 72
Fleming, V.
    The Wizard of Oz 211–12
Fletcher, J. 188
Fowles, J.
    French Lieutenant's Woman, The 66
Freud, S. 12–13, 104, 115, 118, 126, 127, 129, 141, 145, 154

Gaiman, N.
    Fables & Reflections 15, 145–6
Gandy, J. 95
Garber, M. 13, 187
ghosts 13, 15–16, 79, 113, 116–17, 153–73 *passim*, 178–84, 185–8, 202–4
Gielgud, J. 168–171
Ginsberg, R. 78
Glaucus 189, 195
Greene, T. M. 12, 92
Guarini, G. B. 3
Günther of Paris 88

Hansen, W. F. 160
Hardie, P. 86
Hardwick, L. 12
Hart, L. 29–30
Hawke, E. 171, 189
Heaney, S. 3
Hinds, S. 5, 6, 7, 12, 156
Hitchcock, A.
  Dial M for Murder 146
  Rear Window 145
  Vertigo 10, 15, 115, 140, 141, 142–4, 146
Hoban, R.
  Riddley Walker 191
  Some Episodes in the History of Miranda and Caliban 191–3, 195
Hoffmann, E. T. A.
  'Sandman, The' 10, 115, 140–2, 143, 145
Hogg, J. 13, 34, 37, 40, 41
  Private Memoirs and Confessions of a Justified Sinner, The 20–2, 23, 24, 25, 30, 51, 64
  'Strange Letter of a Lunatic' 21–2
Hollander, J. 3, 87, 163
Homer 15, 201, 205
  Iliad, The 201
  Odyssey, The 156, 157–9, 160, 161, 164, 180–3
homosexuality 15, 37, 41, 44–6, 53–4, 57–8, 68–9, 114–47 *passim*
Horace 4, 14, 90–1, 94, 103, 188
Hughes, T. 5
  Tales from Ovid 116–17, 126, 185
Huxley, A.
  Brave New World 72
Huysmans, J. -K.
  Against Nature 35–6, 40, 69

Icarus 191
incest 15, 114, 147, 154, 156–7, 158–9, 160–1, 164

inheritance 3–4
intentionality 7–8
intertextuality 9, 163
Iphis 121–2, 124, 134

James, H.
  'Last of the Valerii, The' 15, 133–7, 138, 140
  Turn of the Screw, The 2–3
Jameson, F. 83
Janowitz, A. 93–4
Jauss, H. J. 40
Jefferies, J.
  After London 101–2
Jervis, J. 10
Jonson, B. 3
  Bartholomew Fair 188
  Cynthia's Revels 8–9
  Sad Shepherd, The 20
Joyce, J.
  Ulysses 204

katabasis 15–16, 178–83, 185, 186, 192, 199–201, 204–5, 210
Keats, J. 12
  Endymion 189–91, 192, 193, 195, 204–5
  'This Living Hand' 129–30
Kingsley, C.
  Water Babies, The 211
Koestler, A. 60
Kosofsky Sedgewick, E. 69
Kratzenstein, C. G. 142

Le Fanu, S.
  Rose and the Key, The 66
Lewis, C. S.
  Lion, the Witch and the Wardrobe, The 1–2, 210, 211
  Magician's Nephew, The 2
  Till We Have Faces 12
Llewellyn, P. 88

Loftis, N.
  Black Anima 16, 198–201, 204
Lucan 14
  Pharsalia 85–7, 103
Lyly, J.
  Gallathea 122
Lyne, R. 113–14

Macaulay, R.
  Pleasure of Ruins 80, 82, 104
Mallarmé, S. 180
Marston, J.
  'Metamorphosis of Pygmalion's Image, The' 123
Martindale, C. 12
Marvell, A.
  Upon Appleton House 81–2
Marx, K. 153
McSweeney, K. 3
memory 5–6, 98, 180, 184, 194–5
Mérimée, P. 15
  'Venus of Ille, The' 130–3, 134, 135, 136, 138, 140
Middleton, T. 123
Miller, G.
  Mad Max 102
Miller, K. 22
Milton, J.
  Areopagitica 112–13, 114, 115, 130
  Paradise Lost 2, 3
Mitchell, D.
  Cloud Atlas 14, 71–2
Mozart, W. A.
  Don Giovanni 167–8, 205
Murch, W.
  Return to Oz 212
Myrrha 114

Nabokov, V.
  Despair 51–4, 57, 73
  Lolita 54
Narcissus 42, 124
New Historicism 16

Orpheus 10, 15, 114–47 *passim*
Orwell, G.
  1984 72
Ovid 5, 12, 15
  Metamorphoses, The 114–47 *passim*, 189

Palahniuk, C. 58, 73, 200
  Fight Club 63–4, 68
Pasolini, P. P.
  Edipo Re 78
Philoctetes 105, 202
Plautus
  Amphitryon 20
  Menaechmi 20
Poe, E. A. 13, 39, 40
  'William Wilson' 25, 34, 39, 64–6
Pope, A.
  Dunciad, The 5
  'First Epistle of the Second Book of Horace Imitated' 4, 6, 103
Poulet, G. 112–13
presentism 12
Price, T. 142
Priest, C. 14, 64
  Affirmation, The 59–61
  Prestige, The 58–61, 62, 100
  Separation, The 60–1
prophecy 6, 163, 196, 212
Pygmalion 15, 114–47 *passim*, 199
Pullman, P.
  Northern Lights 1–2, 210, 211
Punter, D. 13

Rainolds, J. 123
reanimation 14–15, 23–6, 112–47
Ricks, C. 3–4, 5, 8, 12
Ross, D. 12
Rowe, N. 87
Royle, N. 13
'Ruin, The' 14, 88–9, 99, 101–2
ruins 14, 77–105, 154

Sajé, N. 30–1
Samuels, R. 143
Saxo Grammaticus 15
   Gesta Danorum 155–61, 164, 165, 173
Schaffner, H. J.
   Planet of the Apes, The 100
Schwenger, P. 13
Schwyzer, P. 84
Scott, R.
   Gladiator 196
Self, W. 14
   Dorian 68–71
Seneca
   Medea 172, 173
Shakespeare, W. 4, 7, 14, 201, 203–4
   Comedy of Errors, The 20
   Hamlet 3, 10, 11, 15, 153–73, 184, 195, 204
   King Lear 11, 185
   Othello 173
   Richard III 187–8
   Sonnets 125
   Tempest, The 16, 105, 113–14, 178, 183–202
   Titus Andronicus 102–4
   Twelfth Night 20
   Winter's Tale, The 15, 23–4, 125–9, 141
Shelley, M.
   Frankenstein 113, 114, 127
   Last Man, The 14, 96–7, 101
   'Reanimated Roman, The' 95–6
Shelley, P. B. 95, 100
Shiel, M. P.
   Purple Cloud, The 101
Sidney, P.
   Old Arcadia, The 124–5
Silverberg, R.
   Man in the Maze, The 105
Sir Orfeo 119–21, 127
Slavitt, D. 11
Smith, H. 95, 100

Sophocles 202
spectral criticism 13
Spenser, E. 14, 185
   Ruins of Rome, The 89–93, 94, 188
Stevenson, R. L. 13, 34, 39, 40
   'Bodysnatcher, The' 24
   Kidnapped 26–7
   Master of Ballantrae, The 22–7, 37, 40, 41, 43
   Strange Case of Doctor Jekyll and Mr Hyde 36–7, 38, 45, 64, 69
Stewart, J. I. M. 126
Stoker, B.
   Dracula 113
Stoppard, T.
   Invention of Love, The 137
   Rosencrantz and Guildenstern are Dead 15, 168–70, 178

'T. M.'
   'Ingling Pyander' 123–4, 144
Tambling, J. 103
Tate, N. 185
Taymor, J.
   Titus 102–4
Tenniel, J. 212
Tennyson, A. 87
Tolkien, J. R. R.
   The Lord of the Rings 212
Torok, M. 115
Tourneur, J.
   Night of the Demon 3

uncanny allusion markers 3, 6–7, 13–16, 23, 27, 78, 83, 113–14, 123, 144, 154, 172, 183, 194, 200
Unsworth, B.
   Sacred Hunger 196–8
Updike, J.
   Gertrude and Claudius 15, 164–7, 169, 196
   Ur-Hamlet 155, 171–2

Index

Virgil, 12, 14, 15, 90, 103, 188, 201
  Aeneid, The 83–7, 89, 92, 93–4,
    96, 104, 180–3, 185–6, 192,
    199–200
Von Chamisso, A. 19

Wagner, R. 213
Walcott, D.
  Omeros 16, 201–5
Waters, S. 14, 58
Fingersmith 66–8
Watts, G. F. 142
Webster, J.
  Duchess of Malfi, The 77–80, 81,
    88, 96, 103
Weir, P.
  Truman Show, The 173
Weir Smyth, H. 163

Wells, H. G.
  Time Machine, The 100
  War of the Worlds, The 99, 100
Welsh, L.
  Bullet Trick 64–6, 73
Wilamowitz-Moellendorff 172
Wilcox, F. M.
  Forbidden Planet 105
Wilde, O. 13, 54
  Picture of Dorian Gray, The 25,
    34–40, 45, 62, 64, 68–71
  'Selfish Giant, The' 69
William of Malmesbury 130
Wolfreys, J. 13
Wright, R.
  Scientific Romance, A 100–2

Yeats, W. B. 180

233